THE INSTITUTE OF
CHARTERED
ACCOUNTANTS

IN ENGLAND & WALES

IFRS Award Programme Manual

certificate level

IFRS Award Programme Manual

certificate level

Copyright 2004 by the Institute of Chartered Accountants in England and Wales (ICAEW)

ISBN 1 84152 250 3

First Edition

For more information about the IFRS Award Programme:

- go to www.icaew.co.uk/ifrs; or

- telephone + 44 (0) 1908 248038; or

- e-mail training@icaew.co.uk.

Designed and produced by Windrush, Witney, United Kingdom.

British Library Cataloguing-in-Publication Data.

A catalogue record for this book has been applied for from the British Library.

IFRS Award Programme Manual

certificate level

The ICAEW would like to thank the following people for their contribution to this manual:

Hazel Powling BSc Cert.Ed. ACA

Hazel is Head of IAS Implementation at the ICAEW where her primary responsibility is to communicate to the members and the wider business community information on International Accounting Standards. Prior to this appointment, Hazel spent a number of years within the technical department of a leading multinational accountancy practice and several years writing and lecturing on continuing professional development.

Nick Scott BSc FCA

Nick is a Senior Lecturer at Manchester Metropolitan University Business School (MMUBS) where he specialises in advanced financial reporting and international accounting. Prior to joining the MMUBS he held senior financial positions in UK multinational enterprises. Nick authored the ICAEW Faculty of Finance and Management Good Practice Guide – 'Managing the change to IAS'.

IFRS Award Programme Manual

certificate level

Complementary learning material

This manual should be used in conjunction with other learning material available.

To enhance your understanding there are frequent references in this manual to the international accounting and reporting standards from the International Accounting Standards Board (IASB). These appear as paragraph references, for example '[IAS 16.7]' refers to paragraph 7 of IAS 16 *Property, plant and equipment*.

The ICAEW has also produced practice assessments for each chapter in this manual. These questions have the same style as those in the Certificate level assessment and can be used to develop your understanding of each international standard. For more information about these and other learning material available from the ICAEW go to www.icaew.co.uk/ifrs.

IAS and IFRS

International Accounting Standards (IAS) are the standards that were published by the predecessor body to the International Accounting Standards Board (IASB) and were subsequently adopted by the IASB. New standards issued by the IASB are called International Financial Reporting Standards (IFRS). The two terms are interchangeable and any reference in these chapters to IFRS should be taken as including IAS, unless there is a specific statement to the contrary.

IFRS Award Programme Manual

certificate level

Currency and convention

The standard currency used in this manual is the 'currency unit' ('CU') comprising 100 sub units. CU's and their sub units are separated by a decimal point, for example CU10.25. The thousand separator used is the comma, for example one million currency units will appear as CU1,000,000.

Definition of an entity

Throughout this manual the term 'entity' is used to describe a body corporate, partnership, or unincorporated association carrying on a trade or business.

IFRS Award Programme Manual

certificate level

Introduction

The global transition to IAS and IFRS means that organisations will need to review and change their financial policies, processes and systems. The impact will not be restricted to the accountancy profession and will affect many sectors including banking, investment, commerce and industry.

This manual has been produced, as part of an overall IFRS Award Programme, to help preparers and users of financial statements and financial information to develop a broad knowledge and understanding of all of the international accounting and reporting standards effective in 2005 – the "2005 Stable Platform". The manual outlines each standard in a broad business context and is packed with illustrations to demonstrate key principles and concepts.

Chapter	Content
The Reporting Environment	
1 Financial Reporting Context	Global Harmonisation
	Principal Regulatory and
	Institutional Structures
2 The IFRS Framework	Preface to International Financial
	Reporting Standards
	Framework for the Preparation and
	Presentation of Financial Statements
Financial Reporting Statements	
3 Presentation of Financial Statements	IAS 1 Presentation of Financial
	Statements
4 Accounting Policies	IAS 8 Accounting Policies, Changes in
	Accounting Estimates and Errors
Revenue Reporting	
5 Revenue	IAS 18 Revenue
Asset Reporting	
6 Inventories	IAS 2 Inventories
7 Property, Plant and Equipment	IAS 16 Property, Plant and Equipment
8 Borrowing Costs	IAS 23 Borrowing Costs
9 Government Grants	IAS 20 Accounting for Government
	Grants and Disclosure of Government
	Assistance
10 Non-current Assets Held for Sale	IFRS 5 Non-current Assets Held for Sale
	and Discontinued Operations (part)
11 Investment Property	IAS 40 Investment Property
12 Intangibles	IAS 38 Intangible Assets
13 Impairment	IAS 36 Impairment of Assets
Liability Reporting	
14 Provisions and Contingencies	IAS 37 Provisions, Contingent
	Liabilities and Contingent Assets
15 Taxation	IAS 12 Income Taxes
16 Leases	IAS 17 Leases
17 Employee Benefits	IAS 19 Employee Benefits
	IFRS 2 Share-based Payment
18 Events After the Balance Sheet Date	IAS 10 Events After the Balance
	Sheet Date
Reporting for Financial instruments	
19 Foreign Exchange	IAS 21 The Effects of Changes in
	Foreign Exchange Rates
20 Financial Instruments	IAS 32 Financial Instruments:
	Disclosure and Presentation
	IAS 39 Financial Instruments:
	Recognition and Measurement

Chapter	Content
Reporting and Disclosure	
21 Cash Flow Statements	IAS 7 Cash Flow Statements
22 Segment Reporting	IAS 14 Segment Reporting
	IFRS 5 Non-current Assets Held for Sale and Discontinued Operations (part)
23 Interim Reporting	IAS 34 Interim Financial Reporting
24 Earnings Per Share	IAS 33 Earnings Per Share
25 Related Party Disclosures	IAS 24 Related Party Disclosures
Sector Reporting	
26 Construction	IAS 11 Construction Contracts
27 Retirement Benefit Plans	IAS 26 Accounting and Reporting by Retirement Benefit Plans
28 Banks and Similar Institutions	IAS 30 Disclosures in the Financial Statements of Banks and Similar Financial Institutions
29 Insurance	IFRS 4 Insurance Contracts
30 Agriculture	IAS 41 Agriculture
Group Reporting	
31 Consolidation	IAS 27 Consolidated and Separate Financial Statements
32 Hyperinflationary Economies	IAS 29 Financial Reporting in Hyperinflationary Economies
33 Business Combinations	IFRS 3 Business Combinations
34 Associates	IAS 28 Investments in Associates
35 Joint Ventures	IAS 31 Interests in Joint Ventures
Reporting Implementation	
36 First-time Adoption	IFRS 1 First-time Adoption of International Financial Reporting Standards

Interpretations published by the Standing Interpretation Committee (SIC) and the International Financial Reporting Interpretation Committee (IFRIC) that form part of the '2005 Stable Platform' are included in the relevant chapters.

Chapter 1
FINANCIAL REPORTING CONTEXT

1 Business Context

The measurement of business and economic activity is essential to the assessment of the performance of the entity. The publication of financial information has provided a means of providing an account of the way in which resources have been utilised within a business.

In modern and sophisticated capital markets, financial reporting has become, for large companies at least, a key raw material on which investors base their decisions to supply funds.

Over time, different practices and regulations have evolved to meet the requirements of national economic, financial and legal systems. The challenge of international harmonisation is to reduce or eliminate the differences, to produce a level playing field for financial reporting and to help create more efficient international capital markets.

2 Chapter Objectives

This chapter looks at the background to the development and application of international harmonisation through financial reporting standards. It includes the process by which harmonisation has arisen and, more specifically, a description of the structure and bodies within which the International Accounting Standards Board (IASB) operates.

On completion of this chapter you should be able to:

- understand the nature, concepts and purposes underlying the international harmonisation of financial reporting;

- demonstrate a knowledge of the regulatory and institutional structure within which the IASB operates and of the major bodies within that structure; and

- understand the structures in the European Union (EU) as they relate to international financial reporting.

3 From National Accounting to International Harmonisation

Accounting standards are effectively the 'user manual' for how to translate an entity's financial performance into a set of coherent and succinct financial statements. The end result is designed to be a set of financial statements that is the basis for a variety of users to make informed economic investment decisions.

Entities across the world prepare financial statements with this same objective in mind. However the 'user manual' in each national jurisdiction may vary to take account of the local environment in which entities operate. Consequently the same business transaction may be accounted for in a number of different ways depending on which version of the 'user manual' is used, for example the one for the UK, for the US, for Australia or for Japan.

Factors influencing these variations in national practices and regulation of financial reporting include:

- differences in the way that legal systems operate;

- different political systems, for example the degree of central government control;

- different capital markets;

- international variation in the type and scale of economic activity, from agricultural to financial services and from developing economies to industrialised economies;

- the degree of international influence and openness of an economy;

- the stability of the economy and inflation rates;

- cultural differences;

- the influence of the accounting profession; and

- national differences in corporate governance (the exercise of power over and responsibility for an entity) structures and practices.

While national variations in accounting practices have endured for many years, more recently there has been pressure to harmonise financial reporting practice and regulation on a global basis in order to reduce such inconsistencies. In short, it is becoming less acceptable to report the same transactions differently according to where they occur. Accounting practices and financial reporting should be a universal language.

Illustration 1 – Daimler Benz

A good example of inconsistent national financial reporting is that of German car manufacturer Daimler-Benz AG (prior to its merger with Chrysler).

Daimler-Benz obtained a listing of its shares in the US in 1993 and in so doing needed to report under both US generally accepted accounting practices (GAAP) and German GAAP.

While one might expect that the profit reported would be similar (as it was exactly the same set of economic transactions being presented), this was not the case. The company reported a huge loss of $1 billion under US GAAP, while at the same time reporting a profit of $370 million under German GAAP.

This difference was simply the result of different accounting practices being used by different countries. Such significant differences undermine the usefulness of financial statements.

There have been a number of primary drivers encouraging worldwide harmonisation of financial reporting including increased globalisation of trade and capital markets. The rapid pace at which information technology has developed has, amongst other things, led to the ease of the electronic movement of funds across national boundaries and increased investor willingness to invest across national borders.

With international barriers being broken down there has been a move to increased internationalisation of non-accounting regulation, for example international banking agreements (such as the Basel Accord) and international agreements by securities regulators.

As a reflection of the movement towards international harmonisation of financial reporting there has been increased usage of International Financial Reporting Standards (IFRS) worldwide. This trend matches the growing internationalisation of business.

IFRS	Number of countries
Require use of IFRS for all listed companies	32
Require use of IFRS for some companies	6
Permit the use of IFRS	32
Will require use of IFRS in 2005	25

With almost 100 countries using or allowing IFRS for the preparation of financial statements, there is significant progress towards the goal of having one set of global standards. Probably the most significant absentee from the list is the US which continues to have its own 'user manual' of accounting standards. However, as explained later, the US accounting standards setter is working closely with the IASB.

4 The Pathway to Financial Reporting Harmonisation

4.1 The International Accounting Standards Committee (IASC)

The IASC, which was the predecessor body to the IASB, was founded in June 1973. It was set up as a result of an agreement by accountancy bodies in ten national jurisdictions which constituted the original board, being Australia, Canada, France, Germany, Japan, Mexico, the Netherlands, the UK, Ireland and the US.

The IASC subsequently expanded to include representatives from over 100 countries and by 2000 the membership included 143 bodies in 104 countries, representing over two million accountants.

The IASC developed and issued International Accounting Standards (IAS).

In 2001, the IASC was superseded by the IASB, which had a new structure of associated bodies and significantly increased financial resources.

The IASB issues IFRS, but has adopted all the IASC's IAS. Any reference in these chapters to IFRS should be taken as including IAS, unless there is a specific statement to the contrary.

4.2 The International Organisation of Securities Commissions (IOSCO)

In 1995, the IASC embarked on a mission to complete what had been defined as the 'comprehensive core set of standards'. This was motivated by an agreement made with IOSCO.

IOSCO is an international body of security commissions, each of which is responsible for regulating investment markets in its own country.

The agreement between the IASC and IOSCO committed the IASC to the completion of revisions to the standards that IOSCO deemed essential if it was to permit IAS-based financial reporting in the securities markets under its members' control.

In 2000, IOSCO endorsed the use of thirty selected IAS for the purposes of cross-border securities registrations and the financial statements of multinational entities.

IOSCO's membership currently stands at 181 members (including the Securities Exchange Commission (SEC) in the US) and continues to grow. The organisation's members regulate more than 90 per cent of the world's securities markets and IOSCO is today the world's most important international cooperative forum for securities regulatory agencies.

4.3 The Norwalk Agreement

A significant milestone towards achieving the goal of having one set of global standards was reached in October 2002 when the Financial Accounting Standards Board (FASB), the US standard setter, and the IASB entered into a Memorandum of Understanding – the 'Norwalk Agreement'.

This Agreement is a significant step towards the US formalising its commitment to the convergence of US and international accounting standards. In the Press Release that announced the Agreement, Robert H. Herz, chairman of the FASB commented *"The FASB is committed to working toward the goal of producing high-quality reporting standards worldwide to support healthy global capital markets"*.

The Agreement sets out a number of initiatives, including a move to eliminate minor differences between US and international standards, a decision to align the two Boards' future work programmes and a commitment to work together on joint projects. IFRS 5 *Non-current assets held for sale and discontinued operations* was issued by the IASB as a result of this Agreement and the FASB is working in partnership with the IASB on a number of projects including one on a performance statement which will report comprehensive income.

Without the convergence between US GAAP and IFRS, entities that have dual listings in Europe and the US will continue to have to prepare reconciliations between the two sets of accounting requirements.

Illustration 2 – GlaxoSmithKline

GlaxoSmithKline plc is an English public limited company that has its shares listed on the London Stock Exchange and the New York Stock Exchange (NYSE).

It prepares its financial statements in accordance with UK requirements, and is required by the NYSE to reconcile this information to the US accounting requirements.

For its year ended 31 December 2003, profits reported of £4,484million under UK GAAP fell to £2,420million under US GAAP and equity shareholders' funds (net assets less minority interests) increased from £7,720million under UK GAAP to £34,116million under US GAAP.

4.4 EU Regulation

EU Accounting Directives were issued to establish a minimum level of harmonisation within Europe for the preparation of financial statements. However, there has been a change of focus recently with the goal being international harmonisation rather than within Europe alone. As a result, the European Commission published an EU Regulation in June 2002 that requires the adoption of IFRS in member states for the preparation of the consolidated financial statements (i.e. the group financial statements) of listed entities.

The Regulation applies to financial periods beginning on or after 1 January 2005 for entities incorporated in a member state and whose securities, debt or equity, are traded on a regulated market in the EU. The significance of this requirement being issued as a Regulation is that it immediately has the force of law in member states. Its adoption is not dependant on it being incorporated into national legislation, so there is consistency in both timing and application of the requirements.

While in favour of harmonisation, the European Commission did not wish to delegate unconditionally the process of accounting standard setting to a private sector organisation over which it had little influence and no control. It therefore set up an endorsement mechanism to assess new standards and approve them for use in the EU.

The body given responsibility for endorsement is the Accounting Regulatory Committee (ARC), which is a statutory body composed of representatives of member states and chaired by a member of the Commission. Technical views are received from EFRAG (the European Financial Reporting Advisory Group), a group composed of accounting experts from the private sector, including preparers, users, members of the accounting profession and national standard setters.

In addition to its Technical Expert Group, EFRAG also has a Supervisory Board which oversees the work of the Technical Expert Group to guarantee the representation of the full European interest.

4.4.1 The Committee of European Securities Regulators (CESR)

If international standards are to be mandatory, then their application should be enforced in some way. Enforcement can take place at a number of different levels, for example through governments, securities regulators or other regulatory bodies where appropriate.

Within the EU it was felt that harmonisation of accounting standards would be improved through the harmonisation of enforcement, hence providing member states with a level playing field.

The European Commission in conjunction with the Committee of European Security Regulators (CESR) has therefore set up a common approach to enforcement. This common approach is based on a number of principles covering key areas such as the definition of enforcement, the selection techniques for the financial statements to be examined and the powers of the enforcers.

5 The Structure of the IASB

The structure of the IASB is designed to demonstrate the attributes that are necessary to establish the legitimacy of a standard-setting organisation, including the independence of its members and the adequacy of technical expertise.

5.1 The IASB

The primary role of the IASB is to issue IFRS.

There are 14 board members on the IASB, with each member having one vote. The foremost qualification for membership is technical expertise, together with relevant experience of international business. The membership selection process ensures that no particular constituency or geographical group dominates IASB decision making.

To achieve a balance of perspective and experience on the Board, its Constitution sets out that there should be a minimum of:

- five members whose background is as practising auditors;

- three members with a background in the preparation of financial statements;

- three members who are users of financial statements; and

- one member with an academic background.

5.2 The Standards Advisory Council (SAC)

SAC is a group of organisations and individuals with an interest in international financial reporting. It is a body set up to participate in the standard-setting process. There are currently 45 members, appointed by the International Accounting Standards Committee Foundation which also appoints members to the IASB. These members are drawn from different geographic locations and have a wide variety of backgrounds.

The SAC's role includes advising on priorities within the IASB's work programme and the IASB is required to consult with the SAC in advance of any board decisions on major projects that it wishes to add to its agenda.

5.3 The International Financial Reporting Interpretations Committee (IFRIC)

IFRIC is the successor to the former Standing Interpretations Committee (SIC) and is responsible for interpreting the application of international standards. IFRIC publishes interpretations of how specific issues should be accounted for under the application of IFRS where the standards do not include specific authoritative guidance and there is a risk of divergent and unacceptable accounting practices. All the SIC Interpretations issued under the supervision of the IASC have been adopted by the IASB.

IFRIC consists of 12 members who are required to operate on the basis of their own independent views and not as representatives of the organisations with which they are associated.

6 Chapter Review

This chapter has been concerned with the factors leading to the development of international harmonisation through financial reporting standards, and the institutions and structures that have developed to implement and enforce these standards.

The chapter has covered:

- the nature, concepts and purposes underlying the international harmonisation of financial reporting;

- the structure of financial reporting within the EU; and

- the regulatory and institutional structures within which the IASB operates and the major bodies within that structure.

Chapter 2
THE IFRS FRAMEWORK

1 Business Context

The way that items and transactions are treated and presented in the financial statements may affect an investor's perception of the position and performance of an entity. In addition, it may directly affect the way in which contracts based on accounting numbers are written and the size of an entity's tax liability. There is therefore a real danger that the accounting standards setting process may be politically influenced or dominated by self-interest groups.

To ensure that this threat does not become a reality, it is important that there is a framework that sets out the wider purposes that accounting standards are intended to achieve and the principles to guide the development of detailed requirements, thereby achieving consistent standards. The IASB's *Framework for the preparation and presentation of financial statements* attempts to do this in the context of IFRS. It sets out consistent principles which form the basis for the development of detailed requirements in IFRS.

2 Chapter Objectives

This chapter explains the standard setting process, and the concepts underpinning the development of IFRS. In particular, it looks at:

- the International Financial Reporting Standard setting process;

- the *Preface to International Financial Reporting Standards* (the 'Preface'); and

- the *Framework for the preparation and presentation of financial statements* (the 'Framework').

On completion of this chapter you should be able to:

- understand the purpose and role of accounting standards;

- understand the standard-setting process applied by the IASB;

- explain:

  - the purposes of financial reporting; and

  - how financial reporting can assist the management of an entity in being accountable to the entity's shareholders and other stakeholders;

- understand the qualitative characteristics of financial information set out in the *IASB Framework* and the constraints on them;

- understand the elements of financial statements set out in the *IASB Framework*; and

- be able to explain how different methods of recognising and measuring assets and liabilities affect income.

3 The Purpose of Accounting Standards

The overall purpose of accounting standards is to identify proper accounting practices for the preparation of financial statements.

Accounting standards create a common understanding between users and preparers on how particular items, for example the valuation of property, are treated. Financial statements should therefore comply with all applicable accounting standards.

4 The Role of Accounting Standards

The content of financial statements is often defined by national laws prescribing what, how, and when disclosures should be made. Such requirements, however, are often high-level with little, if any, detailed guidance on how the requirements should be implemented in practice. The role of accounting standards is therefore to translate high-level principles into reasoned procedures that an entity can apply in practice.

Accounting standards may be based either on what are commonly referred to as the 'rules-based approach' or the 'principles-based approach'.

A rules-based approach is exactly as its name suggests, detailed rules on a subject. The rules are developed to cover every possible eventuality. If an item or transaction is not covered by a detailed rule, discretion is granted as to how to account for it in the financial statements. This leads in practice to long and often convoluted standards and can encourage a process best described as 'loopholing' where preparers of financial statements attempt to find loopholes in the rules which enable them to ignore the accounting requirements. The standard setters as a result are forced to issue more rules to plug the loophole, and so on.

The US standard setting body, the Financial Accounting Standards Board (FASB) has historically issued standards using the rules-based approach.

A principles-based approach involves explaining the general principles that an accounting standard is based on and then providing practical guidance and explanation on how an entity might meet those principles.

While containing many detailed rules, IFRS are set on a principles-based approach.

Illustration 1

IAS 17 *Leases* sets out the general principle that:

"A lease is classified as a finance lease if it transfers substantially all the risks and rewards incidental to ownership."

The standard goes on to describe what the risks and rewards of ownership might be. However, by setting out the general principle first, entities are required to look at the overall substance of a lease transaction and not see whether they can structure a lease that does not fit into one of the specified criteria.

In comparison, the US standard on leasing, Statement of Financial Accounting Standards (SFAS) No. 13 *Accounting for leases* uses the rules-based approach. It sets out that a lease should be classified as a finance lease (US terminology for a finance lease is a 'capital lease') if it meets any one of a list of four criteria. If the lease does not meet one of the specified four criteria, then it should be classified as an operating lease.

Thus whilst a rules-based approach may seem tougher, it could be argued that a principles-based approach leads to more compliance with the overall intention of the standards setters when they wrote the standard.

5 International and National Accounting Standards

An entity is normally required to comply with the accounting requirements for the country in which it is registered. However, many entities are large multi-national groups and they may list their shares on a number of stock exchanges around the world. Where accounting requirements are different in each country in which an entity is listed, the entity may be required to prepare its financial statements on a number of different bases.

In practice, an entity will generally prepare its financial statements using the requirements for the country in which it is registered, but include a list of differences that arise as a result of applying a different set of national standards. For example, BP plc and Vodafone Group plc prepare their financial statements in accordance with UK accounting policies but within their financial statements they provide a full reconciliation of the adjustments that are required under US generally accepted accounting pratices (US GAAP).

There has been increased pressure in recent years for the adoption of a single set of global accounting standards. Indeed the use of IFRS is already widespread, and with countries in the European Union also being required to adopt IFRS from 2005, the number of different sets of accounting standards being used is reducing. The US continues to operate its own accounting standards although the FASB and the IASB have entered a 'memorandum of understanding' (The Norwalk Agreement) stating that they will work together on projects in order to try to converge their accounting standards in the future.

6 Setting International Financial Reporting Standards

6.1 The IASCF

The International Accounting Standards Committee Foundation (IASCF) was formed in March 2001 as a not-for-profit corporation and is the parent entity of the IASB. The IASCF is an independent organisation and its trustees exercise oversight and raise necessary funding for the IASB to carry out its role as standard setter.

6.2 Membership

Membership of the IASCF has been designed so that it represents an international group of preparers and users, who become IASCF Trustees. The selection process for the 19 trustees takes into account geographical factors and professional background. The IASCF trustees appoint the IASB members.

6.3 The standard-setting process

The IASB process for developing new standards is set out in the *Preface* and generally involves the following stages (those marked in *italics* are always required):

- staff review the issues associated with the topic, including the application of the *IASB Framework* and carry out a study of national requirements and practices in relation to an issue;

- exchange views with national standards setters (to establish how acceptable the standard would be in national jurisdictions);

- *consultation with the Standards Advisory Council (SAC) on whether the issue should be added to the IASB's agenda. The SAC is made up of organisations and individuals with an interest in international financial reporting;*

- the formation of an advisory group with specialist interest and knowledge in the topic;

- issue of a discussion paper for public comment;

- *the publication of an exposure draft, together with any dissenting opinions held by IASB members and a basis of conclusions. Its content should be approved by at least eight of the fourteen IASB members;*

- *consideration of all comments received on an exposure draft during the comment period;*

- public hearings about, and field tests of, the exposure draft;

- *issue of a standard together with any dissenting opinions held by IASB members. Its content is required to be approved by at least eight of the fourteen members; and*

- the publication of the standard should include a basis of conclusions and a description of the due process undertaken.

Written contributions are welcomed at all stages in this process. The IASB has a public gallery at its monthly meetings (and observers can log-on to a live web cast of the meetings) which allows interested parties to attend as observers.

The predecessor body to the IASB, the International Accounting Standards Committee (IASC) issued IAS numbers 1 – 41 (although there are gaps in the sequence with some standards being subsequently superseded or withdrawn). The IASB adopted all previously issued standards. Standards issued by the new IASB can be identified as they are prefixed with IFRS rather than IAS.

6.4 Preface to International Financial Reporting Standards

The *Preface* sets out the objectives and due process of the IASB. It also explains the scope, authority and timing of the application of IFRS. These issues have been discussed above and in Chapter 1.

The *Preface* highlights a number of other important matters:

■ that IFRS apply to all general purpose financial statements of all profit-oriented entities and are directed to the common information needs of a wide range of users; [*Preface* 9, 10]

■ the IASB's objective is to require like transactions and events to be accounted for in a like way. It recognises that the IASC permitted different treatments for given transactions and events ('benchmark treatment' and 'allowed alternative treatment') and has the objective to reduce choice; [*Preface* 12, 13] and

■ standards include paragraphs in bold and plain type. Bold type paragraphs indicate the main principles. However, both types have equal authority [*Preface* 14].

7 The Context for Financial Reporting

This section examines the context for financial reporting, including its purpose, the needs of users of financial statements and how these are met, and the key principles underlying financial statements. The main areas addressed are outlined in the following diagram:

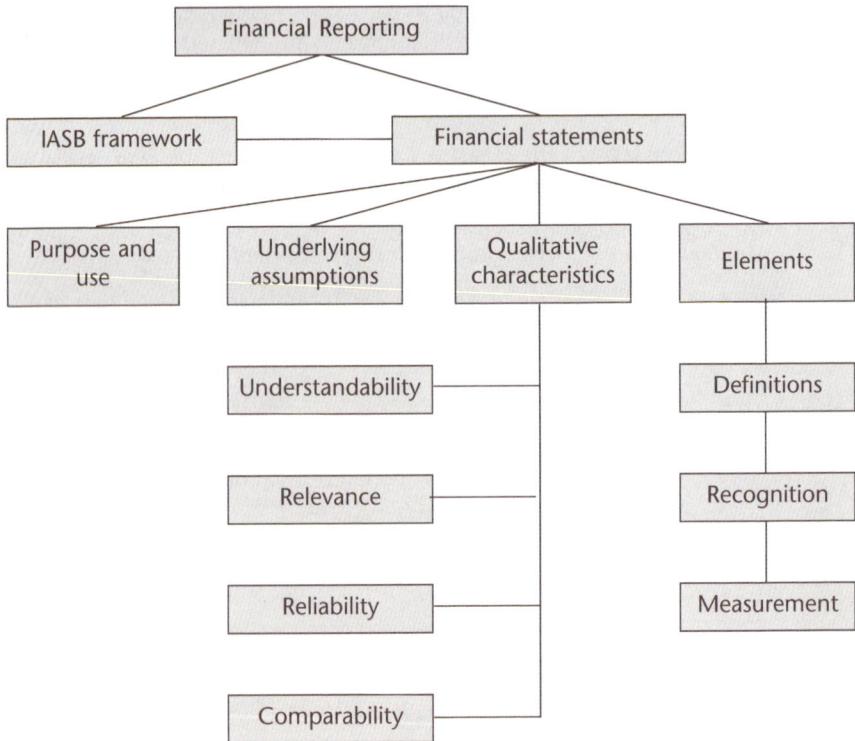

8 What is Financial Reporting?

8.1 Definition

'Financial reporting' is the provision of financial information about an entity to external users that is useful to them in making economic decisions, and for assessing the effectiveness of the entity's management. Typically, this information is made available annually, half-yearly or quarterly and is presented in formats laid down or approved by the governments and other regulators in each national jurisdiction.

8.2 Financial statements

The principal way of providing financial information to external users is through the annual financial statements. Financial statements are the summary of the performance of an entity over a particular period and its financial position at the end of that period. Financial statements are designed to meet the common needs of a wide range of users and therefore are not tailored to the needs of any particular user group.

Financial statements comprise four primary statements and the accompanying notes to these statements, as set out in IAS 1 *Presentation of financial statements*.

9 The Framework for the Preparation and Presentation of Financial Statements

The *IASB Framework* sets out the concepts that underlie the preparation and presentation of financial statements. Such concepts are the foundation on which financial statements are constructed and provide a platform from which standards are developed.

The *IASB Framework* is important because it [*Framework* 1]:

- assists the IASB in the development of new standards and the revision of existing standards;

- provides a rationale for reducing the number of alternative accounting treatments;

- assists national standard setters in developing their national standards on a consistent basis with international principles; and

- assists preparers of financial statements in applying IFRS and general principles, assists auditors in forming their opinions on the financial statements and assists users in their interpretation of financial statements.

The *IASB Framework* is not an accounting standard and it does not contain detailed requirements on how financial statements should be prepared or presented. Specific references to the *IASB Framework* can be found, however, in individual accounting standards dealt with in later chapters.

9.1 Users and their information needs

9.1.1 Economic decisions

The content and presentation of financial statements are influenced by the use to which the financial statements are to be put, for example:

- an investor deciding when to buy, hold, or sell shares;

- employees assessing an entity's ability to provide benefits to them;

- investors assessing an entity's ability to pay dividends and therefore the likely return that they will achieve on their investment; and

- debt providers assessing the level of security for amounts lent to the entity.

9.1.2 Users and specific needs

The *IASB Framework* identifies users of financial statements and their specific information needs as set out in the illustration below. [*Framework 9*]

Illustration 2

Users of financial information and why the information is of interest to them:

1. *Investors*

Investors require information on risk and return on investment and hence an entity's ability to pay dividends.

2. *Employees*

Employees assess an entity's stability and profitability. They are interested in their employer's ability to provide remuneration, employment opportunities and retirement and other benefits.

3. *Lenders*

Lenders assess whether an entity is able to repay loans and its ability to pay the related interest when it falls due.

4. *Suppliers and other trade payables*

Suppliers assess the likelihood of an entity being able to pay them as amounts fall due.

5. *Customers*

Customers assess whether an entity will continue in existence. This is especially important where customers have a long-term involvement with, or are dependent on, an entity, for example where product warranties exist or where specialist parts may be needed.

6. *Governments and their agencies*

Government bodies assess the general allocation of resources and therefore activities of entities. In addition information is needed to determine future taxation policy and to provide national statistics.

7. *The public*

The financial statements provide the public with information on trends and recent developments. This may be of particular importance where an entity makes a substantial contribution to a local economy by providing employment and using local suppliers.

9.2 Accountability of management

Management is accountable for the safekeeping of the entity's resources and for their proper, efficient and profitable use. Shareholders are interested in information that helps them to assess how effectively management has fulfilled this role, as this is relevant to the decisions concerning their investment and the reappointment or replacement of management.

Financial reporting helps management to meet its need to be accountable to shareholders and also to other stakeholders such as employees or lenders, by providing information that is useful to the users in making economic decisions.

9.3 Financial position, performance and changes in financial position

All economic decisions should be based on an evaluation of an entity's ability to generate cash and the timing and certainty of its generation. Information about the entity's financial position, performance and changes in its financial position provides information to support such decisions. [*Framework* 9]

Information about an entity's financial position is provided in a balance sheet.

Profit is used as the measure of financial performance. Information on an entity's financial performance is provided primarily by the income statement but also to a certain extent by the statement of changes in equity.

Cash flow information provides an assessment of changes in an entity's financial position and is largely free from the more judgemental issues that arise when items are included in the balance sheet or performance statements.

9.4 Underlying assumptions

There are two fundamentally important assumptions on which financial statements are based, being the accrual basis of accounting and the going concern basis. Both of these are discussed in IAS 1. However, the fundamental principle of the accrual basis of accounting is that transactions are recorded in the financial statements when they occur, not when the related cash flows into or out of the entity occur. [*Framework* 22]

Under the going concern basis, financial statements are prepared on the assumption that an entity will continue in operation for the foreseeable future. This basis is important, for example, in the assessment of the recoverability of a non-current asset, which is expected to generate benefits in the ongoing business even if its resale value is minimal. [*Framework* 23]

9.5 Qualitative characteristics of financial statements

In deciding which information to include in financial statements, when to include it and how to present it, the aim is to ensure that the information is useful to users of the financial statements in making economic decisions. The attributes that make information useful are known as qualitative characteristics and are described in terms of understandability, relevance, reliability and comparability in the context of the preparation of financial statements. [*Framework* 24]

9.5.1 Understandability

Information in financial statements should be understandable by users. This will, in part, depend on the way in which information is presented.

Financial statements cannot realistically be understandable to everyone and therefore it is assumed that users have:

- a reasonable knowledge of business and accounting; and

- a willingness to study with reasonable diligence the information provided.

9.5.2 Relevance

Information is relevant if it has the ability to influence the economic decisions of users and is provided in time to influence those decisions. Relevance has two characteristics: a predictive value and a confirmatory value. Users can make a reasoned evaluation of how management might react to certain future events, whilst information about past events will help them to confirm or adjust their previous assessments.

Information about an entity's financial position and past performance is often used as the basis for making predictions about its future performance. It is therefore important how information is presented. For example, unusual and infrequent items of income and expense should be disclosed separately.

9.5.3 Reliability

Information may be relevant, but unless it is reliable as well it is of little use. Information is considered to be reliable if it does not contain substantial errors that would affect the economic decisions of users and represents faithfully the entity's transactions.

Faithful representation requires that transactions are accounted for, and presented in accordance with, their substance and economic reality, even where this is different from their legal form.

Management should present information which is neutral, i.e free from bias.

To be reliable, information should also be complete.

9.5.4 Comparability

For financial information to be useful, it is important that it can be compared with similar information of previous periods or to that produced by another entity. For information to be comparable, it should be consistently prepared; this can be achieved by an entity adopting the same accounting policies from one period to the next as explained in IAS 8 *Accounting policies, changes in accounting estimates and errors*.

9.6 Elements of financial statements

The elements included in the financial statements are the building blocks from which financial statements are constructed. These elements are broad classes of events or transactions that are grouped according to their economic characteristics. [*Framework* 47]

9.6.1. Definitions of elements

Examples of elements of financial statements:

Elements	Definition	Comment	Examples
Asset	A resource controlled by an entity "as a result of past events and from which future economic benefits are expected to flow" to the entity	An asset may be utilised in a business in a number of ways, but all will lead to the generation of future economic benefits (i.e. a contribution to cash flowing to the entity).	Cash, inventories, receivables, prepayments, plant, property and equipment.
Liability	A present obligation of the entity "arising from past events, the settlement of which is expected to result in an outflow" of an entity's resources	A liability exists where an entity has a present obligation. An obligation is simply a duty or responsibility to perform in a certain way. It is important to make a clear distinction between a present obligation and a future commitment.	Trade payables, unpaid taxes and outstanding loans.
Equity	The residual interest in an entity's assets after deducting all its liabilities	Equity = ownership interest = net assets (i.e. share capital and reserves)	Share capital, retained earnings, revaluation reserve and other reserves.
Income	Increases in economic benefits not resulting from contributions made by equity holders	Income comprises both revenue and gains. Revenue arises from an entity's normal operating activities. Gains are increases in economic benefits as is revenue and therefore are not separately identified within the *IASB Framework*.	Revenue, revaluations, profit on the sale of a non-current asset and interest received on investments.
Expenses	Decreases in economic benefits not resulting from distributions to equity holders	Expenses include losses, for example write-downs of non-current assets.	Material and labour costs, depreciation, interest paid on loans and a write-down of an asset.

9.6.2 Recognition of elements in financial statements

An item is classed as 'recognised' when it is included in the financial statements. [*Framework* 82]

An item should be recognised if it is probable that there will be an inflow or outflow of economic benefits associated with the asset or liability and the asset or liability can be measured reliably. [*Framework* 83]

The assessment of the outcome of an event as being probable is linked with the uncertainty of the business environment in which an entity operates. There is no precise point that can be identified at which an event is assessed as being probable. An entity is instead required to make an assessment based on the facts at the time of the preparation of the financial statements.

An item to be recognised in the financial statements needs to be capable of reliable measurement; however, this does not mean that the amount must be certain as the use of estimates is permitted.

Revenue should be earned before it is recognised in the income statement. Revenue is earned as increases in assets and decreases in liabilities are recognised from an entity's activities.

Expenses are recognised when there is a decrease in an asset or an increase in a liability.

Matching is a useful concept that encourages the review of all the aspects of a transaction, as it considers whether an asset arises when a liability is recognised and vice versa. It is a concept that matches expenses with income.

9.6.3 Measurement in financial statements

For an item or transaction to be recognised in an entity's financial statements it needs to be measured at a monetary amount. There are several different measurement bases which can be used to recognise items in the financial statements.

The measurement bases referred to in the *IASB Framework* and commonly used in IFRS are: [*Framework* 99]

- *historical cost.* Assets are recorded at their original cost. Liabilities are recorded at their original amount received or the cash expected to be paid out to settle them;

- *current cost.* Assets are recorded at the amount that would have to be paid out at the balance sheet date for an equivalent asset. Liabilities are recorded at the value that they could be settled for at the balance sheet date;

- *realisable or settlement value.* Assets are recorded at the amount that they could be sold for now and similarly liabilities are recorded at the amount expected to be paid out; and

- *present value.* This measurement basis involves discounting future cash flows to take account of the time value of money.

Although the *IASB Framework* includes an explanation of the different measurement options, IFRS are primarily based on historical cost.

10 Chapter Review

This chapter has been concerned with the process by which IFRS are set, thus providing useful background information for understanding the purpose and role of accounting standards.

The *IASB Framework* is an essential element to understanding the chapters in this manual. It deals with the purposes and role of financial reporting.

In summary, this chapter has covered:

- the International Financial Reporting Standard setting process;

- the content of the *Preface* to *international financial reporting standards;* and

- the content of the *IASB Framework for the preparation and presentation of financial statements* in particular looking at:

  - the information needs of different users of financial statements;

  - the qualitative characteristics of financial information;

  - the elements of financial statements; and

  - recognition criteria of the elements in financial statements.

Chapter 3
PRESENTATION OF FINANCIAL STATEMENTS

1 Business Context

To ensure that financial statements are prepared to an adequate level it is important that entities are provided with a basic framework for the preparation of their financial statements. Financial statements should provide users with relevant information. To meet this requirement a number of key statements have been identified which allow users to assess the financial performance, the financial position and the liquidity of an entity. The broad structure of financial statements is standardised so that this information is presented in a similar manner by all entities, allowing meaningful comparisons to be made across different entities.

Although a basic framework has been identified in IAS 1 *Presentation of financial statements* entities also have the flexibility to adapt formats and headings to present their information in a way that aids understanding.

2 Chapter Objectives

This chapter deals with:

- the purpose of financial statements;

- the various components that make up a set of financial statements;

- the overall considerations when preparing financial statements; and

- the structure and content of the financial statements.

On completion of this chapter you should be able to:

- identify the components of a set of financial statements and the items which appear in each component;

- demonstrate an understanding of the key concepts of fair presentation, going concern, accrual, consistency, materiality, aggregation and offsetting; and

- demonstrate a knowledge of which items should be presented on the face of the key statements.

3 Objectives, Scope and Definitions of IAS 1

The purpose of financial statements is to provide information about financial position, financial performance and cash flows.

The objective of IAS 1 is to set out the basis for the presentation of financial statements and to ensure comparability with previous periods and with other entities. The standard identifies a minimum content of what should be included in a set of financial statements as well as guidelines as to their structure, although rigid formats are not prescribed. Examples of the key statements are presented in an appendix to IAS 1, but are clearly identified as being for illustrative purposes only.

IAS 1 applies to all general purpose financial statements prepared and presented in accordance with international standards. [IAS 1.2]

"General purpose" financial statements are statements that have been prepared for general usage; they do not include specifically tailored reports that have been prepared to meet the needs of an identified audience. General purpose financial statements do not have to be presented as a standalone document and can instead form part of a wider report, such as the annual report or a prospectus.

IAS 1 requires that the financial statements should be presented at least annually. If, for example, the entity changes its year end and therefore reports a shorter or longer period, the entity should explain why such a change has been made. Where a shorter or longer period is reported, comparative information will not be entirely comparable and it is important that this is clearly highlighted.

4 The Components of Financial Statements

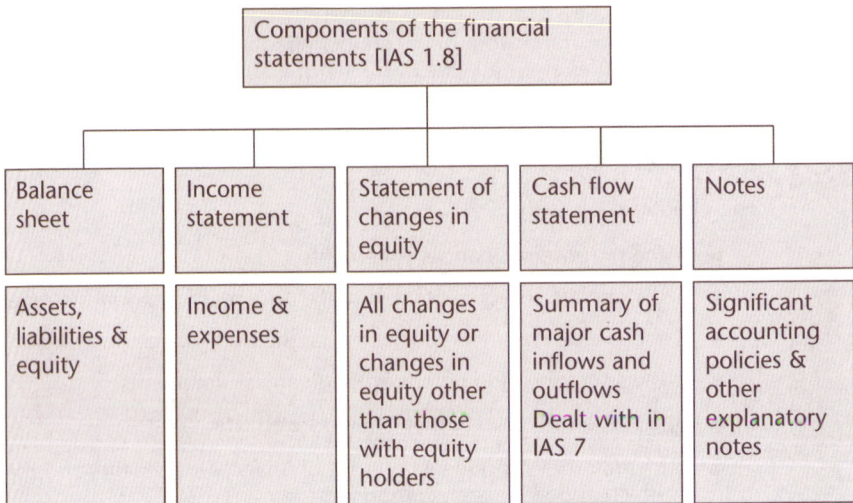

Components of the financial statements [IAS 1.8]				
Balance sheet	Income statement	Statement of changes in equity	Cash flow statement	Notes
Assets, liabilities & equity	Income & expenses	All changes in equity or changes in equity other than those with equity holders	Summary of major cash inflows and outflows Dealt with in IAS 7	Significant accounting policies & other explanatory notes

As well as setting out the main components that make up a set of financial statements, as shown above, IAS 1 also highlights items that have been identified as being of significant importance and therefore should be disclosed on the face of a particular statement, for example the balance sheet.

Although the financial statements may be included as part of a wider document, IAS 1 requires that they should be clearly identified and distinguished from other information presented, to ensure that there is no confusion over what is within their scope. Additional information is identified in IAS 1 as being important to ensure the correct interpretation of information presented. Such information includes, for example, the name of the reporting entity, whether the financial statements are for an individual entity or a group, the period which the financial statements cover, the currency used to present the financial statements and the level of rounding used, for example, thousands or millions.

4.1 The balance sheet

Although no prescribed format for the balance sheet is required by IAS 1, it does set out the minimum information which is required to be presented on the face of the statement, as set out below: [IAS 1.68]

- property, plant and equipment;
- investment property;
- intangible assets;
- financial assets not disclosed in other headings below;
- investments accounted for using the equity method;
- biological assets;
- inventories;
- assets/disposal groups classified as held for sale;
- trade and other receivables;
- cash and cash equivalents;
- liabilities included in disposal groups classified as held for sale;
- trade and other payables;
- provisions;
- financial liabilities not disclosed in other headings above;
- liabilities and assets for current tax;
- deferred tax liabilities and assets;
- minority interest, presented within equity; and
- issued capital and reserves attributable to equity holders of the parent.

The above information is considered to be sufficiently different in nature or function to warrant separate presentation. The descriptions used and the ordering of items may be amended if by doing so the new presentation provides more relevant information to the users of the financial statements. Additional line items, headings and subtotals should be added where relevant to the understanding of the financial statements. Generally an entity will separate current and non-current assets and liabilities (see below for information on these categorisations) on the face of the balance sheet. Where this presentation is followed, IAS 1 specifically states that deferred tax balances should be reported as non-current items. [IAS 1.69, 1.70]

Further sub-classifications of headings should be presented either on the face of the balance sheet or within the notes and are generally necessary to meet the requirements of other standards. For example, IAS 16 *Property, plant and equipment* requires information to be disaggregated into classes of assets, for example freehold buildings, plant and machinery and office equipment.

IAS 1 also requires that specific information is presented in relation to the share capital of the entity. These disclosures include identifying: [IAS 1.76]

- the number of shares authorised;

- the number of shares issued and fully paid, and issued but not fully paid; and

- the par (nominal) value per share, or that the shares have no par value.

In addition, a full reconciliation of the movement during the year in the number of shares outstanding is required, specifying any rights, preferences and restrictions attaching to the shares. Disclosure should also be made of any shares in the entity, held by the entity or by its subsidiaries or associates and any shares reserved for issue under options and contracts for the sale of shares.

Where an entity does not have share capital, equivalent information should be disclosed.

4.2 The income statement

IAS 1 states that, as a minimum, the following information is required to be presented on the face of the income statement: [IAS 1.81, 1.82]

- revenue;

- finance costs;

- share of the profit or loss of associates and joint ventures accounted for using the equity method;

- tax expense;

- an aggregate figure for the profit or loss of discontinued operations and the gain or loss in relation to the remeasurement, or disposal, of discontinued operations;

- profit or loss for the period;

- the profit or loss attributable to minority equity holders; and

- the profit or loss attributable to equity holders of the parent.

In addition, information should be disclosed either on the face of the income statement or statement of changes in equity or in the notes, in respect of the amount of dividends recognised in the period and the related earnings per share. [IAS 1.83]

As explained above, for the balance sheet presentation, additional line items, headings, sub-classifications and subtotals should be added where relevant to the understanding of the financial statements. If an item of income or expenditure is important to the fundamental understanding of the performance of the entity during the period this item should be disclosed separately. Examples of such items include a significant write down (a loss in value) of property, disposals of investments or where the entity has discontinued some of its operations during the period.

A choice of formats for the income statement is offered in IAS 1. The format should be based either on the nature of expenses, highlighting the main types of expenditure incurred, for example staff costs and raw materials or on the function of expenses. The latter format allocates expenses under headings such as cost of sales or administration; this format generally requires considerable judgement to ensure that allocations of the expenditure are appropriate. [IAS 1.88]

An illustrative income statement is set out in the Guidance accompanying the standard.

4.3 Current/non current distinction

IAS 1 requires that both assets and liabilities should be classified separately as current and non-current. For most businesses it will be appropriate to identify this classification with reference to their operating cycle. This separate classification identifies how an item will be utilised within a business. For example, a motor dealer sells motor vehicles whereas another business may hold such assets for use by the directors over a number of years. [IAS 1.51]

The operating cycle of a business is the period between the commencement of work on behalf of a customer and the receipt of the final payment against outstanding invoices. For a manufacturing entity the operating cycle begins with the purchase of raw materials, spans the work in progress, finished goods and delivery stages and finishes when the payment is received. For some businesses this may be a relatively short period while in others it may not be possible to identify clearly when the cycle starts and finishes; in these circumstances it is taken to be twelve months. That is not to say that an operating cycle cannot be more than twelve months in length; for contractors working on large construction projects, such as Terminal 5 at London's Heathrow Airport, the operating cycle may be much longer.

IAS 1 specifically sets out four criteria which identify when an asset should be disclosed as current. Items falling outside of these criteria should be classified as non-current. The criteria are that the item is expected to be used or sold within the entity's normal operating cycle, it is held primarily for trading rather than long-term usage within the business, it is cash or a cash receivable (or something that is readily convertible into cash within twelve months of the balance sheet date) or it is expected to be realised, for example sold for cash, within twelve months of the balance sheet date. So the motor vehicles held by the motor dealer should be classed as current assets whereas the vehicles used by the directors should be classed as non-current assets. [IAS 1.57]

There are very similar criteria for identifying a current liability, for example, the item is used for trading purposes, expected to be settled within the normal operating cycle, due to be settled within twelve months of the balance sheet date and there are no unconditional rights to defer payment beyond twelve months of the balance sheet date.

Illustration 1

An entity supplies seasoned timber to furniture manufacturers. The operating cycle is clearly defined and timber is matured over a three to five year period.

The cost of the timber inventories would be classified as a current asset as they are realised within the normal operating cycle. The entity should disclose the amount of inventories to be realised more than twelve months after the balance sheet date, to assist users in assessing its liquidity and solvency.

4.4 The statement of changes in equity

A statement of changes in equity is required to be presented as part of the financial statements. Changes in equity reflect the increase or decrease in net assets during the period (except for transactions that have taken place directly with the shareholders). Such a statement should include: [IAS 1.96]

- the profit or loss for the period;
- each item that has been reported directly in equity rather than in the income statement;
- the total income or expense for the period, being the sum of the first two items listed above, with any allocation to the minority shareholders clearly separated; and
- where there has been a change in accounting policy, or the correction of an error, during the period the effect of these changes.

In addition, IAS 1 requires that a full reconciliation of each reserve, including retained earnings, is presented and the amount of any transaction that has taken place with the shareholders should be separately identified, specifically separating out distributions (e.g. dividend payments) made. [IAS 1.97]

An illustrative statement of changes in equity is included in the Guidance accompanying the standard.

4.5 The cash flow statement

Cash flow information provides users of the financial statements with information to assess an entity's ability to generate cash and how it utilises the cash in its operations. Reqirements for the preparation of a cash flow statement are set out in IAS 7 *Cash flow statements*.

4.6 Notes to the financial statements

The notes to the financial statements provide additional relevant information to ensure that users fully understand the financial statements of an entity. Notes can be in a number of forms, for example, narrative disclosures, disaggregation of information presented on the face of the component statements or additional information which has not been recognised in the balance sheet but is relevant to the understanding of the financial statements. [IAS 1.103]

The notes to the financial statements should present information about the basis of preparation of the financial statements and set out the specific accounting policies followed and judgements made by management in applying them. In addition, information should be provided on the key assumptions concerning the future and the uncertainty of estimates that have been made, which may lead to significant adjustments having to be made in the future. In such circumstances information should be provided on the nature of these items and their carrying amount at the balance sheet date. The notes should be presented in a systematic order, for example following the order in which items are presented in the component statements and there should be full cross referencing between the main component statements and the notes.

Specific information should be included in the notes to the financial statements about the overall entity, for example the country of incorporation, domicile, the legal form of the entity and its registered address. A description of the nature of the entity's operations and its principal activities along with the name of its parent, and where appropriate, the ultimate parent of the group should be provided. Information should also be provided on dividends that were proposed or declared before the financial statements were authorised for issue but have not been recognised as a distribution in the period, with disclosure of the related amount per share and the amount of any cumulative preference dividend not recognised. [IAS 1.125, 1.126]

5. Overall Considerations

Much of the material covered in the rest of this chapter on IAS 1 details the specific application within financial statements of the general principles dealt with in the *IASB Framework*.

5.1 Fair presentation and compliance with IFRS

IAS 1 requires that the financial statements should present fairly the financial position, performance and cash flows of the entity.

Fair presentation is defined as representing faithfully the effects of transactions, other events, and conditions in accordance with the definitions and recognition criteria in the *IASB Framework*. Under IAS 1 application of international standards along with any relevant interpretations and disclosures is presumed to result in a fair presentation. [IAS 1.13]

If a set of financial statements complies with International Financial Reporting Standards (IFRS), then those financial statements should include an explicit and unreserved statement to that effect. Such disclosure can only be made when the financial statements comply with all IFRS requirements; management is not permitted to cherry pick requirements. [IAS 1.14]

IAS 1 sets out procedures to be followed when management concludes that compliance with an IFRS would be so misleading as to conflict with the objectives of the financial statements as set out in the *IASB Framework*. It is thought that in practice such circumstances are likely to be extremely rare. If, however, such circumstances did exist, then management should depart from the particular requirement, provided that to do so would not be inconsistent with the regulatory framework in which the entity operates. If there has been a departure from an international standard, then this should be fully explained, setting out the circumstances that led to the departure, quantifying the effect on all periods reported and stating specifically what the departure is. [IAS 1.17-19]

5.2 Offsetting

Assets and liabilities should not be offset against each other unless this is specifically required or permitted by a standard. This is because the offsetting or netting of items is assumed to make it more difficult for the users of financial statements to understand past transactions and assess future cash flows.

5.3 Other considerations

In order for financial statements to be comparable certain overall considerations need to be followed in the preparation of the financial statements, as set out below.

5.3.1. Going concern

When preparing a set of financial statements management should assume, unless there are specific reasons to believe otherwise, that the business will continue to operate for the foreseeable future. This is known as the going concern concept. This is particularly relevant when management make estimates about the expected outcome of events, such as the recoverability of trade receivables and the useful lives of non-current assets. [IAS 1.23]

5.3.2 Accrual concept

Financial statements should be prepared by applying the accrual concept. In its simplest form the accrual concept means that assets are recognised when they are receivable rather than when physically received, and liabilities are recognised when they are payable rather than when actually paid. This is not relevant for the preparation of the cash flow statement which is based purely on cash flows. [IAS 1.25]

5.3.3 Consistency of presentation

To aid comparability of financial statements year on year and across different entities it is important that a consistent presentation and classification of items is followed. The presentation should only be changed where a new or revised standard requires such a change or where there has been a significant change in the nature of the entity's operations and a new presentation would therefore be more appropriate. [IAS 1.27]

5.3.4 Materiality and aggregation

IAS 1 requires that items that are of importance to the users of the financial statements in making economic decisions should be separately identified within the financial statements. Such items are defined as being "material". In assessing whether items are considered to be material, the entity should consider both the nature and size of the item. For example, the purchase of large tangible assets may be common for a particular entity, and therefore it would generally be appropriate to aggregate such items together as the purchase of plant. However, a fairly small transaction with a director may be considered as important information for users of the financial statements. [IAS 1.11, 1.29]

5.3.5 Comparative information

Comparative information for the previous period should be disclosed for all amounts reported in the financial statements unless a particular standard does not require such information. This includes the requirement to show comparative information in narrative disclosures where it is relevant to the full understanding of the explanation. [IAS 1.36]

6 Chapter Review

This chapter has been concerned with the presentation of financial statements and has covered:

- IAS 1's objective, scope, definitions and disclosure requirements;

- the components of the financial statements;

- the notes to the financial statements; and

- the overall considerations that need to be addressed in preparing a set of financial statements.

Chapter 4
ACCOUNTING POLICIES

1 Business Context

The ability to compare financial statements year on year for an individual entity and between different entities is a fundamental process for investors and businesses alike. Effective comparisons allow an entity to benchmark itself within a particular sector. Useful comparisons could not be undertaken if financial statements were prepared on different bases.

It is also imperative that companies are restricted in their ability to select different ways of treating the same information period on period. Such an ability would allow entities to choose the most beneficial outcome in that period.

IAS 8 *Accounting policies, changes in accounting estimates and errors* provides the guidelines under which accounting policies can be changed and therefore represents the structure that underpins the successful comparison of financial statements.

2 Chapter Objectives

This chapter reviews IAS 8 which is primarily concerned with the income statement.

On completion of this chapter you should be able to:

- understand the objectives and scope of IAS 8;

- interpret the important terminology and definitions which relate to the treatment of accounting policies, estimates and errors in financial statements;

- understand the key principles relating to the recognition and measurement of retrospective and prospective adjustments;

- demonstrate knowledge of the principal disclosure requirements of IAS 8; and

- apply knowledge and understanding of IAS 8, in particular circumstances, through basic calculations.

3 Objectives, Scope and Definitions of IAS 8

The objective of IAS 8 is to enhance the relevance, reliability and comparability of financial statements and it should be applied by an entity to select and apply its accounting policies. In addition, IAS 8 should be applied where an entity changes its accounting policies or estimates, and for the correction of errors arising in prior periods.

The *IASB Framework* identifies comparability as one of the key qualitative characteristics of financial information. Comparability allows both the identification of trends over time in relation to a single entity and the evaluation of comparative performance across different entities.

To facilitate comparability, it is important that:

- different entities take account of the same types of income and expenditure in arriving at the profit or loss for the period;

- information is available about the accounting policies adopted by different entities;

- different entities treat changes in accounting policies or estimates and the accounting for errors in the same way; and

- the scope for accounting policy changes is constrained.

Accounting policies are defined by IAS 8 as the specific principles, bases, conventions, requirements and practices used by an entity in preparing and presenting its financial statements. In summary, accounting policies explain the way that an entity treats items within its financial statements.

Accounting standards set out the required recognition and measurement principles that an entity should follow in preparing its financial statements and will often prescribe the accounting policy to be adopted. However, in the absence of a standard which specifically applies, management will be required to use its judgement in developing the most appropriate accounting policies. It is important that such policies should be based on the *IASB Framework* to ensure wider comparability of the financial information published. Such policies should reflect the economic substance of transactions and provide relevant information so that users of the financial statements are able to make informed investment decisions. [IAS 8.5, 8.10, 8.11, 8.12]

IAS 8 requires that accounting policies are applied consistently to similar transactions. [IAS 8.13]

4 Changes in Accounting Policies

An existing accounting policy should only be changed where a new accounting standard requires such a change or where the new policy will result in more relevant and reliable information being presented. [IAS 8.14]

It is important to note how restricted the powers of management are in relation to accounting policies. Accounting policies should be based on the recognition and measurement requirements laid down in international standards. Some standards provide choices which provide management with more flexibility.

A change of an existing accounting policy to another policy of equal relevance is not permitted on the grounds that, in these circumstances, comparability should take precedence.

IAS 8 requires changes in accounting policies to be accounted for retrospectively except where it is not practicable to determine the effect in prior periods. [IAS 8.22]

Retrospective application is where the financial statements of the current period and each prior period presented are adjusted so that it appears as if the new policy had always been followed. This is achieved by restating the profits in each period presented and adjusting the opening position by restating retained earnings (i.e. cumulative profits held in the balance sheet as part of equity). [IAS 8.5]

Where it is not practicable to determine either the specific effect in a particular period or the cumulative effect of applying a new policy to past periods, the new policy should be applied from the earliest date that it is practicable to do so. [IAS 8.24]

The reasons for and effects of a change in accounting policy should be disclosed. [IAS 8.28, 8.29]

Where a new standard has been issued but an entity is not yet required to implement it and the entity has not implemented it early, it should disclose this fact. The information provided should quantify the effect on future periods if this can be reasonably estimated. This provides useful information to users of the financial statements about an entity's future reported performance. [IAS 8.30]

Illustration 1

Multi Ltd commenced trading two years ago, on 1 January 2002. Its draft balance sheet at 31 December 2003, and its final balance sheet for the previous year are as follows:

	2003 CUm	2002 CUm
Property, plant and equipment	301	250
Other assets	899	900
	1,200	1,150
Share capital	100	100
Retained earnings		
year ended 2002	50	50
year ended 2003	50	
Liabilities	1,000	1,000
	1,200	1,150

Additional information is available as follows:

Property, plant and equipment include interest of CU10 million capitalised, in accordance with IAS 23 *Borrowing Costs* in 2002, and CU10 million in 2003. Due to changes in the way the entity obtains its funding the directors now believe that it would be more appropriate not to capitalise interest. The decision has therefore been made to change the accounting policy and to recognise all interest costs in profit or loss in the year in which they were incurred.

Property, plant and equipment are depreciated on a straight-line basis over their useful life of ten years. They have no residual value.

This change in accounting policy should be applied retrospectively as follows (the tax implications as a consequence of this change have been ignored for the purposes of this illustration):

	2003 CUm	Restated 2002 CUm
Property, plant and equipment (301-9-8) / (250-9) W1	284	241
Other assets	899	900
	1,183	1,141
Share capital	100	100
Retained earnings		
year ended 2002 (50-9) W1	41	41
year ended 2003 (50-8) W1	42	
Liabilities	1,000	1,000
	1,183	1,141

Workings

W1 Adjustment re capitalised borrowing costs

	2003 CUm	2002 CUm
Amount capitalised in the year	10	10
Depreciation: 2002 10% x 10		(1)
Depreciation: 2003 10% x (10 + 10)	(2)	
Profit adjustment / assets write-down	8	9

5 Changes in Accounting Estimates

The preparation of financial statements requires many estimates to be made on the basis of the latest available, reliable information. Key areas in which estimates are made include, for example, the recoverability of amounts owed by customers, the obsolescence of inventories and the useful lives of non-current assets.

As more up-to-date information becomes available estimates should be revisited to reflect this new information. These are changes in estimates and are not changes in accounting policies or the correction of errors. [IAS 8.5]

Illustration 2

An entity is considering the recoverability of its receivables, consistent with its accounting policy to recognise assets at no more than their recoverable amount.

It decides that, as the economy is entering a period of recession, it should raise its provision from 2% of the total to 3%.

This is not a change in accounting policy. What has changed is the level of the receivables that are recoverable. This is a change in estimate.

By its very nature the revision of an estimate to take account of more up to date information does not relate to prior periods. Instead such a revision is based on the latest information available and therefore should be recognised in the period in which that change arises. The effect of a change in an accounting estimate should therefore be recognised prospectively, i.e. by recognising the change in the current and future periods affected by the change. [IAS 8.5, 8.36]

Illustration 3

A machine tool with an original cost of CU100,000, has an originally-estimated useful life of ten years, and residual value of nil. The annual straight-line depreciation charge will be CU10,000 per annum and the carrying amount after three years will be CU70,000.

If in the fourth year it is decided that, as a result of changes in market conditions, the remaining useful life is only three years (so a total of six years), then the depreciation charge in that year (and in the next two years) will be the carrying amount brought forward divided by the revised remaining useful life, CU70,000/3 = CU23,333. There should be no change to the depreciation charged for the past three years.

The effect of the change (in this case an increase in the annual depreciation charge from CU10,000 to CU23,333) in the current year, and the next two years, should be disclosed.

6 Prior Period Errors

Financial statements do not comply with international standards if they contain errors made intentionally to achieve a particular presentation in the financial statements. A prior period error is where an error has occurred even though reliable information was available when those financial statements were authorised for issue and could reasonably be expected to have been taken into account at that time.

Examples of such errors are:

- mathematical errors;
- mistakes in applying an accounting policy;
- oversights or misinterpretation of facts; and
- fraud.

As such errors may relate to a number of past periods reported IAS 8 requires that these errors are adjusted in those past periods to which the error arose rather than in the current period. Adjustment in the current period would lead to a distorted result in the period in which the error was identified. [IAS 8.42]

Retrospective restatement corrects the financial statements as if the prior period error had never occurred. [IAS 8.5]

If it is impracticable to determine the effect on an individual period of an error, then the adjustment should be made to the opening balance of the earliest period in which it is possible to identify such information. [IAS 8.43, 8.45]

It is important to distinguish between prior period errors and changes in accounting estimates. Accounting estimates are best described as approximations, being the result of considering what is likely to happen in the future, for example how many customers will pay their outstanding invoices and the period over which non-current assets can be used productively within the business. By their very nature estimates result from judgements made on the basis of information available at the time they are made, so they may need to be adjusted in the future, in the light of additional information becoming available.

Prior period errors, on the other hand, result from discoveries which undermine the reliability of the previously published financial statements, for example unrecorded income and expenditure, fictitious inventory or the incorrect application of accounting policies such as classifying maintenance expenses as part of the cost of non-current assets. Prior period errors should be rare.

7 Chapter Review

This chapter has covered IAS 8, and the key issues covered are:

- the link between the *IASB Framework's* qualitative characteristic of comparability, and the objectives of IAS 8, which tries to ensure comparability between companies;

- how an entity should choose an accounting policy, the circumstances in which a entity may change an accounting policy and how changes in accounting policies are accounted for;

- the distinction between accounting policies and estimates and how changes in estimates are accounted for;

- the nature of prior period errors and how they are accounted for; and

- the difference between an estimate and an error.

Chapter 5
REVENUE

1 Business Context

Revenue recognition and measurement is crucial to reporting financial performance. In recent years, different entities operating within the same business sector have adopted varying pratices for revenue recognition which has led to marked variations in the timing and measurement of revenue and hence profit. Aggressive earnings management policies have resulted in questionable revenue recognition practices.

Many of the high profile accounting scandals of recent years have involved the manipulation of revenue, with revenue being recognised in an inappropriate manner leading to hugely inflated reported profits. In part the dot.com boom was fuelled by similarly aggressive revenue recognition policies.

An effective and credible accounting standard on revenue is essential to ensure capital market confidence in corporate reporting, which is the purpose of IAS 18 *Revenue*

2 Chapter Objectives

This chapter deals with:

- the recognition, measurement and disclosure of revenue in the income statement; and

- the different types of revenue, that arising from the sales of goods, the rendering of services and in other forms such as interest, royalties and dividends.

On completion of this chapter you should be able to:

- demonstrate a knowledge of the objectives and scope of IAS 18;

- demonstrate a knowledge of the important terminology and definitions which relate to revenue;

- demonstrate an understanding of the key principles of revenue recognition; and

- apply IAS 18 knowledge and understanding in particular circumstances, through basic calculations.

3 Objectives, Scope and Definitions of IAS 18

Income is defined in the IASB's *Framework for the preparation and presentation of financial statements* as 'increases in economic benefits in the form of inflows or enhancements of assets or decreases of liabilities that result in increases in equity.'

Revenue is simply income that arises in the course of the ordinary activities of the entity and is often known by different names, including sales, turnover, fees, interest, dividends, and royalties. [IAS 18.7]

The primary issue in accounting for revenue is one of timing. When should an entity recognise revenue? The timing of the recognition is critical to the timing of profits.

Financial statements are prepared on the underlying assumption of the 'accrual basis' of accounting. Under this basis, the effects of transactions or events are recognised when they occur rather than when the cash is received or paid.

IAS 18 states that revenue should be recognised when it is probable that the economic benefits associated with the transaction will flow to the entity and these benefits can be measured reliably.

IAS 18 applies to: [IAS 18.1]

- the sale of goods, which includes both goods produced by the entity for sale and goods purchased directly for resale;

- the rendering of services, which typically involves the performance of a contractually agreed task over an agreed period of time; and

- revenue earned from the use by others of the entity's assets including interest, royalties and dividends earned by the entity.

Amounts collected on behalf of others, including sales taxes, value added taxes and amounts collected as agent on behalf of a principal, are excluded from the revenue figure.

4 Measurement

IAS 18 sets out that revenue should be measured at the fair value of the payment, which may take a number of different forms (i.e. it is not limited to cash), received or receivable. [IAS 18.9].

The amount of the payment will normally be expressed in the agreement between the buyer and the seller. Revenue is measured net of trade discounts or volume rebates that are given.

Generally cash will be paid on receipt of the goods or services, or within a short credit period of, say, 30 days. However, where payment is deferred for a long period of time to provide the buyer with an interest-free credit period the deferred cash payment includes a form of financing.

A typical example is a retail outlet selling furniture or household electrical equipment on a year's interest-free credit. In such cases the entity will need to assess what the fair value of the payment is. This is determined by estimating what value the debt could be exchanged for between willing parties. The difference between the fair value and the actual amount paid will be classified as interest revenue.

Illustration 1

A company sells goods to a customer for CU2,500 on 5 July 2004. Although delivery will take place as soon as possible, the company has given the customer an interest-free credit period of 12 months.

The fair value of the consideration receivable is CU2,294. In other words, if the company tried to sell this debt to a debt factoring company it would expect to receive CU2,294 rather than CU2,500.

The balance of CU206 represents interest revenue.

Therefore the company should split the CU2,500 between revenue and interest.

Revenue of CU2,294 should be recognised on 5 July 2004, with the balance of CU206 being recognised as interest revenue over the 12-month credit period.

Where the entity receives similar goods or services as payment this is essentially a 'swap' transaction. The entity is replacing one asset with another similar asset. In such cases no revenue is generated, with no additional cost reported. Such transactions are quite common in the sale of commodities, for example milk, with suppliers exchanging inventories to fulfil demand in a particular location.

When the payment is receivable in the form of dissimilar goods or services, revenue is generated and costs should be recognised. In such cases the transaction is measured based on the fair value of what will be received. If it is not possible to measure the value of the goods or services received reliably, then the revenue should be based on the fair value of the goods or services supplied.

5 Recognition of the Sale of Goods

IAS 18 sets out five criteria that need to be met before revenue from the sale of goods should be recognised. The five criteria are that: [IAS 18.14]

1. the significant 'risks and rewards' of ownership have been transferred from the seller to the buyer. In a simple scenario this will be when the legal title or actual possession of the goods passes between the two parties. The retention of insignificant risks and rewards would not necessarily prevent the recognition of the revenue. This might be the case in the retail industry where an item may be returned and a refund provided;

2. the seller no longer has management involvement or effective control over the goods;

3. the amount of the revenue can be measured reliably;

4. it is probable that payment for the goods will be received by the entity. The effect of this is that the revenue in relation to credit sales is recognised before actual payment is received; and

5   the costs incurred, or to be incurred, in relation to the transaction can be measured reliably. It may be difficult to estimate the costs in relation to a transaction in certain circumstances; however that does not prevent a reliable estimate being made, and therefore should not stop revenue being recognised. The provision of a warranty is an example of this. If, however, it is not possible to estimate reliably the costs to be incurred, this precludes the recognition of revenue and therefore any payment received should be recognised as a liability.

As stated above in criteria 1 revenue should not be recognised until the 'risks and rewards' of ownership have been transferred to the buyer. The seller may retain significant risks and rewards of ownership in a number of ways. Examples of these are as follows:

(a)   the seller retains some obligation for unsatisfactory performance which is outside a normal warranty cover; and

(b)   the particular goods, although shipped, may require installation by the seller as part of the contract before the buyer can utilise the goods (revenue should not be recognised until the full installation process has been completed).

In (a) the seller retains a significant risk that the goods will not perform, and in (b) the buyer is not yet able to gain the rewards associated with using the goods. In both cases no revenue would be recognised.

Illustration 2

A motor car is sold for CU20,000 on 1 March 2004, and includes a two-year manufacturer's warranty. As a special promotion a deferred payment option is being offered by the manufacturer – 'buy now, pay in 12 months' time'. The dealer has a 31 December year end.

The following steps are needed to account for the sale:

- split the CU20,000 payment between the cash sale price and the effective interest;

- recognise the cash sale price as revenue on 1 March;

- recognise interest income for the 10 months' credit given in the accounting period in which the sale is recognised;

- recognise the remaining 2 months' interest in the following period;

- production and selling costs will be recognised in the same period that the revenue relating to the sale of the motor car is recognised;

- a warranty provision will be set up in the period in which the revenue relating to the sale of the motor car is recognised for expected costs under the warranty provision (in accordance with IAS 37 *Provisions, contingent liabilities and contingent assets*); and

- costs incurred under the warranty provision will be charged to the warranty provision to the extent that the provision covers the costs. Any excess costs incurred will be charged directly to the income statement, and any balance remaining on the provision at the end of the second year will be released to the income statement.

6 Recognition of the Rendering of Services

The criteria for the recognition of revenue in relation to the rendering of services are similar to those for the sale of goods. However, the criteria which refer to ownership are clearly not relevant where services are being provided. Criteria 3 - 5 above are, however, equally relevant to the rendering of services. In addition, the entity should be able to assess accurately the stage of completion of the transaction. [IAS 18.20]

Issues in relation to completion arise when a contract for services extends beyond the end of the current accounting period. Some part of the total revenue needs to be recognised in the current period, with the remainder being carried forward to the future periods. This split of revenue is usually made by reference to the stage of completion of the contract. IAS 18 specifically mentions three methods of assessing the stage of completion but does not prohibit the use of other methods. The three methods are:

1. surveys of work performed;

2. assessing the services performed to date against the total services to be performed under the contract; and

3. assessing the costs incurred to date against the total costs to be incurred under the contract.

It is generally not appropriate to recognise revenue based on payments received under the contract, as often stage payments set out under the terms of the contract bear little resemblance to the actual services performed.

If the overall outcome of a service transaction cannot be estimated reliably, then revenue is only recognised to the extent that costs incurred to date are recoverable from the customer. If costs are not recoverable under the contract, revenue should not be recognised although costs incurred should be expensed.

Illustration 3

An entity enters into a CU210,000 fixed price contract for the provision of services. At the end of 2001, the first accounting period, the contract is assessed as being one-third complete, and costs incurred to date are CU45,000.

If costs to complete can be estimated reliably at CU90,000, the overall contract is profitable as the total revenue of CU210,000 exceeds total costs (CU45,000 plus CU90,000). Revenue to be recognised in the first accounting period will be CU70,000, calculated as one-third of the total contract revenue. Costs of one-third of total estimated costs i.e. CU45,000 would also be recognised and matched against the related revenue.

If the costs to complete cannot be estimated reliably, then the outcome of the total contract cannot be estimated reliably, and revenue is recognised to the extent that the costs incurred are believed to be recoverable from the client.

7 Recognition of Revenue Generated on Entity Assets

Assuming an entity is able to measure reliably the revenue and that it expects to receive payment, the recognition of revenue generated on the use by others of the entity's assets should be accounted for as follows: [IAS 18.30]

- interest should be recognised on a time basis;

- dividends should be recognised when the entity, as a shareholder, has a right to receive payment. This is usually when the dividends are declared, rather than when they are proposed; and

- royalties should be recognised on an accrual basis, i.e. they should be recognised as they fall due under the terms of the relevant agreement.

8 Disclosure Requirements

The entity should clearly set out its accounting policy for the recognition of revenue in the notes to the financial statements. This description should include any methods used to assess the stage of completion of transactions. If revenue has been recognised from the exchange of goods or services, this amount should be clearly identified for each category of revenue. [IAS 18.35]

Revenue should be analysed into a number of different categories where the amount recognised is significant. Categories include, for example, the sale of goods, the rendering of services, interest, dividends and royalty payments. [IAS 18.35]

9 Practical Application and Examples

IAS 18 includes an appendix of illustrations of how to apply its concepts in a variety of particular circumstances. What follows is a selection of the more commonly encountered applications.

9.1 Consignment sales

Under such arrangements, the buyer takes delivery of the goods and undertakes to sell them on, on behalf of the original seller. Although the buyer takes delivery of the goods, he is in such circumstances really acting as an agent on behalf of the original seller. The original seller only recognises his sale when his buyer sells the goods on to a third party, since it is only at this point that the seller passes on the significant risks and rewards of ownership.

This treatment is also relevant in sale and return transactions, i.e. revenue should not be recognised until the goods are sold to third parties.

Illustration 4

An entity sells recorded music from emerging artists through a number of retail outlets. The outlets can return any unsold material within three months of receipt. The artists are unproven in a commercial market and it is unclear if the sale of the music will be successful.

There is uncertainty about the timing of receipts from the retailers. This uncertainty is only removed when the retailer sells the music or the three-month period has expired. The risks and rewards of ownership do not pass until the retailer has sold the music.

Revenue should be recognised at the end of the three-month return period, or when the retailer has sold the music if earlier (this could be based upon monthly returns demanded from the retailer).

9.2 Subscriptions to publications

Where a series of publications are subscribed to and each publication distributed is of similar value, revenue should be recognised on a straight-line basis over the period of the subscription. Where the value of each publication varies, revenue is recognised based on the value of the individual publication compared with the total subscription paid.

9.3 Servicing fees included in the price of the product

When the sale price for goods includes an amount in relation to the ongoing servicing of the product, and the servicing element is identifiable, it should be deferred and recognised as revenue over the period of the service contract.

Illustration 5

On the last day of the current accounting period an entity completes the handover of a new system to a client at an agreed price of CU800,000. The price includes after-sales support for the next two years. The cost of providing the support is estimated at CU48,000 per annum, and the entity earns a gross profit of 20% on support contracts.

The after-sales support revenue should be deferred and recognised over the next two years and should include a reasonable element of profit. This is often computed by reference to similar contracts. The revenue deferred on the after-sales contract will be CU60,000 (cost and the 20% gross profit on selling price) per annum.

The revenue to be recognised on the handover of the system will be CU680,000 (CU800,000 - (2 x CU60,000)).

9.4 Advertising commissions

Revenue should be recognised for media commissions, for example running a series of advertisements, when the related advertising appears before the public.

9.5 Franchise fees

Fees which are received for the use of continuing rights, granted as part of a franchise agreement, should be recognised as revenue as the services are provided, or the rights are used.

9.6 Agency transactions

No revenue is recognised when the party is acting as agent for another (the principal). In such transactions, the sale does not represent revenue of the agent who is, in fact, acting as 'intermediary' for another party. The agent is often paid a commission in such transactions, and it is this commission receivable which is, instead, recorded as revenue for the agent.

10 SIC-31 Barter Transactions Involving Advertising Services

As mentioned earlier, some entities have been criticised in the past for adopting aggressive revenue recognition policies. One way this was done was by one entity exchanging advertising space on its website for advertising space on another entity's website. Although no cash or other consideration changed hands, each entity would recognise revenue and costs in relation to these items, boosting their revenues and their perceived worth in the eyes of investors.

SIC-31 *Revenue – Barter transactions involving advertising services* states that unless specific conditions are met no revenue should be recognised in these circumstances as it is not normally possible to measure reliably the fair value of such transactions; this means that the definition of revenue is not met.

11 Chapter Review

This chapter has been concerned with the key issues relating to how, and when, revenue should be recognised in the income statement.

The chapter has covered:

- the objectives, scope, definitions and disclosure requirements of IAS 18;

- how revenue should be measured;

- recognition of the sale of goods, services and other items such as commissions and fees; and

- the treatment of interest portions of the revenue in the case of 'interest-free purchases'.

Chapter 6
INVENTORIES

1 Business Context

Inventories, which include goods purchased and held for resale, work-in-progress and finished goods, are of major significance to some businesses. The level and hence significance of inventories depends not only on the type of industry and market within which an entity operates, but also the manner in which they are managed. For example, inventories in the retail sector consist of goods held for resale and present few valuation problems. On the other hand, manufacturing businesses have materials or supplies, goods in process of production and finished goods held for sale, all of which can be made up of a variety of costs and present more difficult measurement issues often involving judgement and uncertainty.

In terms of the management of inventories, insignificant levels of inventories may be expected in many service industries, where just-in-time inventory management is used (i.e. only ordering goods when they are needed) or where goods are supplied-to-order. Conversely, manufacturing entities typically have inventories amounting to 10%-20% of total assets, forming a major part of the business.

Risk is a potential business issue in respect of inventories. Entities operating in a dynamic environment, such as the technology industry, can experience problems with volatile inventory prices and obsolescence. These business uncertainties also cause issues for the valuation of inventory for accounting purposes.

Accounting for inventories requires an element of management judgement particularly in manufacturing businesses, where the costs attributable to specific inventory items may be uncertain. The determination of cost and its subsequent recognition as an expense will have an effect on the profit or loss reported for the period and is therefore an important consideration. Consequently, the measurement, presentation and disclosures required by IAS 2 *Inventories* provide important information to users of the financial statements.

2 Chapter Objectives

On completion of this chapter you should be able to:

- demonstrate a knowledge of the objectives and scope of IAS 2;

- demonstrate a knowledge of the important terminology and definitions which relate to the measurement of inventories;

- understand the key principles relating to the measurement of inventories; and

- apply this knowledge and understanding in particular circumstances through basic calculations.

3 Objectives, Scope and Definitions of IAS 2

The objective of IAS 2 is to prescribe the accounting treatment for inventories.

Inventories can take a number of different forms which include assets purchased and held for resale in the ordinary course of business, raw materials, partly processed assets and finished goods that have undergone the full production process. [IAS 2.6]

Inventories should be recognised when they meet the defintion of an asset as set out in the *IASB Framework*. No additional guidance on the timing of recognition is provided in IAS 2.

IAS 2 applies to all types of entity but some types of inventory are excluded from IAS 2, for example: [IAS 2.2]

1 work in progress arising under construction contracts (dealt with by IAS 11 *Construction contracts*);

2 financial instruments (dealt with by IAS 32 *Financial instruments: disclosure and presentation* and IAS 39 *Financial instruments: recognition and measurement*); and

3 biological assets related to agricultural activities and agricultural produce at the point of harvest (dealt with by IAS 41 *Agriculture*).

4 IAS 2 and Measurement

Inventories should be measured at the lower of cost and net realisable value. Net realisable value (NRV) is the selling price expected to be achieved less an estimate of the costs to complete the production of the finished good and of the costs to be incurred in making the sale. [IAS 2.9]

Valuing inventory at the lower of cost and NRV ensures that any profit to be earned on their sale is not recognised before the sale takes place although any loss is recognised as soon as it is identified.

Illustration 1

Manufacturing costs in 2003 for inventory held at the year-end are CU60 million.

All goods held at the year-end were sold in January 2004, for CU50 million.

The selling costs incurred for the goods sold in January 2004 were CU4 million.

The value of inventories held at the year ended 31 December 2003 is CU46 million (NRV) (i.e. CU50m less CU4 million) since this is less than the cost of CU60 million.

4.1 Cost of inventories

In most businesses inventories will be sold at a profit so they will be measured at cost (since this is lower than NRV).

Many of the provisions of IAS 2 result from the commonsense application of the principle that the cost of inventory is expenditure incurred in bringing items to their present location and condition. Such costs will include the purchase price of goods acquired for resale or the raw materials that are to be used in a production process. Any discounts or rebates that have been received should be deducted from the cost.

It is only the costs that are directly attributable to bringing the goods to their current state which should be included. These may include import duties, transport and other handling costs. For inventory that is subject to some form of production or conversion process, additional costs will be incurred as part of this process which should also be included in the cost of inventory. Such amounts may include direct manufacturing and direct labour costs as well as a systematic allocation of fixed (costs that will be incurred regardless of the level of output) and variable (costs determined based on the level of output) overheads that are incurred as part of the production process.

Fixed overheads should be allocated to each production process on a systematic basis. It will generally be appropriate to allocate an element of fixed overheads based on normal levels of production.

It is not appropriate to allocate to inventory abnormal costs or administrative costs that do not contribute to bringing the inventory to their current state; instead such amounts should be expensed in the income statement in the period in which they are incurred.

Illustration 2

The costs set out below are those typically incurred by manufacturing business. The costs have been identified as either being part of the costs of inventories or those that should be expensed as incurred.

Include in cost of inventory

Supplier's gross price for raw materials
Quantity discounts allowed by supplier (deduct from cost)
Costs of transporting materials to the business premises
Labour costs directly incurred in the processing of raw materials
Variable costs, such as power, incurred in the processing of raw materials
Fixed production costs/overheads, such as rent for the processing factory
Depreciation charges on the plant used in the processing

Expensed as incurred

Costs of transporting goods to customers on sale
Non-recoverable purchase taxes charged to customers on sale
Non-recoverable sales taxes
Commission payable to salesmen on the sale of the goods
Provisions for bad and doubtful debts in relation to trade receivables
Costs of the accounts department
Head office costs relating to the overall management of the business

Costs recoverable (neither inventory or expensed)

Purchase taxes and duties charged by the supplier and are recoverable from the taxing authorities

Illustration 3

A business plans for fixed production overheads of CU50,000 and annual production is estimated at 100,000 items in its financial year. The planned overhead recovery rate is CU0.50 per item (CU50,000 per 100,000 items).

A fire at the factory results in production being only 75,000 units although there is no saving in the level of fixed production overheads.

Inventory should still be valued on the basis of CU0.50 per item, leading to a recovery of CU37,500 of overheads with the balance of CU12,500 being expensed directly in the year.

In the retail industry it is common practice to value inventory at selling price less the normal gross profit margin. This practice is permitted because it is often impracticable to use other valuation methods due to the large volume of rapidly changing items and it generally results in a valuation which is very close to actual cost.

4.2 Cost formulae

Where inventories are not freely interchangeable because, say, they have been made to an individual customer specification the cost should be the actual expenditure incurred. [IAS 2.23]

Where inventories are interchangeable, for example cases of nails bought and put into a single storage bin, individual cost identification is not necessary or indeed practicable. In this scenario cost formulae should be used.

Two cost formulae are allowed. [IAS 2.25]. These are:

- first-in, first-out, known as FIFO: this method assumes a physical flow of items whereby those purchased or produced earliest are the first to be sold. The items purchased or produced most recently are the ones in inventory, to be valued at the most recent cost; and

- weighted average cost: this method calculates an average cost of purchase or production (calculated either on a periodic basis or after each shipment has been received or new batch has been produced), and values inventory at that average cost.

An entity shall use the same cost formula for all inventories of a similar nature.

Illustration 4

A business produces and sells the following quantities of a product:

Date		Tonnes	CU Total	CU per tonne
1 July	Opening inventory	10	200	20
4 July	Production	8	176	22
6 July	Sale	(9)		
15 July	Production	6	144	24
18 July	Sale	(11)		
23 July	Production	4	104	26
31 July	Closing inventory	8		

The FIFO cost formula will result in closing inventory being made up of the most recent production, i.e. the 4 tonnes produced on 23 July (costing CU104) and 4 of the 6 tonnes produced on 15 July (at CU24 = CU96 cost). So closing inventory will be valued at CU200.

Using the weighted average cost formula, and recalculating the average cost after each new batch has been produced, results in the following:

Date		Tonnes	CU Total	CU per tonne
1 July	Opening inventory	10	200	20
4 July	Production	8	176	22
	Recalculation	18	376 ⟶	20.89
6 July	Sale	(9)		↓
	Inventory	9	188 ⟵	20.89
15 July	Production	6	144	24
	Recalculation	15	332 ⟶	22.13
18 July	Sale	(11)		↓
	Inventory	4	89 ⟵	22.13
23 July	Production	4	104	26
31 July	Recalculation and closing inventory	8	193 ⟶	24.12

In the example, average production costs are rising and therefore the weighted average cost formula, which smoothes different costs out, results in a slightly lower inventory value (and therefore period profit), than the FIFO formula which does not include any smoothing.

4.3 Net realisable value (NRV)

The key points to note with regard to NRV are:

- in the case of incomplete items, NRV takes account of the costs to complete;

- in making the assessment of whether NRV is lower than cost of inventory it may be appropriate to group items together. However, items should only be grouped together when the individual items cannot be valued separately. It is not appropriate to treat a whole class of inventory, for example all goods held for sale, as a group. If NRV is less than cost the write down of inventory will also be made on a group basis;

- in the absence of a contractually agreed selling price, the best estimate is the likely selling price, less appropriate deductions; and

- materials to be incorporated into a finished good should only be written down if the eventual finished good will be sold for less than the total cost.

5 Recognition as an Expense and Disclosure

Once an item has been sold, it is removed from inventory as it no longer meets the *IASB Framework* definition of an asset. Its cost is therefore treated as an expense in the accounting period in which the item is sold and the related revenue recognised.

The amount of any write-downs of inventory to NRV should be recognised as an expense in the period when the write-down occurs. [IAS 2.34]

There are a number of disclosure requirements in relation to inventory, designed to provide the users of the financial statements with information on the level and turnover of inventory during a period. Specific disclosure requirements include, an explanation of the accounting policy followed in measuring inventory, the amount of inventory held at the year end, and how much of this has been valued based on fair value less costs to sell (where appropriate) and details of inventory related expenditure that has been recognised in the income statement during the year. Amounts recognised in the income statement will be for inventories sold during the year and amounts written-down where the NRV is less than cost (or reversals). If there has been a reversal of a previous write down, then the circumstances leading to the increase in NRV should be explained. In addition, if inventory has been pledged as security for liabilities, this should be disclosed and quantified.

6 Chapter Review

This chapter has been concerned with the key issues relating to how goods produced for sale are measured in inventory prior to their sale to customers.

The chapter has covered:

- the objectives, scope, definitions and disclosure requirements of IAS 2;
- the measurement rule: measure at the lower of cost and realisable value;
- what constitutes cost;
- the FIFO and weighted average cost formulae for inventory; and
- the disclosure requirements for inventory.

CHAPTER 7
PROPERTY, PLANT AND EQUIPMENT

1 Business Context

Businesses operating in certain industries, for example manufacturing, typically have ownership of substantial items of property, plant and equipment (PPE) in their balance sheets. PPE are tangible assets such as freehold and leasehold land and buildings, plant and machinery and are being held for use in the production or supply of goods or services or for administrative purposes. The management of these resources underpins the continued viability of a business and therefore represents a key feature of business prosperity. It is important therefore that users of financial statements understand how a business uses its PPE and how such assets are treated in the financial statements.

The relevant reporting principles are set out in IAS 16 *Property, plant and equipment*. To aid comparability the standard is applied across all industry sectors.

Although financial statements have typically been based on historic cost, being the value at which the original transaction took place, recently there has been a move towards including items at their fair value. IAS 16 permits either treatment; although this choice leads to reduced comparability across entities, it reflects the fact that the use of historic cost information may not always provide the most accurate picture of the entity's financial position.

2 Chapter Objectives

This chapter deals with accounting for property, plant and equipment (PPE).

On completion of this chapter you will should able to:

- demonstrate a knowledge of the objectives and scope of IAS 16;

- demonstrate a knowledge of the important terminology and definitions relating to PPE;

- demonstrate an understanding of the key principles relating to the recognition, valuation and depreciation of PPE; and

- apply IAS 16 knowledge and understanding in particular circumstances through basic calculations.

3 Objectives, Scope and Definitions of IAS 16

IAS 16's objective is to set out the accounting treatment for PPE. The principal issues in accounting for PPE and addressed in IAS 16 are the recognition of assets, the determination of their carrying amounts and the charging of depreciation. The standard should be applied in accounting for all PPE except where another international standard specifically requires a different approach to be applied. [IAS 16.2]

PPE are tangible assets (they have physical substance) that are held for use in the production or supply of goods or services, for rental to others, or for administrative purposes and are expected to be utilised in more than one period. [IAS 16.6]

The key issue in terms of whether an asset should be classified as PPE is the use to which an asset is being put. Many items may be either non-current or current assets (i.e. utilised in more than one period or in only one period) depending on how they are used. For example, cars held for resale by a motor dealer are inventories (a current asset), whereas cars held for use by employees on entity business, or as a benefit in kind, are PPE (a non-current asset).

The cost of an item of PPE should be recognised as an asset, if the cost can be measured reliably and it is probable that the asset will generate future economic benefits for the entity. It is important to note that legal ownership of the item of PPE is not required for recognition by the entity. [IAS 16.7]

IAS 16 does not prescribe 'the unit of measurement' for an item of PPE, but instead leaves this to the discretion of management. Where an individual item, a tool for example, qualifies for recognition as PPE but is individually insignificant, it may be appropriate to aggregate it with other similar items.

3.1 Initial recognition and elements of cost

If an item of PPE qualifies for recognition, it should initially be recognised at its cost. Cost is defined as 'the amount of cash or cash equivalents paid and the fair value of other consideration given to acquire an asset at the time of its acquisition or construction' and includes: [IAS 16.6, 16.16]

- the purchase price, including all non-refundable duties and taxes, but net of any trade discounts received;

- costs 'directly attributable' to bringing the asset to the location and condition necessary for it to be capable of operating in the manner intended by management; and

- the initial estimate of the cost of dismantling and removing the item and site restoration costs, where the entity has an obligation to return the site to its original condition, for example the decommissioning of a nuclear power plant.

Directly attributable costs include: [IAS 16.17]

- costs of employee benefits arising directly from the construction or acquisition of the item; and

- site preparation, initial delivery and handling costs, installation and assembly costs, costs incurred in testing that the asset is functioning properly, for example flight testing of a new aircraft and professional fees, for example legal costs and architects' fees.

Costs that are not directly attributable to the item cannot be recognised as part of the PPE asset. Such costs are expensed as they are incurred, unless it is appropriate to recognise them under another accounting standard. Examples of costs that should normally be expensed as they are incurred include the cost of opening a new facility, introducing new products, conducting business in a new location or with a new class of customer and administration and general overheads.

3.2 Self-constructed assets

The cost of a self-constructed asset is determined using the same principles as for an acquired asset. It is therefore not appropriate to include, as part of the cost of constructing the asset, an allocation for internal profit. Any abnormal costs incurred by the entity, for example those arising from design errors, wastage or industrial disputes, should be expensed as they are incurred and do not form part of the capitalised cost of the PPE asset.

Borrowing costs incurred may form part of the asset in accordance with IAS 23 *Borrowing costs*.

3.3 Ceasing recognition of costs

The recognition of costs as part of a PPE asset should stop when the item is capable of operating in the manner intended by management. In the case of an asset being built, this will be when it has been fully constructed and tested and is installed in the location intended, even if the asset has not yet been put into use. Any operating losses that are incurred during the early part of an asset's life whilst demand is being built up, should not be recognised as part of the asset, for example the opening of a new hotel complex.

Illustration 1

An entity is constructing a new production facility. The cost of the materials used was CU20,000, consultancy fees were CU1,000 and site preparation costs were CU2,000. All of these are direct costs which should be included as part of the cost of the asset.

The production facility will require dismantling in 5 years time at a cost of CU800. This cost should be included as part of the cost. If the effect of the time value of money is significant, the cost of dismantling the facility should be recognised at its present value.

Operating losses of CU350 were incurred in the start up period between the asset becoming ready for use and full production commencing. The start up losses cannot be capitalised.

4 Measurement of Cost

Cost is measured as the cash price at the time of recognition of the asset. If payment is deferred beyond normal credit terms then the cost recognised is discounted to take account of the time value of money. The difference is recognised as interest.

If instead of paying cash to acquire an asset, the entity exchanges one of its assets, the new asset should be recognised at 'fair value'. Fair value is defined as 'the amount for which an asset could be exchanged between knowledgeable, willing parties in an arm's length transaction'. This treatment assumes that the exchange transaction is commercially viable and fair value can be measured reliably. [IAS 16.24]

4.1 Subsequent expenditure

Routine repairs and maintenance and servicing costs should normally be expensed in the income statement when the costs are incurred. However, in circumstances where subsequent expenditure enhances the value of the asset to the extent that additional economic benefits will flow to the entity, the additional expenditure should be recognised as part of the asset's cost.

Where an asset is made up of many distinct parts, these should be separately identified, as shown in illustration 3 below. Therefore, where part of an asset is replaced at regular intervals, for example replacing the seats within an aircraft, the additional cost will replace the cost of the original part of the asset.

IAS 16 also sets out that where major inspections or overhauls take place, the cost of such inspections should be recognised as part of the carrying amount of the item of PPE, assuming that the overhaul meets the recognition criteria. An example is where an aircraft is required to undergo a major inspection after so many flying hours. Without the inspection the aircraft would not be permitted to continue flying.

5 Measurement after Initial Recognition

Once an item of PPE has initially been recognised at cost, the entity has a choice of how to account for it in subsequent periods. The entity may use a 'cost model' (whereby the item of PPE continues to be carried at cost less accumulated depreciation and accumulated impairment losses), or a 'revaluation model' (whereby the item is carried at its fair value at the date of revaluation less accumulated depreciation and accumulated impairment losses). [IAS 16.29, 16.30]

6 Cost Model and Depreciation

The cost model requires the initial cost of the asset less its residual value, described as its depreciable amount, to be depreciated over its useful life. This is a way of charging part of the net cost of an asset in each period, so that at the end of the asset's useful life to the entity, the whole of its net cost has been charged to the income statement. In each period the carrying amount of the asset in the balance sheet is reduced by the depreciation charged.

The asset will continue to be depreciated until its carrying amount is zero or the value for which the entity expects to be able sell the asset at the end of its useful life, i.e. its residual value. Residual value should be assessed each period on the assumption that the asset is already at the end of its useful life for the entity. [IAS 16.51]

The useful life of an asset is the period of time over which an asset is expected to be available for use within the entity. [IAS 16.6]

The carrying amount of an asset is the amount at which it is recognised in the balance sheet; in this case, it represents the cost of the asset less the accumulated depreciation charged in relation to the asset to date.

Depreciation does not relate to the value of an asset, because it is a way of writing off its cost over its useful life. Therefore an increase in the current value of an asset does not itself justify not depreciating the asset.

A systematic basis should be used to allocate the depreciation on an item of PPE over its useful life. This basis should reflect the pattern in which future economic benefits are enjoyed by the entity. For example, if it is expected that an item of machinery will have broadly the same production levels throughout its useful life, then a constant charge for depreciation would be appropriate (this is known as the straight-line method). [IAS 16.50, 16.60]

IAS 16 also specifically mentions two other methods of depreciation. The first is the units of production method. This is where an estimate is made of the number of units of production that will be achieved over the life of the asset. Each period, the amount charged to the income statement is based on the level of production in the period. The third method is known as 'diminishing balance'. Using this method, the amount of depreciation that is charged each year reduces as the asset gets older. This is achieved by charging a constant percentage against the reducing carrying amount of the asset. This method is sometimes used for new motor vehicles.

The depreciation charge for each period should usually be recognised in the income statement. [IAS 16.48]

Illustration 2

An entity acquires an asset for CU10,000. It is expected to have a useful life of ten years, after which time the asset will be scrapped. The asset has no residual value.

Straight-line method

The depreciation charged in each of the ten years of the asset's life will be:

CU10,000 / 10 years = CU1,000 per annum.

Units of production method

It is estimated that the asset will produce 100,000 units over its ten-year life. The production plan is as follows:

Year	Production	Depreciation	
1	5,000	CU10,000 x (5/100 units) =	CU500
2	8,000	CU10,000 x (8/100 units) =	CU800
3	10,000	CU10,000 x (10/100 units) =	CU1,000
4	12,000	CU10,000 x (12/100 units) =	CU1,200
5	16,000	CU10,000 x (16/100 units) =	CU1,600
6	16,000	CU10,000 x (16/100 units) =	CU1,600
7	12,000	CU10,000 x (12/100 units) =	CU1,200
8	9,000	CU10,000 x (9/100 units) =	CU900
9	7,000	CU10,000 x (7/100 units) =	CU700
10	5,000	CU10,000 x (5/100 units) =	CU500

Diminishing balance method

Depreciation is charged at 25% per annum on a diminishing balance basis. In this scenario it is assumed that the asset will have a small, but insignificant, value at the end of the ten-year estimated life.

Year	Carrying value at start of Year	Depreciation	
1	10,000	CU10,000 x 25% =	CU2,500
2	7,500	CU7,500 x 25% =	CU1,875
3	5,625	CU5,625 x 25% =	CU1,406
4	4,219	CU4,219 x 25% =	CU1,055
5	3,164	CU3,164 x 25% =	CU791
6	2,373	CU2,373 x 25% =	CU593
7	1,780	CU1,780 x 25% =	CU445
8	1,335	CU1,335 x 25% =	CU334
9	1,001	CU1,001 x 25% =	CU250
10	751	CU751 x 25% =	CU188

Each significant part of an item of PPE should be depreciated separately. For example, an aircraft's engines will be depreciated separately from its airframe, when they have different useful lives. [IAS 16.43]

Land and buildings are separable assets and should therefore be accounted for separately even where they were acquired together. Land usually has an infinite life, with some exceptions such as quarries and landfill sites, whereas buildings do not and should therefore be depreciated.

Illustration 3

An entity has acquired a new freehold building with a useful life of 50 years for CU7,000,000. The entity has identified the following components and calculated the depreciation charge per annum using a straight-line method as follows.

Component	Useful Life (years)	Cost	Depreciation (per annum)
Land	Infinite	CU2,000,000	Nil
Roof	25	CU1,000,000	CU40,000
Lifts	20	CU500,000	CU25,000
Fixtures	10	CU500,000	CU50,000
Remainder of building	50	CU3,000,000	CU60,000
		CU7,000,000	CU175,000

When the roof requires replacement at the end of its useful life the carrying value will be nil. The cost of replacing the roof should be recognised as a new component.

An entity is required to review at least once a year the depreciation methods used and the estimated useful life of its assets. If a change in the depreciation method or in the asset's useful life is made, the new method, or life, is used from that date. The carrying amount of the asset at the date of change will be depreciated over the new life, or by using the revised method in future periods. No restatement is made for the accounting treatment used in earlier periods. Such a change is known as a change in accounting estimate and is addressed in IAS 8 *Accounting policies, changes in accounting estimates and errors*. [IAS 16.51, 16.61]

Illustration 4

A machine is acquired for CU60,000 and is estimated to have a useful life of 15 years. Depreciation is being calculated on a straight-line basis. The asset has no residual value. The depreciation charge each year and the carrying amount of the asset at the end of year 5 is:

Asset cost CU60,000. Straight-line depreciation over a useful life of 15 years with no residual value.

Annual depreciation in years 1 to 5 is:

CU60,000 / 15 years = CU4,000.

Carrying amount of the asset at the end of year 5 is:

CU60,000 – (CU4,000 x 5 years) = CU40,000.

The entity revises the machine's useful life at the end of year 5, because of changes in technology, and estimates that it only has a further 4 years' life before it will need replacing.

At the end of year 5, the remaining life is estimated to be 4 years.

Annual depreciation charge in years 6 to 9 is:

CU40,000 / 4 years = CU10,000.

The charging of depreciation should begin when the asset is ready for use and should stop only when the asset is derecognised. During periods when the asset is standing idle, depreciation continues to be charged. If the units of production method of depreciation is being used, then during idle periods the charge may be zero.

7 Revaluation Model

Following initial recognition of an item of PPE, it may be carried at a revalued amount, assuming that its fair value can be measured reliably. If the revaluation model is used, then valuations should be carried out at regular intervals to ensure that the valuation remains up to date. [IAS 16.31]

Fair value would generally be market value and is usually assessed by a professionally qualified valuer. However, for some specialised property, such as an oil rig, there is no ready market because such items are rarely sold except as part of a continuing business. In these circumstances, the standard sets out that the fair value should be estimated using an income, or a depreciated replacement cost approach. A depreciated replacement cost approach looks at what the replacement cost of an asset would be and then depreciates that value for the current age of the asset held. [IAS 16.6]

Illustration 5

An entity acquires a specialised piece of machinery for CU200,000. Due to the specialised nature of the machinery, there is no active resale market for it. The entity revalues its plant and machinery.

The machine is currently a quarter of its way through its life and therefore its carrying amount would have been CU150,000 using a cost model and assuming a straight-line method of depreciation with no residual value. To replace the asset new would cost CU300,000. The estimated depreciated replacement cost would, therefore, be 75% of the CU300,000, i.e. CU225,000.

If an entity decides to use the revaluation model, then it should do so for the entire 'class' of assets, it may not revalue individual assets. Examples of classes of assets include: [IAS 16.36]

- land and buildings;
- machinery;
- fixtures and fittings; and
- motor vehicles.

7.1 Upward valuations

The general principle is that an increase in value on the revaluation of an asset is recognised directly in equity (in the revaluation surplus on the balance sheet). [IAS 16.39]

However, if an upward valuation reverses an earlier downward valuation (see below) which was recognised directly in the income statement, the upward valuation is recognised in the income statement to the extent that it reverses the previous decrease. Any excess above the previous decrease in value should be recognised in equity under the general principle. This treatment puts the entity back to the original position as if the original decrease in value recognised in the income statement had not arisen.

7.2 Downward valuations

The general principle is to account for a downward valuation of an item of PPE by recognising the decrease as an expense directly in the income statement. However, where there has been a previous upward valuation of the asset that was recognised in equity and part of that surplus remains in the revaluation surplus, the decrease in valuation should first be charged against this surplus. Any excess should then be recognised in the income statement. [IAS 16.40]

7.3 Depreciation and revalued assets

Depreciation is still applicable to revalued assets since, as discussed above, it is a way of charging the cost (or revalued amount) of an asset in each period, so that at the end of the asset's useful life the whole of its cost (or revalued amount), less any residual value, has been charged to the income statement. Where the asset has been revalued, the depreciation is based on the revalued amount rather than on its cost. Depreciation on a revalued asset is still charged directly to the income statement.

On revaluation of an asset, the depreciation should be based on the new valuation over the number of remaining years of the asset's useful life at the time of the latest valuation.

Illustration 6

An entity acquires an item of PPE for CU50,000, which is depreciated over 20 years. Three years later, the asset is revalued to CU60,000. The useful life has not changed.

On revaluation the depreciation will be based on CU60,000 over the remaining 17 years.

The amount transferred to the revaluation surplus should represent the difference between the carrying amount of the asset at the date of revaluation and the new revalued amount.

Illustration 7

An entity acquires an item of PPE for CU50,000, which is depreciated over 20 years. Three years later, the asset is revalued to CU60,000.

Depreciation of (CU50,000 / 20 years) x 3 years = CU7,500 has been set against the gross cost of the asset to give a carrying amount of CU50,000 less CU7,500 (i.e. CU42,500) at the date of the valuation.

Compare the carrying amount of CU42,500 with the revalued amount of CU60,000 and recognise the difference of CU17,500 in the revaluation surplus.

The revaluation surplus included in equity in respect of an item of PPE may be transferred to retained earnings when the asset is derecognised. This may occur upon sale. However, some of the surplus may be transferred as the asset is used by the entity. The amount transferred is the difference between the depreciation based upon the revalued amount and that based upon historical cost. [IAS 16.41]

Illustration 8

An entity owns a building which originally cost CU200,000. The property is depreciated over 50 years on a straight-line basis with no residual value. The entity adopts a policy of revaluation for property. The property has so far had three valuations as follows.

At the start of year 2 – valuation CU230,000.

At the start of year 4 – valuation CU260,000.

At the start of year 6 – valuation CU300,000.

In year 1 depreciation, based on the cost of the property, is CU4,000 (i.e. CU200,000 / 50 years).

In following years the depreciation charge is based on the valuation at the start of the year.

Annual depreciation:

Year 1 - CU200,000 / 50 years = CU4,000.

Year 2 - CU230,000 / 49 years = CU4,694.

Year 3 - CU230,000 / 49 years = CU4,694.

Year 4 - CU260,000 / 47 years = CU5,532.

Year 5 - CU260,000 / 47 years = CU5,532.

Year 6 - CU300,000 / 45 years = CU6,667.

Revaluation surpluses:

Start Year 2:

Carrying amount of the property is CU200,000 - CU4,000 = CU196,000. Revalued amount is CU230,000.

Balance transferred to revaluation surplus is CU34,000.

Start Year 4:

Carrying amount of the property is CU230,000 – (CU4,694 x 2) = CU220,612. Revalued amount is CU260,000.

Balance transferred to revaluation surplus is CU39,388.

Start Year 6:

Carrying amount of the property is CU260,000 – (CU5,532 x 2) = CU248,936. Revalued amount is CU300,000.

Balance transferred to revaluation surplus is CU51,064.

The amounts transferred from the revaluation surplus to retained earnings as the revaluation surplus is realised through depreciation are:

Year 1 – nil.

Year 2 – CU4,694 - CU4,000 = CU694.

Year 3 – CU4,694 - CU4,000 = CU694.

Year 4 – CU5,532 - CU4,000 = CU1,532.

Year 5 – CU5,532 - CU4,000 = CU1,532.

Year 6 – CU6,667 - CU4,000 = CU2,667.

8 Impairment of PPE

IAS 36 *Impairment of assets* requires that an item of PPE is reviewed to ensure that there has not been an impairment of the asset. Impairment arises when the carrying amount of the asset is higher than its recoverable amount. For example, a car has a carrying amount of say CU10,000, but due to a new model being released by the manufacturer, the amount that could be recovered through, say, the sale of the car is only CU7,000.

IAS 36 sets out when an entity should review items of PPE for impairment, how impairments are calculated and the accounting treatment required for them.

Compensation may be received from a third party for an item of PPE when it is impaired, lost, or given up, for example an insurance payment where an asset has been damaged by fire. IAS 16 states that the impairment or loss of an asset, any compensation received in relation to the asset and any subsequent purchase to replace the asset are all separate events and hence should be accounted for individually. Any compensation received for an impaired, or lost, asset should therefore be recognised in the income statement when the amount becomes receivable. [IAS 16.65]

9 Derecognition of an Item of PPE

An item of PPE should be removed from the balance sheet (i.e. derecognised) when it is disposed of or when no future economic benefits are expected from its use. On removal from the balance sheet, a gain or loss should be recognised in the income statement. The gain or loss is calculated by comparing the carrying amount of the asset with the net disposal proceeds received after deducting selling costs. The gain or loss is calculated in the same way, regardless of whether the asset is revalued or not. Any gain should not be classified as part of the entity's revenue. [IAS 16.67, 16.68, 16.71]

The date of disposal and presentation of an asset held for resale should be determined by considering the criteria set out in IAS 18 *Revenue* and IFRS 5 *Non-current assets held for resale and discontinued operations*.

If on disposal of a revalued asset there remains a balance on the revaluation surplus relating to the asset, this balance should be transferred to retained earnings. This transfer is shown as a movement between reserves and does not form part of any profit or loss on disposal of the item recognised in the income statement.

10 Disclosure Requirements

IAS 16 requires that a reconciliation of the carrying amount at the beginning and end of each period is disclosed in relation to the movement in PPE. The reconciliation should show all movements during the period, including additions, assets classified as held for sale and other disposals, impairment losses, revaluations, depreciation and acquisitions made as part of a business combination. The most practical way to meet these disclosure requirements is to present the information in the form of a table. The reconciliation should be set out for each class of assets. [IAS 16.73]

In addition to a full reconciliation, the entity should disclose its depreciation policy and rates (or length of the useful lives). Where the entity adopts a policy of revaluation, this should be explained along with information on when the last valuation exercise was carried out, whether the valuation was carried out by an independent valuer, the major assumptions used in the valuation and on what basis the fair value was determined, for example by reference to an active market. In addition, the carrying amount of the revalued asset based on cost should be set out, along with the amount of the revaluation surplus, with any movements during the period highlighted. [IAS 16.77]

Information is also required to be disclosed on a number of ancillary items which involve PPE. These disclosures include the existence and amount of any restrictions on the title of PPE (where PPE has been pledged as security over some of the entity's liabilities), the amount of any expenditure recognised in respect of assets in the course of construction, the amount of any contractual commitments for the future acquisition of items of PPE and the amount of any compensation received in respect of impaired or lost assets. [IAS 16.74]

11 Chapter Review

This chapter has been concerned with the key issues relating to how PPE is recognised, valued and depreciated.

The chapter has covered:

- the objectives, scope, definitions and disclosure requirements of IAS 16;

- cost model versus revaluation model;

- different methods of depreciation;

- an overview of impairment;

- derecognition;

- when to start and cease recognition; and

- what cost can be recognised as part of the asset and what should be expensed.

Chapter 8
BORROWING COSTS

1 Business Context

Inventories that require a number of manufacturing processes or the construction of non-current assets such as investment properties or a cruise liner can take a significant time to complete. In addition, they typically require substantial capital expenditure and are therefore often financed through borrowings on which the entity incurs finance costs.

The issue is whether borrowing costs specifically incurred on the construction of such assets form part of the cost of such assets. The treatment can have a significant effect on the results and capital employed for an entity.

2 Chapter Objectives

This chapter deals with the treatment of costs of financing the construction, production or acquisition of a qualifying asset.

On completion of this chapter you should be able to:

- demonstrate a knowledge of the objectives and scope of IAS 23 *Borrowing costs*;

- demonstrate an understanding of the principles relating to the treatment of borrowing costs; and

- apply IAS 23 knowledge through basic calculations.

3 Objectives, Scope and Definitions of IAS 23

The objective of IAS 23 is to set out the permitted accounting treatment for borrowing costs.

The principal issue is whether finance costs on borrowings incurred during the construction of the asset are, in effect, part of the cost of the asset. The recognition of borrowing costs as part of the cost of the related asset is known as 'capitalising' costs.

The benchmark treatment in IAS 23 for borrowing costs is to expense them in the income statement in the period in which they are incurred. [IAS 23.7]

However, IAS 23 allows an alternative treatment of capitalising borrowing costs as part of a qualifying asset in specific circumstances. The finance costs on the relevant borrowings become part of the overall asset and are therefore charged to the income statement as the asset is depreciated over its useful life, rather than as incurred.

3.1 Allowed alternative treatment

Borrowing costs that are directly attributable to the acquisition, construction, or production of a qualifying asset may be capitalised as part of that asset. [IAS 23.11]

A 'qualifying asset' is defined as one that necessarily takes a substantial period of time to get ready for its intended use or sale. The definition is wide and therefore may cover assets accounted for under IAS 11 *Construction contracts* and IAS 2 *Inventories* as well as property, plant and equipment under IAS 16 *Property, plant and equipment*. [IAS 23.4]

3.1.1 Which costs can be capitalised?

Borrowing (or finance) costs are interest and other costs incurred by an enterprise in connection with the borrowing of funds. [IAS 23.4]

This definition encompasses interest on all types of borrowings including finance leases and ancillary costs incurred in connection with the arrangement of borrowings. [IAS 23.5]

Only borrowing costs directly attributable to the acquisition of the asset may be capitalised. The principle is that the amount to be capitalised under the allowed alternative treatment is the borrowing costs which would have been avoided if the expenditure on the qualifying asset had not been made. [IAS 23.11]

Illustration 1

An entity has a bank overdraft of CU500,000 and a loan of CU1 million which was taken out to finance the expansion of the entity several years ago. The entity has just commissioned the construction of a new factory to expand the business. The factory will cost CU2 million to build and this will be financed by a new loan.

If the entity has a policy of capitalising borrowing costs, then the finance costs on the new loan only (CU2 million) will be capitalised as part of the cost of the new factory. The entity may also capitalise the ancillary costs incurred in connection with setting up the new borrowing facility.

Where funds are specifically borrowed to finance the construction of an asset, the specific borrowing costs incurred can be readily identified. However, the asset may also be financed from borrowings made for general use within the entity or group. The amount of borrowings that may be capitalised is calculated by reference to a weighted average of the costs of all the 'general use' borrowings. The weighted average calculation will exclude any borrowings used to finance a specific purchase or building. [IAS 23.15, 23.17]

Illustration 2

An entity already has a number of general loan arrangements:

Loan 1 of CU800,000, interest paid at 9%;

Loan 2 of CU2 million, interest paid at 8%; and

Loan 3 of CU400,000, interest paid at 7.5%.

The entity has commissioned a new printing press to be constructed on its behalf. The total cost will be CU800,000 and the entity expects that it will be able to fund the purchase from its existing borrowings since it has arranged for stage payments to be made.

The entity has adopted a policy of capitalisation of borrowing costs.

The existing borrowings are utilised to fund the purchase.

The construction takes six months.

The weighted average is calculated as follows

$$\frac{(800,000 \times 0.09) + (2,000,000 \times 0.08) + (400,000 \times 0.075)}{(800,000 + 2,000,000 + 400,000)} = 8\%$$

Cost of asset: CU800,000

Borrowing costs to be capitalised:

800,000 x 8% x 6/12 = CU32,000

Where the funds specifically borrowed to finance the asset are not wholly utilised immediately but are instead invested until they are required, the finance cost to be capitalised should be reduced by any investment income received on the excess funds invested. [IAS 23.15]

Illustration 3

An entity borrowed CU5 million to fund the construction of a new building. Interest is payable on the loan at 8%. Stage payments were due throughout the construction period and therefore excess funds were reinvested during that period. By the end of the project investment income of CU150,000 had been earned and the construction took twelve months to complete. The entity capitalises borrowing costs.

Interest capitalised as part of the cost of the asset is the actual interest cost less income earned on the temporary investment of the surplus funds.

Interest cost: CU5,000,000 x 8% = CU400,000

Total borrowing costs capitalised: CU400,000 - CU150,000 = CU250,000

The amount of borrowing costs that may be capitalised is limited so that the total value of the asset (including borrowing costs) should not exceed the asset's recoverable amount.

3.1.2 When can capitalisation of borrowing costs commence?

Borrowing costs of the asset may be capitalised when the following three conditions have been met: [IAS 23.20]

- expenditure on the acquisition, construction, or production of the asset is being incurred;
- borrowing costs are being incurred; and
- activities are taking place that are necessary to prepare the asset for its intended use or sale.

Activities necessary to prepare the asset for use include more than just the actual construction and may include, for example, drawing up plans and obtaining permits for a building where the land has been purchased. However, merely holding assets for use or development without any associated development activity does not qualify for capitalisation.

3.1.3 Suspension of capitalisation

There may be periods when the development of an asset is temporarily suspended. During such inactive periods the capitalisation of borrowing costs should be discontinued and instead finance costs incurred during this period should be immediately recognised in the income statement. [IAS 23.23]

It is possible that a temporary delay is part of the production or construction process, and during such periods borrowing costs should continue to be capitalised. Examples include where the maturity of an asset is an essential part of the production process or where there is expected non-activity due to geological features (such as periods of very high tides).

Illustration 4

The following events took place:

- An entity buys some land on 1 December.

- Planning permission is obtained on 31 January.

- Payment for the land is deferred until 1 February.

- The entity takes out a loan to cover the cost of the land and the construction of the building on 1 February.

- Due to adverse weather conditions there is a delay in starting the building work for six weeks and work does not commence until 15 March.

In the above scenario the key dates are:

- Expenditure on the acquisition is incurred on 1 February.

- Borrowing costs start to be incurred from 1 February.

- Although work was being undertaken on planning permission etc. during December and January, no borrowing costs were incurred during this period. During the six-week inactive period capitalisation of borrowing costs would not be permitted.

- Capitalisation of borrowing costs could commence from 15 March.

3.1.4 Ceasing capitalisation

Capitalisation should cease when substantially all the activities necessary to get the asset ready for its intended use or sale are complete. It is the availability for use which is important, not when the asset is actually brought into use. An asset is normally ready for its intended use or sale when its physical construction is complete. [IAS 23.25]

Some assets are completed in parts. Where each part is capable of being used separately while other parts continue to be constructed, the cessation of capitalising borrowing costs should be assessed on the substantial completion of each part, for example the construction of separate buildings within a new business park. [IAS 23.27]

4 Disclosure

The entity should disclose the accounting policy adopted for borrowing costs. Where the alternative treatment of capitalising borrowing costs is adopted the entity should separately identify those costs capitalised and the capitalisation rate used to determine the amount of borrowing costs eligible for capitalisation. [IAS 23.9, 23.29]

5 Chapter Review

This chapter has been concerned with the key issues relating to how borrowing costs incurred are accounted for and disclosed in the purchase or construction of qualifying assets.

The chapter has covered:

- the objectives, scope, definitions and disclosure requirements of IAS 23;

- the benchmark and allowed alternative treatments of borrowing costs; and

- when the capitalisation of borrowing costs may commence, when it should cease and when it should be suspended.

CHAPTER 9
GOVERNMENT GRANTS

1 Business Context

It is common practice amongst governments around the world to offer some form of selective financial assistance to certain entities. There are various motives for governments to provide such aid, including:

- geographical – to stimulate employment in poorer regions;

- industrial – to support key industries (such as defence, IT and energy);

- inward investment – to promote investment from overseas; and

- new start-ups – to help infant entities gain a foothold in a market.

To ensure that the objective of providing the assistance is met by the recipient entity in its application of such amounts there are often a variety of criteria and conditions attached to their receipt. Conditions, for example, may require a minimum investment to be provided or a minimum level of employment to be sustained over a specified period by the entity.

In a financial reporting context it is important to disclose adequate information in relation to government assistance, to ensure that an entity's performance is accurately interpreted. The identification of government assistance allows a fair comparison to be made with other entities in a similar industry that have not received such assistance.

2 Chapter Objectives

This chapter deals with the accounting treatment of government grants and in particular the issue of when revenue from such grants should be recognised. It also considers the distinction between asset-related and income-related grants.

On completion of this chapter you should be able to:

- understand the scope of IAS 20 *Accounting for government grants and disclosure of government assistance*;

- interpret the important terminology and definitions which relate to the treatment of government grants in financial statements;

- understand the key principles relating to the recognition and measurement of government grants;

- demonstrate knowledge of the principal disclosure requirements of IAS 20; and

- apply knowledge and understanding of IAS 20 in particular circumstances through basic calculations.

3 Objectives, Scope and Definitions of IAS 20

IAS 20 sets out the accounting requirements when an entity receives a form of government assistance. The reference to 'government' is quite wide and includes, for example, government agencies and similar local, national or international bodies. [IAS 20.1, 20.3]

IAS 20 does not deal with:

- the issues that arise in accounting for government grants in financial statements reflecting the effect of changing prices;

- the accounting treatment of tax-related government assistance;

- government participation in the ownership of the enterprise; or

- government grants received in relation to an entity's agricultural activities and accounted for in accordance with IAS 41 *Agriculture*.

Government assistance is action by governments to provide economic benefits to one or more entities. Government grants are assistance in the form of the transfer of resources, usually in the form of cash, to an entity for a specific purpose. Conditions of receipt are commonplace, although they do not form an essential part of receipt. Government assistance provided indirectly to an entity by, for example a general provision of infrastructure in a development area, does not meet the definition of government assistance. [IAS 20.3]

Government grants that cannot reasonably have a value placed on them (for example the provision of free services by a government department) are excluded from the definition of government grants. The definition also excludes "transactions with government which cannot be distinguished from the normal trading transactions" of the entity. The benefit of receiving an interest free loan, although classed as a form of government assistance, should not be recognised by calculating an imputed rate of interest. [IAS 20.3, 20.37]

4 Recognition and Measurement

Government grants should only be recognised when there is reasonable assurance that any conditions attaching to the grant will be complied with and the grant will actually be received. These conditions equally apply to non-monetary (i.e. non-cash) grants that are measured at fair value. [IAS 20.7]

As stated above, one of the conditions for recognition is that the grant will be received. Actual receipt of the grant does not necessarily meet this requirement since circumstances may exist where the grant will have to subsequently be repaid. Government grants should not be recognised on a cash basis as this is not consistent with the general accounting concepts addressed in IAS 1 *Presentation of financial statements*.

The general principle is that a government grant should be recognised as income in the periods in which the costs that it is intended to compensate are recognised. Where the grant has been received towards the cost of, say, a piece of machinery, the grant should be recognised as income when depreciation is charged in respect of the asset. The purpose of this treatment is to provide a matching effect in the income statement. A systematic basis should be used to recognise the grant income. [IAS 20.12]

If the receipt of a government grant represents compensation for expenses already incurred by the entity, the grant should be recognised as income in the period in which it becomes receivable. Immediate recognition will also be appropriate where the grant is given to provide immediate financial support and there are no future related expenses expected to be incurred. [IAS 20.20]

4.1 Non-monetary government grants

Where a grant is received in the form of a non-monetary asset (i.e. not in the form of cash) it is usual to recognise both the grant and the asset at fair value (although nominal value is also permitted as an alternative).

Illustration 1

The following government grants should be recognised in the income statements of the relevant entities according to IAS 20 as follows:

(1) The government makes a grant to a start-up entity writing teaching software for children with learning difficulties. The purpose of the grant is to help with general financing on start up and there are no further conditions attaching to the grant.

The grant should be recognised in full immediately that it is receivable. This grant has been provided for the purpose of giving immediate financial support to the entity.

(2) A manufacturing entity sets up a plant in an area of high unemployment. A grant of CU4 million is receivable if it continues to employ at least 100 people over a period of four years. It is highly probable it will do so. CU2 million of the grant is to be received immediately and a further CU2 million is receivable in four years' time.

Since there is reasonable assurance that the conditions attaching to the grant will be met, the grant is recognised as income evenly over the four year period in which the entity incurs the costs of employing the 100 people.

(3) An agricultural research entity is given land that belonged to the government to set up a new laboratory and to investigate new farming methods.

This is a grant related to a non-monetary asset and, as such, it should probably be recognised when the costs of constructing the laboratory are incurred. Treatment will depend on the specific circumstances and whether there are conditions relating to the gift of land.

(4) Free technical advice is provided by government employees to help an export entity to market its new technology in North America.

Free technical advice is likely to be a grant that cannot reasonably have a value placed upon it and therefore should not be recognised.

5 Government Grants Related to Assets and Income: Presentation

5.1 Grants related to assets

Government grants related to assets are those provided so that an entity can acquire or construct specific long-term assets. [IAS 20.3]

In such circumstances the grant should be presented in the balance sheet either by recognising the grant as deferred income and systematically recognising it in the income statement over the assets' useful life or by deducting the grant (netting it off) directly from the asset's carrying value. The netting off approach equally recognises the grant in the income statement over the period of use of the asset by reducing the amount of depreciation charged. [IAS 20.24]

This treatment is also appropriate for the receipt of non-monetary grants measured at fair value. [IAS 20.24]

Illustration 2

An entity purchased an item of equipment for CU100,000 on 1 January 2004. It will depreciate this machinery on a straight-line basis over its useful economic life of five years, with a zero residual value. Also on 1 January 2004, the entity received a government grant of CU10,000 to help finance this equipment.

Under the netting-off method the grant and the equipment should be shown in the income statement for the year to 31 December 2004 and in the balance sheet at that date as follows:

Balance sheet

	CU	
Fixed asset		
Cost	90,000	(CU100,000 less grant of CU10,000)
Depreciation	(18,000)	(CU90,000 / 5 years)
Net book value	72,000	

Income statement

Expense:	Depreciation	CU18,000

Under the deferred income method the grant and the equipment should be shown in the income statement for the year to 31 December 2004 and in the balance sheet at that date as follows:

Balance sheet

	CU	
Fixed asset		
Cost	100,000	
Depreciation	(20,000)	(CU100,000 / 5 years)
Net book value	80,000	
Deferred income	8,000	(CU10,000 less amount recognised in income statement in year of CU2,000)

Income statement

Expense:	Depreciation	CU20,000	
Income:	Deferred income	CU2,000	(CU10,000 / 5 years)

Note: The overall profit effect is the same with each method but the presentation is different.

5.2 Grants related to income

A government grant related to income is simply defined as one not related to an asset. Such grants should be recognised in the income statement when any conditions for their recognition have been met. Income related government grants may be presented as income and shown separately, or under 'other income' or deducted from the expenditure to which they relate.

6 Government Grants: Other Issues

6.1 Repayment of government grants

A government grant that becomes repayable, for example because conditions of receipt have not been met, should be accounted for as a change in an accounting estimate accounted for in accordance with IAS 8 *Accounting policies, changes in accounting estimates and errors.* [IAS 20.32]

6.2 No specific relation to operating activities

SIC-10 *Government assistance – No specific relation to operating activities* considers the situation where government assistance is given but there are no conditions that relate specifically to the entity's operating activities. Such government assistance is given, for example, to encourage an entity to operate in a particular industry or area.

Although such government grants do not relate to specific activities of the entity, they meet the definition of a government grant and should therefore be recognised in accordance with the general requirements of IAS 20.

7 Disclosure

IAS 20 requires that information is disclosed to provide sufficient detail in an entity's financial statements so that a user is able to understand the impact that government grants have had on the entity's financial statements.

An entity should disclose the accounting policy, including presentation, adopted for the treatment of government grants and the nature and extent of government grants recognised in the financial statements. This disclosure should include an indication of any other form of government assistance that, although not recognised in the financial statements, the entity has received a direct benefit from, for example the provision of free services by the government. [IAS 20.39]

An entity should also explain the existence of any unfulfilled conditions or other contingencies that relate to recognised government assistance. [IAS 20.39]

8 Chapter Review

This chapter has been concerned with the accounting and presentation requirements for government grants and assistance. The key issues relate to the recognition and measurement of both asset and income based grants.

This chapter covered:

■   the scope and key definitions included in IAS 20 on government grants;

■   forms of government assistance that should be recognised in the financial statements of the recipient entity;

■   the alternative permitted methods of measurement of asset related government grants in the balance sheet;

■   the manner in which grants should be recognised in the income statement; and

■   the principal disclosure requirements of IAS 20.

Chapter 10
NON-CURRENT ASSETS HELD FOR SALE

1 Business Context

One of the main purposes of financial statements is to provide users with sufficient information so that they are able to make informed economic decisions. It is therefore important that the financial statements not only present information about the entity's past performance but also enable a user to make an assessment about its future performance and its ability to generate future cash flows.

An asset is held for sale when the entity does not intend to use it as part of its ongoing business but instead intends to sell it. The separate identification of assets that are held for sale rather than to generate continuing economic benefits for the entity on an ongoing basis substantially improves the information made available to users. It provides information on the entity's likely future performance.

IFRS 5 *Non-current assets held for sale and discontinued operations* not only provides additional useful information on assets held for resale but has also led to the same classification and measurement requirements of such assets as under US accounting requirements (SFAS 144 *Accounting for impairment or disposal of long-lived assets*). This promotes convergence of accounting standards.

2 Chapter Objectives

IFRS 5 deals with two related topics: the accounting for assets classified as held for sale which is covered in this chapter and discontinued operations which are covered as part of segment reporting. This chapter sets out the processes to be followed when an item of property, plant or equipment (PPE) or a group of assets and liabilities are set aside for sale.

On completion of this chapter you should be able to:

- understand the objectives and scope of IFRS 5;

- interpret the important terminology and definitions which relate to the treatment of IFRS 5 in financial statements;

- understand the key principles relating to the recognition and measurement of non-current assets held for sale;

- demonstrate knowledge of the principal disclosure requirements of IFRS 5; and

- apply knowledge and understanding of IFRS 5 in particular circumstances, through basic calculations.

3 Objectives, Scope and Definitions of IFRS 5

IFRS 5 sets out the treatment of assets held for sale and the presentation and disclosure of discontinued operations. It applies to all non-current assets and to groups of assets and associated liabilities which will be disposed of in a single transaction, described as a disposal group. But it does not apply to those assets which are required to be measured in accordance with another international standard. The assets excluded from the scope of IFRS 5 are either those that are already carried at fair value, with changes in their fair value being reported directly in the income statement, or where there are difficulties in establishing a reliable fair value.

Assets which specifically fall outside the scope of IFRS 5 are:

- deferred tax assets accounted for in accordance with IAS 12 *Income taxes*;

- employee benefit assets accounted for in accordance with IAS 19 *Employee benefits*;

- financial assets accounted for in accordance with IAS 39 *Financial instruments: recognition and measurement*;

- non-current assets accounted for in accordance with IAS 40 *Investment property* under the fair value model option;

- non-current assets accounted for in accordance with IAS 41 *Agriculture* at fair value less point-of-sale costs; and

- contractual rights as defined in accordance with IFRS 4 *Insurance contracts*.

A disposal group is a related group of assets and their associated liabilities that will be disposed of in a single transaction. The definition includes, but is not limited to, a cash-generating unit of the entity, i.e. a group of assets which generates economic benefits which are largely independent of other activities of the entity, although this is not a requirement.

4 Non-current Assets Held for Sale

Non-current assets may be measured, following their initial recognition, at cost or a revalued amount. These measurement bases are relevant when such assets are held for ongoing use in the business.

IFRS 5 requires that a non-current asset, or disposal group, should be classified as 'held for sale' when the entity does not intend to use the asset as part of its on-going business but instead intends to sell it and recover its carrying amount principally through sale. [IFRS 5.6]

To be classified as held for sale the asset or disposal group should be available for immediate sale. This means that the asset's current condition should be adequate to be effectively 'sold as seen'. The likelihood of a sale taking place should also be considered to be highly probable and normally completed within one year of the date of its classification. For a sale to be considered as highly probable there should be a committed plan and management should be actively trying to find a buyer. The commitment by management that a sale will take place should be such that withdrawal from the plan is unlikely.

If the entity decides to abandon, rather than sell, such an asset, it will not meet these criteria and should not be classified as held for sale, since any benefit flowing to the entity will be through its continuing use.

Where an entity acquires a non-current asset, or disposal group, solely on the basis that it intends to sell it on rather than use it as part of its ongoing activities, it should be classified as a held for sale asset at the date of acquisition only where the condition that it be sold within one year of the acquisition date is met. The asset should also meet all other conditions for classification within a short period of its acquisition, which is normally considered to be three months.

The conditions for sale should be met before the balance sheet date if the asset or disposal group is to be recognised as a held for sale asset in the current reporting period. If the conditions are only met after the balance sheet date, there should be full disclosure in the notes to the financial statements.

A non-current asset, or disposal group, that meets the recognition criteria to be classified as held for sale should be measured at the lower of its carrying amount (the value at which it is currently recognised in the balance sheet) and the fair value less costs to sell. [IFRS 5.15]

Costs to sell are the incremental costs that the entity will incur as a result of the disposal of the assets, for example transport costs and costs to advertise that the asset is available for sale.

By applying this measurement basis the entity will recognise any anticipated loss on the sale as an impairment loss as soon as the decision to sell the asset has taken place.

Non-current assets classified as held for sale should not be depreciated.

On ultimate disposal of an asset classified as held for sale, any difference between its carrying amount and the disposal proceeds is treated as a loss or gain under IAS 16 *Property, plant and equipment* and not as an adjustment to any impairment previously recognised.

Illustration 1

An entity with a 31 December year-end acquired an item of PPE on 1 January 2001 at a cost of CU100,000. The asset has an estimated residual value of CU10,000 and a useful life of 10 years. On 1 January 2004 the asset was classified as held for sale. Its fair value was estimated at CU40,000 and the costs to sell at CU2,000.

The asset was sold on 30 June 2004 for CU38,000.

(a) Upon re-classification as held for sale on 1 January 2004:

(i) The asset is removed from its PPE category within non-current assets into the held for sale category

(ii) The carrying amount of the asset immediately before the reclassification is CU73,000 (CU100,000 – ((CU100,000 – CU10,000) x 3/10))

(iii) The fair value less costs to sell of the held for sale asset is CU38,000 (CU40,000 less CU2,000 costs). The asset is now measured at this value, which is lower than its carrying amount

(iv) A loss of CU35,000 is recognised in the income statement as an impairment loss, the difference between the current carrying value and the fair value less costs to sell (i.e. its recoverable amount)

(b) Upon sale on 30 June 2004, there is no profit or loss to be recognised in the income statement. The loss was recognised when the asset was classified as held for sale.

Illustration 2

Assume the facts are as in Illustration 1, except that on classification as held for sale, the fair value was estimated at CU80,000 and the costs to sell at CU3,000.

The asset was sold on 30 June 2004 for CU77,000.

(a) Upon re-classification as held for sale on 1 January 2004:

(i) The asset is removed from its PPE category within non-current assets into the held for sale category

(ii) The fair value less costs to sell of the held for sale asset is CU77,000
(CU80,000 - CU3,000 = CU77,000). This is higher than the asset's current carrying value (calculated in illustration 1 as being CU73,000), so the asset remains measured at CU73,000

(iii) The gain is not recognised in the income statement at this time, since any gain should not be anticipated at the point of reclassification.

(b) Upon sale on 30 June 2004, a profit of CU4,000 is recognised in the income statement
(Proceeds of CU77,000 received less current carring value of CU73,000)

Where an entity adopts the revaluation model for the measurement of assets, any asset classified as held for sale should be revalued to fair value immediately prior to the revaluation. Upon reclassification the costs to sell are deducted and recognised as an impairment loss in the income statement.

Illustration 3

An entity carries its land at fair value. One piece of land had a carrying value of CU60,000. On 1 January 2004 the asset was classified as held for sale, its fair value being estimated at CU70,000 and the costs to sell at CU2,000. The asset was sold on 30 June 2004 for CU67,000.

On 1 January 2004 the land is revalued to CU70,000. The gain of CU10,000 is recognised in a revaluation reserve. The land is then classified as held for sale and the costs to sell of CU2,000 are recognised in the income statement as an impairment loss. The carrying amount is now CU68,000.

Upon sale a further loss of CU1,000 is recognised as a loss on sale as the sale proceeds are less than the carrying amount. The balance on the revaluation reserve is now realised and it will be transferred to retained earnings.

4.1 Changes of plan

If a non-current asset classified as held for sale no longer meets the specific recognition requirements for such classification then it should be reclassified. Should reclassification be necessary, the asset should then be measured at the lower of the carrying amount that it would have been recognised at had it not been reclassified and its recoverable amount. The carrying amount that the asset would have been recognised at, is its carrying amount at the date of the original classification as held for sale was made, adjusted for depreciation or valuations that would otherwise have taken place. Recoverable amount is determined at the date the decision not to sell is made.

It is possible for individual assets or liabilities within a disposal group no longer to be considered to be part of that group and therefore should be reclassified. Such an event will not lead to the remaining part of the disposal group having to be reclassified provided that it continues to meet the recognition criteria.

5 Presentation and Disclosure

An asset classified as held for sale should be presented in the balance sheet separately from other assets. Typically a separate heading 'non-current assets – held for sale' would be appropriate.

Where a disposal group is held for sale, the assets and liabilities within it should also be separately identified. Such assets and liabilities should not be netted off for disclosure purposes and presented as a single line item. The major classes of assets and liabilities of the disposal group should be presented separately either on the face of the balance sheet or within the notes to the financial statements. This disclosure is not, however, required where the disposal group was classified as held for sale when it was newly acquired.

The separate presentation is required when the assets are classified as held for sale. It is therefore not appropriate to restate prior period balance sheet figures to reflect the current classification.

An entity should also provide a description of any non-current assets, or a disposal group, classified as held for sale or sold including details of any sale and expected time scales for disposal. If a sale has taken place within the reporting period, then the gain or loss on disposal should be separately identified either on the face of the income statement or within the notes to the financial statements.

Where held for sale assets have been included within a segment as part of the segmental analysis presented in accordance with IAS 14 *Segment reporting* this information should be highlighted.

6 Chapter Review

This chapter has been concerned with the accounting requirements for non-current assets and disposal groups that have been identified as being held for sale.

The chapter has covered the:

- scope of IFRS 5 in relation to held for sale assets;

- criteria for assets to be classified as held for sale;

- appropriate measurement basis; and

- disclosure requirements in relation to held for sale assets.

Chapter 11
INVESTMENT PROPERTY

1 Business Context

Investment properties are properties that are held by their owners for their investment potential. This potential may be realised either through the receipt of rental income or by continuing to hold the properties for their capital appreciation. Investment properties are not held by an entity for use in the production or supply of goods and services. The risks and returns associated with an investment property are different to those that result from an entity using the property for its own occupation.

While rental income presents few problems, the issue of capital gains raises both commercial and accounting issues. Gains can be viewed as either a year on year increase in the property's value or as one total gain over the period of ownership.

Since an investment property is an investment of the entity it is not necessarily appropriate to recognise the consumption of the asset as a charge in the income statement each period on a systematic basis. It is generally the current value of investment properties which is of prime importance and therefore recognising such properties in the financial statements at their market value may be seen as more appropriate.

2 Chapter Objectives

This chapter deals with IAS 40 *Investment properties.* The key issue is the identification of properties which should be treated as investment properties. Other important areas include the recognition and measurement of investment properties at different stages (i) initial recognition, (ii) whilst held for rental purposes or capital appreciation and (iii) on disposal. Disclosure issues are also relevant.

On completion of this chapter you should be able to:

- demonstrate a knowledge of the types of properties that fall within the scope of IAS 40;

- demonstrate an understanding of, and be able to apply, recognition and measurement criteria to investment properties;

- demonstrate the correct treatment on the change in use of an investment property;

- demonstrate an understanding of and be able to apply, the correct treatment on the disposal of an investment property;

- demonstrate a knowledge of the disclosure requirements of IAS 40; and

- apply IAS 40 knowledge and understanding in particular circumstances through basic calculations.

3 Objectives, Scope and Definitions of IAS 40

3.1 Nature of investment properties

An investment property is land or buildings, or both, that is held by an entity to earn rentals and/or for its capital appreciation potential. [IAS 40.5]

In summary, an investment property generates cash flows largely independent of the other assets held by an entity. This distinguishes investment property from owner-occupied property, which is held by the owner for use in the production or supply of goods or services, for administrative purposes or for sale in the ordinary course of business. The definition of an investment property includes a building that is currently vacant but is held with a view to it being let out and an existing investment property that is being redeveloped with a view to its continued use as an investment property. [IAS 40.5]

IAS 40 makes it clear that where a property is being constructed for future use as an investment property it does not meet the investment property definition until the construction or development is complete. During construction the property should be accounted for in accordance with IAS 16 *Property, plant and equipment.*

A property held under an operating lease may be classified by the lessor as an investment property if certain conditions are met. [IAS 40.16]

3.2 Scope

IAS 40 applies to the recognition, measurement and disclosure of investment properties. It does not deal with areas that are more specifically dealt with in other international standards. For example, the recognition of rental income is accounted for under IAS 18 *Revenue.*

Illustration 1

Which of the following should be treated as an investment property according to IAS 40?

(1) An entity has a factory which due to a decline in activity is no longer required and is now being held for resale.

This is a property held for sale in the ordinary course of business and is not an investment property.

(2) Farming land is purchased for its investment potential. Planning permission has not been obtained for building constructions of any kind.

This is land held for long-term capital appreciation and therefore is an investment property. The lack of planning permission is not relevant as values can appreciate in the absence of permission to build.

(3) A factory is in the process of being constructed on behalf of the government.

This is property being constructed for a third party and would therefore be dealt with under IAS 11 Construction contracts.

(4) A new office building used by an insurance entity as its head office which was purchased specifically in the centre of a major city in order to exploit its capital gains potential.

This building generates cash flows as part of a larger organisation. This is therefore an owner-occupied property dealt with under IAS 16 rather than IAS 40.

4 Recognition and Measurement

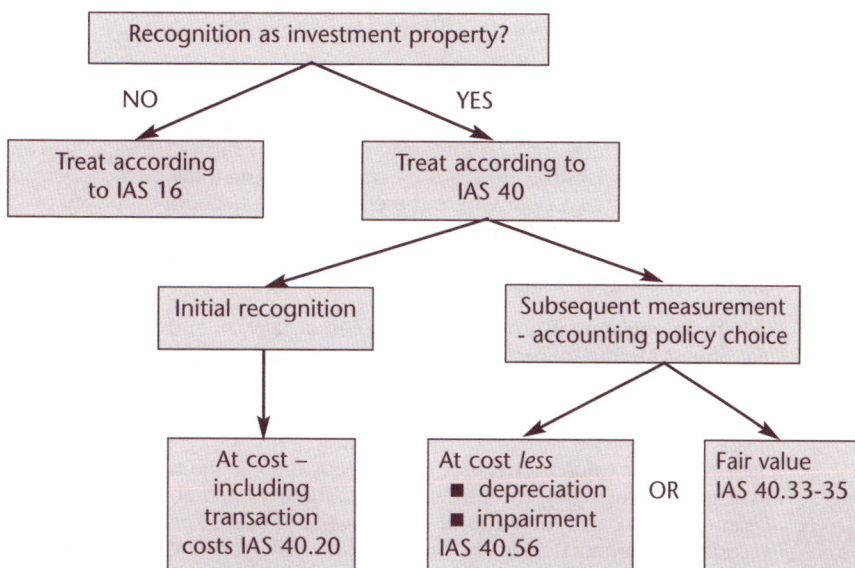

```
                   ┌─────────────────────────────────┐
                   │ Recognition as investment property? │
                   └─────────────────────────────────┘
              NO                              YES
   ┌──────────────────┐          ┌──────────────────┐
   │ Treat according  │          │ Treat according to │
   │   to IAS 16      │          │     IAS 40        │
   └──────────────────┘          └──────────────────┘

        ┌──────────────────┐        ┌────────────────────────┐
        │ Initial recognition │     │ Subsequent measurement   │
        └──────────────────┘        │ - accounting policy choice │
                                     └────────────────────────┘

   ┌──────────────┐     ┌──────────────┐         ┌──────────────┐
   │ At cost –    │     │ At cost less │         │ Fair value   │
   │ including    │     │ ■ depreciation│  OR     │ IAS 40.33-35 │
   │ transaction  │     │ ■ impairment │         │              │
   │ costs IAS 40.20 │  │ IAS 40.56    │         │              │
   └──────────────┘     └──────────────┘         └──────────────┘
```

4.1 Initial recognition

An investment property should be recognised when the normal conditions for asset recognition are satisfied. These are when:

- it is probable that the future economic benefits associated with the investment property will flow to the entity; and

- the cost of the investment property can be measured reliably. [IAS 40.16]

An investment property should initially be measured at its cost. Cost includes transaction costs; these are expenses that are directly attributable to the investment property, for example professional fees and property transfer taxes. Cost does not include activities that, whilst related to the investment property, are not directly attributable to it, for example start up costs, relocation costs and the normal servicing of the property. [IAS 40.20]

Self-constructed investment properties should be held at the cost recognised in accordance with IAS 16 at the date when the construction or development is completed. Only on completion can the property be recognised as an investment property in accordance with IAS 40.

Where a property held under a lease is classified as an investment property, IAS 17 *Leases* requires the property to be recognised at the lower of fair value and the present value of the minimum lease payments under the lease. [IAS 40.25]

4.2 Measurement after recognition

Following initial measurement at cost, investment properties are either held at cost less accumulated depreciation (the cost model) or measured at fair value. (the fair value model). Where the cost model is chosen the property should be accounted for in accordance with IAS 16. [IAS 40.33, 40.56]

The chosen accounting policy should generally be consistently applied to all of the entity's investment properties (i.e. it is not permitted to measure one property at cost and another at fair value). There is an assumption that an entity will be able to determine an investment property's fair value reliably. However, in exceptional cases this may not be possible, so the individual property should be measured at cost even where the entity has an accounting policy of measuring investment properties at fair value. Where an entity has this mixed accounting for investment properties, it should disclose why this has arisen and if possible provide a range of estimates for fair value. [IAS 40.53, 40.78]

Where an investment property is measured at fair value, the entity should continue to apply this accounting policy to it. [IAS 40.55]

4.3 Fair value model

Where the fair value model is adopted following the initial recognition of investment properties, the properties should be valued at fair value at each balance sheet date. Changes in the fair value of investment properties should be recognised immediately in the income statement, forming part of the profit or loss for the period in which the remeasurement occurred. [IAS 40.35]

The fair value of an investment property is the price at which the property could be exchanged between knowledgeable and willing parties in an arm's length transaction. [IAS 40.5]

Fair value should reflect the market conditions at the balance sheet date. The best evidence of fair value is given by current prices in an active market for similar properties in the same location and condition. It is important to appreciate that fair value is time specific (since market conditions change), so the valuation should take place at each balance sheet date. [IAS 40.38]

Illustration 2

An entity owns two investment properties, X and Y, the fair values of which are:

	At 31 December 2002	At 31 December 2003
	CUm	CUm
Property X	15	20
Property Y	10	8

The original cost of the properties was CU9 million each when they were acquired on 1 January 2001.

The entity uses the fair value model to value all its investment properties.

The following amounts should be recognised in the financial statements for the year ended 31 December 2003:

Income statement

	CUmillion
Property X (income)	5
Property Y (charge)	2
Net credit in year	3

Balance sheet	CUmillion
Property X	20
Property Y	8
Total	28

5 Transfers Following a Change in Usage

A change in the use of a property may lead to it no longer being recognised as an investment property. The following table sets out where there might be evidence that a change in use has occurred and how the property should be treated following the change in use. [IAS 40.57]

Evidence of change in use	Accounting treatment
Occupation of the property by the entity itself.	The property is now owner-occupied and should therefore be recognised as a property in use by the entity in accordance with IAS 16. Where the investment property was measured at fair value, its fair value at the date of change in use should be treated as the deemed cost for future accounting. [IAS 40.60]
Development of the property commences with the intention that it will then be sold by the entity.	The property is being held for sale in the normal course of business and should therefore be reclassified as inventory and accounted for in accordance with IAS 2 *Inventories*. Where the investment property was measured at fair value, its fair value at the date of change in use should be treated as the deemed cost. [IAS 40.60]
Development of the property commences with the intention that it will continue to be let after completion of the development works.	The property should continue to be held as an investment property under IAS 40.

A building that was occupied by the entity is vacated so that it can be let to third parties.	The property is no longer owner-occupied and therefore should be transferred to investment properties and accounted for in accordance with IAS 40. Where investment properties are measured at fair value the property should be revalued at the date of change in use and any difference should be recognised as a revaluation under IAS 16. [IAS 40.61]
A property that was originally held as inventory has now been let to a third party.	The property is no longer held for resale and is instead held to generate future rental income and therefore should be transferred to investment properties in accordance with IAS 40. Where investment properties are measured at fair value the property should be revalued at the date of change in use and any difference should be recognised immediately in the income statement. [IAS 40.63]
An entity has constructed a property that it now intends to let out to a number of third parties.	Whilst the property is being constructed it is accounted for in accordance with IAS 16. However, on completion it should be transferred to investment properties. Where investment properties are measured at fair value the property should be revalued at the date of change in use and any difference should be recognised immediately in the income statement. [IAS 40.65]

6 Disposal of Investment Properties

An investment property should be eliminated from the balance sheet when it is disposed of, either through sale or by entering a finance lease. An investment property which is permanently withdrawn from use and will not generate any future economic benefits, even on its ultimate disposal, should be eliminated from the balance sheet. [IAS 40.66]

When an investment property is disposed of or permanently withdrawn from use and no future benefit will accrue to the entity, a gain or loss should be calculated and recognised directly in the income statement in the period in which the disposal or 'retirement' takes place. The gain or loss should normally be determined as the difference between the net disposal proceeds and the carrying amount of the asset. [IAS 40.69]

Illustration 3

An entity purchased an investment property on 1 January 2001, for a cost of CU400,000. The property has a useful life of 50 years, with no residual value and at 31 December 2003 had a fair value of CU560,000. On 1 January 2004 the property was sold for net proceeds of CU540,000.

The amount that should be recognised in the income statement for the year ended 31 December 2004 regarding the disposal of the property is shown below:

	CU
The cost model	
(a) Carrying amount 400,000 - (400,000/50 years x 3) =	376,000
Net proceeds	540,000
Profit on sale	164,000
The fair value model	
(b) Fair value	560,000
Net proceeds	540,000
Loss on sale	20,000

7 Disclosure

The disclosures required in relation to investment properties are in three broad groups:

- those applicable to both the fair value model and the cost model;
- those applicable only to the fair value model; and
- those applicable only to the cost model.

7.1 Applicable to both the fair value model and the cost model

An entity should disclose which measurement basis it uses for its investment properties, so whether it uses the cost model or fair value model. When it has been particularly difficult to establish whether the property is an investment property or an owner-occupied property, the entity should set out the criteria that it considered in making its decision. [IAS 40.75]

An entity should separately identify the amount of rental income recognised in the period along with any related operating expenses attributable to the rentals.

If restrictions exist on the realisation of income, either through rentals or sale proceeds, or if the entity has a contractual obligation to purchase or construct an investment property, these facts should be disclosed.

7.2 The fair value model

Where an entity applies the fair value model it should present a detailed reconciliation, showing all movements, between the carrying amount of investment property at the beginning and the end of the period. [IAS 40.76]

An entity should disclose the methods and significant assumptions made, including whether there was market evidence or not, in determining the fair value of investment property and whether the valuation was carried out by an independent qualified valuer. [IAS 40.75]

It is possible that significant fixtures, such as lifts and office furniture, within an investment property have been separately recognised in the financial statement as property, plant and equipment under IAS 16. A property will generally be valued as a whole and therefore the valuation will include such fixtures. To avoid the double counting of these items, the fair value of the property should be adjusted. Where such an adjustment has been made, this fact should be disclosed. [IAS 40.77]

7.3 The cost model

An entity that applies the cost model should disclose the depreciation methods and rates, or useful life, used.

A detailed reconciliation should be presented for the gross cost of investment properties and the related accumulated depreciation showing all movements during the year. The carrying amount (i.e. the cost less the accumulated depreciation) should be clearly disclosed for both the beginning and end of the period.

In addition an entity is required to disclose the fair value of investment properties where possible. If it is not possible, this fact should be explained and a range of estimates should be provided instead. [IAS 40.79]

8 Chapter Review

This chapter has been concerned with the accounting for investment properties. A key issue is the identification of properties that should be treated as investment properties. Once identified as an investment property the entity should address recognition and measurement issues. These include: (i) initial recognition, (ii) ongoing measurement and (iii) on disposal.

This chapter has covered:

- the nature of investment properties and the scope of IAS 40;

- recognition and measurement criteria for investment properties, including the fair value model and the cost model;

- treatment on the change in use of an investment property;

- treatment on the disposal of an investment property; and

- the disclosure requirements of IAS 40.

Chapter 12

INTANGIBLES

1 Business Context

Brand names such as Coca-Cola and Microsoft, are in many cases, an entity's most valuable asset but they are extremely difficult to value when they have been generated internally and over a period of time. Brands are one example of an intangible asset. Internally generated brands that cannot be measured reliably are not recognised in the balance sheet because of the difficulties that surround their valuation.

However, an entity that has acquired as opposed to internally generated an equally valuable brand will recognise it, since a fair value can be attributed to it. As the acquirer has paid a price to acquire this brand, that price provides a reliable measurement.

This inconsistent treatment has in the past led to some companies writing off acquired brands (i.e. removing the asset from the balance sheet and charging this amount to the income statement).

2 Chapter Objectives

This chapter deals with IAS 38 *Intangible assets* which sets out the reporting requirements relating to intangible assets.

On completion of this chapter you should be able to:

- demonstrate a knowledge of the objectives and scope of IAS 38;

- demonstrate a knowledge of the important terminology and definitions which relate to intangible assets;

- demonstrate an understanding of how to identify, measure, disclose and account for the disposal of intangible assets; and

- apply IAS 38 knowledge and understanding in particular circumstances through basic calculations.

3 Objectives, Scope and Definitions of IAS 38

An intangible asset is defined as an identifiable non-monetary asset that does not have physical substance. Non-monetary assets are those which are not 'monetary assets' (monetary assets are defined as items whose value is fixed in money terms, for example, a receivable or cash). [IAS 38.8]

The objective of IAS 38 is to prescribe the accounting treatment for intangible assets that are not dealt with specifically in other standards. It requires an entity to recognise an intangible asset if certain criteria are met. It also specifies how to measure the carrying amount of intangible assets and the nature of the disclosures required.

Examples of assets specifically excluded from IAS 38 include: [IAS 38.2]

■ goodwill which is accounted for under IFRS 3 *Business combinations*;

■ financial assets as defined in IAS 39 *Financial instruments: recognition and measurement*; and

■ mineral rights, related exploration and development expenditure incurred.

One of the principal distinctions between property, plant and equipment, and intangible assets is that while the former have physical substance, the latter do not.

The distinction can sometimes be blurred, where, for example an item itself does not have physical substance but it is held in or on something that does. Examples of this are computer software held on compact disc, a licence or patent written into a legal document, or a film held on tape. In such cases judgement will be needed to assess whether the item should be accounted for in accordance with IAS 16 *Property, plant and equipment* or IAS 38. If software forms an integral part of the related hardware then it will be accounted for as part of the hardware under IAS 16; if, however, it is a piece of independent software then it should be accounted for under IAS 38.

IAS 38 specifically applies to expenditure incurred on activities such as advertising, training, start-up activities, and research and development. The standard also applies to rights under licensing agreements for items such as motion pictures, video recordings, plays, manuscripts, patents and copyrights.

An intangible asset should be initially measured at cost. [IAS 38.24]

4 The Definition of Intangible Assets

4.1 Identifiability

The definition of an intangible asset, as set out above, includes the requirement for the asset to be identifiable. The reason for this requirement is to distinguish it from goodwill, which arises on the acquisition of a subsidiary. Goodwill represents the excess of the acquisition cost over the sum of the identifiable net assets acquired. Goodwill is not identifiable itself since it represents future economic benefits arising from assets not capable of individual identification and separate recognition.

For an intangible asset to be determined as identifiable it should either be: [IAS 38.12]

■ separable; or

■ arise from contractual or other legal rights.

An asset is separable if it can be sold, licensed, or rented to another party on its own, rather than as part of the business. Rights to films, airport landing slots, fishing or milk quotas, taxi licences, patents, copyrights and trademarks are all examples of separable assets and therefore fall within the definition of intangibles.

4.2 Control

One of the characteristics of an asset is that it is under the control of the entity. Control results in the entity being able to obtain the future economic benefits generated by using an asset and to restrict other parties from obtaining them. This would normally arise where there are legal rights enforceable in a court of law, for example trademarks, copyrights and patents. The existence of legal rights is not, however, an essential element in determining control, although it is more difficult to assess without their presence.

Staff is a common example of an asset that is not controlled by the entity and does not therefore meet the definition of an intangible asset. Although the entity expects that staff skills and knowledge will lead to increased economic benefits flowing to it, it has insufficient control over them, since they can usually leave at short notice. Without the protection of a legal right, the entity has insufficient control over the expected future economic benefits from customer relationships to meet the definition of an intangible asset. However, it is possible for an entity to sell part of a customer list, such a sale is not a business combination. The ability to exchange, for example a customer relationship is evidence that the entity has control over the future economic benefits flowing from that relationship, and therefore meets the definition of an intangible asset.

Future economic benefits flowing from an intangible asset may result in increased revenue, but may also result in the reduction of costs as a result of, for example a legal right to use a new technology.

5 Initial Recognition and Measurement

Before an intangible asset can be recognised on the balance sheet, not only does it need to meet the definition discussed above but it also needs to meet certain recognition criteria.

The recognition criteria are that: [IAS 38.21]

- it is probable that future economic benefits from the asset will flow to the entity; and

- the cost of the asset can be measured reliably.

IAS 38 provides examples of where expenditure is incurred to provide future economic benefits to the entity, but where no intangible asset should be recognised. Such expenditure should instead be recognised as an expense directly in the income statement. Examples include expenditure on start-up activities, staff training costs (even where this is directly related to a new asset), advertising and promotional activities, and expenditure on relocating an activity.

5.1 Separately acquired intangible assets

In most cases separately acquired intangible assets, for example brands, licences, computer software and patents, meet the above recognition criteria.

An intangible asset should be initially recognised at its cost. Cost includes the net amount paid for the asset after taxes, trade discounts and other directly attributable costs. Other directly attributable costs might include, for example, professional fees, or costs incurred to test the functionality of the asset. Such costs do not include the cost of incorporating the new asset into the existing business, or general administrative and overhead costs.

The requirements for the recognition and timing of costs capitalised as part of the cost of the intangible asset are similar to those set out in IAS 16. Capitalisation of costs should cease when the asset is ready for use even if the asset has not yet been put into use, or is operating at below expected levels.

Illustration 1

A entity acquires new technology that will revolutionise its current manufacturing process. The costs are set out below:

	CU
Original cost of the new technology	1,000,000
Discount provided	100,000
Staff training incurred in operating the new process	50,000
Testing of the new manufacturing process	10,000
Losses incurred whilst other parts of the plant stood idle	20,000

The cost that should be capitalised as part of the intangible asset is:

Cost	1,000,000
Less discount	(100,000)
Plus testing of process	10,000

5.2 Exchanges of assets

Where one non-monetary asset is exchanged for another, the intangible asset acquired is normally measured at its fair value. Where it is not possible to fair-value the asset acquired, for example where the fair value is not reliably measurable, then it should be recognised at the carrying amount of the intangible asset given up.

5.3 Intangible assets acquired as part of a business combination

The cost of an intangible asset acquired as part of a business combination should be assessed at its fair value at the date it was acquired. Fair value is defined as *the amount for which an asset could be exchanged between knowledgeable, willing parties in an arm's length transaction*. [IAS 38.8]

Fair value may be observable from an active market or recent similar transactions. Other methods may also be used, but if no means are available of ascertaining its fair value reliably, then the asset does not meet the recognition criteria. In such circumstances no separate intangible asset would be recognised. However, the value of goodwill would increase.

There is an assumption that where an intangible asset acquired as part of a business combination is considered to have a finite useful life, i.e. it will be used in the business for a finite number of years, then its fair value is capable of reliable measurement.

6 Internally Generated Intangible Assets

Internally generated goodwill should not be recognised as an asset. [IAS 38.48]

The key difficulties in deciding whether an internally generated asset should be recognised are pinpointing exactly when it comes into existence and measuring its costs reliably. It is difficult to distinguish the costs of generating an intangible asset from those of maintaining or enhancing the day-to-day operations of the business.

In order to assist in defining an internally generated asset, its evolution is thought of in terms of a research phase and a development phase. These phases relate to all intangible assets and are not limited to the area of research and development expenditure.

6.1 The research phase

All expenditure identified as arising during the research phase should be recognised as an expense as it is incurred. An intangible asset should not be generated during the research phase. [IAS 38.54]

During this phase the probability that future economic benefits will be generated for the entity is too low.

Examples of activities within the research phase include:

(i) the search for alternative materials, devices, products, processes, systems or services; and

(ii) the formulation, design, evaluation and final selection of possible alternatives for new or improved materials, devices, products, processes, systems or services.

6.2 The development phase

During the development phase it may be possible to identify an intangible asset which should be recognised. The development phase of a project is further advanced than the research phase; it is the next stage and therefore the probability of determining whether economic benefits will be generated is more likely. The development phase will typically see the design and development of a new product, tool, process or system.

To be recognised as an intangible asset arising from development, or the development phase, a number of stringent conditions should be satisfied. The characteristics that should be demonstrated if an intangible asset is to be recognised are: [IAS 38.57]

1. the technical feasibility to complete the asset, and the intention and ability to use or sell it (these requirements relate to the completion of the process to be able to obtain future economic benefits);

2. the means by which the probable future economic benefits will be generated and the availability of the resources to complete the development (this relates to both the definition of an asset and the recognition criteria); and

3. the ability to measure the development expenditure reliably (to meet the recognition criteria).

All three characteristics should be present. The second of these criteria specifically requires that the entity can demonstrate the existence of a market for the output of the intangible asset or, if it is to be used internally, the usefulness of the intangible asset.

IAS 38 explicitly states that internally generated brands, mastheads, publishing titles, customer lists and similar items should not be recognised as intangible assets. Such items cannot be identified separately from the cost of developing the business as a whole. Instead such items are seen as being component parts of internally generated goodwill, the recognition of which is prohibited. [IAS 38.63]

6.3 The cost of internally generated intangible assets

If an internally generated intangible asset is recognised, it should be measured at its cost. This is the directly attributable cost necessary to create, produce, and prepare the asset for its intended use. Such costs include, among other things:

- materials and services consumed;

- employment costs of those directly engaged in generating the asset; and

- legal, patent or licence registration fees.

It is important to note that it is only expenditure incurred after the project has entered its development phase that can be included as part of the cost. It is not possible at the time of recognition to go back to recognise expenditure which occurred during the research phase.

Illustration 2

An entity is developing a new pharmaceutical ingredient. In the previous year the entity recognised CU1,000 as an expense. During the current year expenditure incurred was CU1,200. Of this CU800 was incurred before the entity was able to demonstrate that the pharmaceutical ingredient met the criteria for recognition as an intangible asset.

The pharmaceutical ingredient is recognised as an intangible asset at a cost of CU400 being the expenditure incurred since the recognition criteria were met. The CU1,800 incurred before this should not form part of the cost of the intangible asset recognised in the balance sheet.

6.4 Web site development costs

A web site has many of the characteristics of both tangible and intangible assets. An interpretation was issued SIC 32 – *Intangible assets – web site costs* to provide guidance on how such costs should be treated to ensure that they are treated in a consistent manner.

SIC 32 is consistent with IAS 38 but provides the link between the standard and the specific characteristics of the development of a web site. SIC 32 makes it explicit that a web site that has been developed for the purposes of promoting and advertising an entity's products and services does not meet the requirement in IAS 38 to generate probable future benefits and therefore costs incurred in its development should be expensed as incurred.

7 Measurement After Initial Recognition

Measurement of intangible assets, following initial recognition, is similar to that in IAS 16.

An entity can choose to follow a cost model, whereby intangible assets are held at their cost less amortisation and impairment, or to use a revaluation model.

The revaluation model may, however only be used if fair value can be determined by reference to an active market. Such active markets are uncommon in practice, but do exist, for example freely transferable taxi licences.

Intangible assets with finite useful lives should be amortised over their useful life. [IAS 38.97]

Amortisation is a way of charging the cost of an intangible asset in each period, so that at the end of the asset's useful life to the entity, the whole of its cost has been charged to the income statement. At the end of its useful life the intangible asset will be stated at nil or its residual value.

The residual value of an intangible asset will normally be assumed to be nil unless certain criteria are met. These include where an active market exists for these items and is likely to exist at the end of the useful life of the asset to the entity, or there is a commitment by a third party to buy the asset at the end of its useful life. [IAS 38.100]

The carrying value of an intangible asset is the amount recognised in the balance sheet for each item: in this case it represents the cost of the intangible asset less the accumulated amortisation charged in relation to it to date.

Amortisation of an intangible asset should commence when the asset is ready and available for use within the entity. The amortisation method should reflect the pattern in which the asset's future economic benefits are expected to be used by the entity. Amortisation methods mentioned in IAS 38 include the straight-line method, the diminishing balance method and the unit of production method. If it is not possible to identify the pattern in which the economic benefits are expected to be utilised by the entity, then the straight-line method should be used.

Where an intangible asset is revalued, subsequent amortisation is based on the revalued amount.

The standard sets out a number of factors that should be considered in determining what the useful life of an intangible asset is. These factors include:

- expected usage of the asset by the entity, typical product life cycles for similar assets and dependence on other assets of the entity;

- the stability of the industry in which the company is operating, and the expected actions of competitors; and

- the speed of technological change and expected obsolescence.

Amortisation should normally be recognised in the income statement. An entity should review its amortisation periods and methods, and the residual value of intangible assets in each reporting period.

An intangible asset has a useful life that is indefinite if there is no foreseeable limit to the period over which it is expected to generate benefit for the entity. A conclusion that a useful life is indefinite should not depend on planned future expenditure that is expected to increase the performance of the asset.

An intangible asset that has been identified as having an indefinite life should not be amortised. Instead the asset is reviewed annually to assess whether there has been a fall in its value in accordance with IAS 36 *Impairment of assets.* [IAS 38.107]

8 Disposals of Intangible Assets

Intangible assets should be removed from the balance sheet when they are sold, or when no future economic benefits are expected from them. When the intangible asset is removed from the balance sheet, a profit or loss should be calculated based on any proceeds received and the current carrying amount of the asset. This gain or loss should be recognised directly in the income statement. [IAS 38.112–113]

Illustration 3

An entity acquires a brand for CU300,000. It estimates that the brand will generate cash flows for the entity over the next 15 years, at which time it is thought that the market will have increased, and the brand will be diluted in value.

The brand is therefore amortised straight-line over 15 years. Annual amortisation of CU20,000 is charged (CU300,000 / 15 years).

A third party makes an offer to buy the brand for CU250,000 at the end of the fifth year. The carrying amount of the brand is CU200,000 (CU300,000 less CU20,000 x 5 years).

The entity accepts the offer and the brand is sold. The carrying amount of the brand is removed from the balance sheet, the CU250,000 cash is received, and a profit of CU50,000 (the difference between the carrying amount of CU200,000 and the proceeds of CU250,000) is recognised directly in the income statement.

9 Disclosure

A number of detailed disclosures are required for each class of intangible assets to enable users to determine the mechanisms and factors affecting intangible asset values. If the entity has recognised internally generated intangible assets, then the disclosure information should be shown separately for these assets. [IAS 38.118]

Disclose:

1. the amortisation rates for intangible assets and the methods used;

2. the identification of the line item in the income statement where amortisation has been charged, and separate disclosure of any impairment losses incurred (with any reversals);

3. a full reconciliation of movements in the carrying amount of intangible assets, for example additions, amortisation, impairment and disposals;

4. net exchange differences that arose on translation; and

5. the aggregate amount of research and development expenditure recognised as an expense during the period.

In addition to these disclosures, if an intangible asset has been assessed as having an indefinite life, its carrying value and the reasons supporting the indefinite life assessment should be disclosed.

If an individual intangible asset is considered to be significant to the entity's financial statements, a description of the asset should be provided, along with its carrying amount and, in the case of an asset with a finite useful life, the remaining amortisation period should be set out.

Disclosure is required where the title of an intangible asset is restricted in some way, or the asset is pledged as security for the entity's liabilities. If the entity is contractually committed at the period end to acquiring intangible assets, the amount of this commitment should be disclosed.

For intangible assets that have been revalued, information should be disclosed about the effective date of the last valuation, the methods and assumptions used in calculating fair value, the current carrying amount for the class of intangibles, and what the carrying amount would have been had the entity continued to use the cost method. A reconciliation of the revaluation reserve should be set out to the extent that it contains balances in relation to revalued intangible assets.

10 Chapter Review

This chapter has been concerned with key issues relating to intangible assets and how they are measured and recognised in the financial statements.

This chapter has covered:

- the objectives, scope, definitions and disclosure requirements of IAS 38;

- recognition and measurement;

- different classes of intangibles and their treatments;

- purchased versus internally generated intangibles;

- cost versus revaluation approaches; and

- disposals of intangibles.

Chapter 13

IMPAIRMENT

1 Business Context

Asset availability and usage in the business is one of the key drivers to business success. Any assessment, therefore of assets should consistently reflect their worth to the business. At the very least, an asset recognised in the balance sheet should not be reported at a value above the amount that could be recovered from using or selling the asset. During periods where general prices are increasing there is an assumption that recoverability of the reported value of such assets will not be an issue.

It is important that all assets utilised within the business are considered. For example, some intangible assets which are highly technical in nature may attract premium valuations which may not be recoverable as technology continues to be developed or competitors enter the market.

Illustration 1

Businesses in the European telecoms sector invested over $100bn in third generation (3G) mobile phone operating licences but had to reduce the reported value of the licences very quickly when they realised that the market for the related services was significantly lower than expected. The reduction in the reported value had a major impact on their income statements, their overall value and, in some cases, their ability to continue in business.

It is therefore important that an entity considers the values its assets are measured at in the context of not only the individual entity but also the wider industry in which it operates.

Whenever an asset's recoverable amount falls to an amount less than its carrying amount, it is said to be impaired. Its value on the balance sheet is therefore reduced to this recoverable amount and, in most instances, an expense is recognised in the income statement.

2 Chapter Objectives

This chapter deals with 'impairment', which is a loss in the value of an asset i.e. its carrying amount recognised in the balance sheet is greater than its recoverable amount. The recoverable amount of an asset is that which can be recovered through continuing to use the asset or by selling it. Impairment usually arises where a substantial change has come about which adversely affects the way in which an asset is being used in the business. A simple example is where there have been technological advances that limit the planned use of an asset.

Judgement is required by management to establish when an asset's value is impaired, and how to measure the impairment. IAS 36 *Impairment of assets* provides guidance on identifying indicators that suggest impairment may have occurred and how to measure the extent of that impairment. It also considers the circumstances in which impairments may be reversed.

On completion of this chapter you should be able to:

- demonstrate a knowledge of the objectives and scope of IAS 36;

- demonstrate a knowledge of the terminology and definitions relating to impairment of assets;

- understand the key principles relating to the identification and measurement of impairment;

- understand in which circumstances and to what extent impairments can subsequently be reversed; and

- apply IAS 36 knowledge and understanding in particular circumstances through basic calculations.

3 Objectives, Scope and Definitions of IAS 36

IAS 36 applies to all assets apart from those specifically excluded from the standard. It most commonly applies to assets such as property, plant and equipment accounted for in accordance with IAS 16 *Property, plant and equipment* and intangible assets accounted for in accordance with IAS 38 *Intangible assets*. The standard also applies to some financial assets, namely subsidiaries, associates and joint ventures. Impairments of all other financial assets are accounted for in accordance with IAS 39 *Financial instruments: measurement and recognition*. [IAS 36.2]

An entity is required to assess at each reporting date whether there is an indication of an impairment. If such an indication is identified, the asset's recoverable amount should be calculated and compared to its carrying amount.

In addition, regardless of whether there have been any indicators of an impairment during the period, there are three specific situations where the recoverable amount of the asset should be assessed for impairment annually.

The three scenarios are: [IAS 36.10]

- where the entity has intangible assets that have been identified as having indefinite lives;

- where the entity has an intangible asset that is not yet ready for use; and

- where goodwill has been recorded as a result of a business combination.

The impairment test in these circumstances may be carried out at any time during the period, provided that it is carried out at the same time each period.

4 Key Stages in the Impairment Process

The stages in the process of identifying and accounting for an impairment loss are as follows:

(i) assess whether there is an indication that an asset may be impaired. Note that if there is no such indication, subject to the exceptions listed above, then no further action is required;

(ii) if there is an indication of impairment, then measure the asset's recoverable amount; and

(iii) reduce the asset's carrying amount to its recoverable amount, usually by treating the loss as a separately disclosed expense in the income statement.

4.1 Stage 1 – Indicators of impairment

IAS 36 identifies two sources of information that may indicate that an impairment has occurred. [IAS 36.12]

(i) *External sources* including:

- a significant decline in the asset's market value. This may arise, for example, as a result of a new competitor entering the market;

- significant changes in the technological, market, economic or legal environment in which the entity operates. This could be as simple as a change in customer tastes; and

- increases in market interest rates.

(ii) *Internal sources* including:

- obsolescence or physical damage to the asset;

- significant changes in how an asset is used or is expected to be used, including the asset becoming idle and plans to discontinue or restructure the division in which an asset is used; and

- performance of the asset being below that planned, for example actual net cash flows generated by the asset being below that budgeted.

4.2 Stage 2 – Measuring recoverable amount

If the carring amount of an asset (i.e. the cost of an item of plant less the accumulated depreciation charged in relation to it to date) is greater than its recoverable amount, then an impairment has taken place. There has been a loss in the value of the asset.

The recoverable amount of an asset is the higher of its fair value less costs to sell and its 'value in use'. Fair value is the amount obtainable from a sale in an arm's length transaction between a willing buyer and seller. [IAS 36.6]

The 'value in use' calculation is a measure of the future cash flows expected to be derived from an individual asset or a cash-generating unit. Since cash flows are likely to be over several periods, they should be discounted to take account of the time value of money, i.e. based on their present value. The calculation needs to take into account the specific risks associated with the asset and the entity.

There are two steps involved in calculating the value in use of an asset. The first is to estimate the future cash inflows and outflows that are expected to arise in relation to the asset. Inflows should include an estimate for the ultimate disposal of the asset.

The second step is to discount the scheduled cash flows to arrive at a present value. The discount rate to be used should be the risk-free rate of interest adjusted to reflect the risk associated with the particular asset and entity. This risk-adjusted rate of interest should reflect the return that an investor would require if he/she were to make an investment with cash flows similar to those expected from the asset. Risk-adjusted rates are used in the discounting process and are an indication of the risk/return profile of an entity.

It is not always necessary to calculate both the asset's fair value and its value in use. If either one of these figures is greater than the asset's current carrying amount then there is no impairment. This is particularly useful in cases of property where there is an active market and it is relatively straightforward and inexpensive to calculate the fair value.

The recoverable amount should be determined on an individual asset basis as far as possible. If, however, the individual asset does not generate cash flows largely independent from other assets, then the asset is grouped with other assets to form what is referred to in IAS 36 as a 'cash-generating unit'. This is the smallest group of assets for which it is possible to identify separately independent cash flows.

Illustration 2

A bus company has a contract with a local education authority to transport children to and from school. There are ten routes contracted to this particular bus company. One of the routes is making losses because it collects children from remote areas and, as a result, the number of children collected is much lower than on the highly populated routes.

The bus company does not have the ability to withdraw from individual routes. The ten routes are contracted for as a group. The ten routes should therefore be grouped together as one cash-generating unit.

4.3 Stage 3 – Recognising an impairment loss

If the recoverable amount of an asset is less than its carrying amount, the asset should be reduced to its recoverable amount. The difference is an impairment loss. [IAS 36.59]

An impairment loss is recognised immediately in the income statement unless the impairment is in relation to a revalued asset. An impairment loss on a revalued asset is treated as a decrease in valuation in accordance with IAS 16. To the extent that the asset has previously been revalued upwards, and there remains a balance on the revaluation reserve for that upwards valuation, any impairment loss will first be charged against this surplus. If the impairment is greater than a previous valuation surplus then the excess is charged directly to the income statement.

Illustration 3

An entity has a property that was originally acquired for CU500,000. The property was revalued to CU800,000, and the CU300,000 was recognised in the revaluation reserve in accordance with IAS 16.

The current carrying amount for the property is CU750,000. Due to finding that the land on which the property stands is contaminated, the entity has undertaken an impairment review.

The fair value of the property is now estimated to be only CU300,000 and the value in use of the property is calculated as being CU400,000. The recoverable amount of the property is therefore CU400,000.

An impairment of CU350,000 has occurred, being the difference between the current carrying amount of CU750,000 and the recoverable amount of CU400,000.

As the property was previously valued upwards, this part of the impairment loss should be set against the revaluation reserve. Consequently, CU300,000 is recognised in the revaluation reserve, i.e. it reduces the revaluation reserve balance to zero. The remaining loss of CU50,000 is recognised directly in the income statement.

Following the recognition of an impairment loss, any depreciation charged in respect of the asset in future periods will be based on the revised carrying amount, less any residual value expected, over the remaining useful life of the asset as per IAS 16.

Illustration 4

A piece of machinery was originally acquired for CU100,000. It was expected to have a useful life of ten years and no residual value. At the start of year six, there was a downturn in demand due to a competitor product entering the market, and this has led to an impairment of the asset. The impairment has been calculated as being CU20,000, although it is expected that the asset will continue to have a remaining five-year life.

At the end of year five, the asset had a carrying value of CU50,000 (CU100,000 x 5/10 years). The impairment reduces the carrying amount of the asset to CU30,000 (CU50,000 less CU20,000) which should be depreciated over the remaining life of five years.

If the recoverable amount has been calculated on a 'cash-generating unit', rather than on an individual asset basis, it is important that it is compared with the carrying amount applicable to the whole of the 'cash-generating unit'. If some of the assets that generate the cash inflow are excluded, the carrying amount will be understated. Although it may therefore appear that the cash-generating unit is fully recoverable an impairment has actually arisen.

It is sometimes difficult to allocate central assets, such as the head office and goodwill, to individual assets or cash-generating units, but these are still relevant in assessing asset carrying amounts.

Goodwill does not itself generate cash flows that are independent of other assets, since it represents part of a payment made to acquire a business anticipated to generate future economic benefits from the assets acquired.

However, goodwill does represent an asset that contributes towards the generation of cash flows. Goodwill will often contribute towards a number of cash-generating units rather than a single unit. If it is not possible to allocate the goodwill across the cash-generating units, then it should be allocated to a group of units for the purpose of determining carrying amounts.

If an impairment loss has been identified for a group of cash-generating units to which goodwill has been allocated, then the impairment loss should in the first instance be allocated against the carrying amount of the goodwill of the group of cash-generating units. If the impairment loss is greater than the carrying amount of the relevant goodwill, the excess should be allocated to the other assets of the group of cash-generating units on a pro-rata basis of the carrying amount of each asset in the group of cash-generating units.

Illustration 5

A cash-generating unit contains:

	CU
Property, plant and equipment	60
Patent	40
Goodwill	20
	120

An annual impairment review is required as the cash-generating unit contains goodwill. The most recent review assesses its recoverable amount to be CU90. An impairment loss of CU30 has occurred and is charged to the income statement.

Firstly, the entity reduces the carrying amount of the goodwill. As the impairment loss exceeds the value of goodwill within the cash-generating unit, all goodwill is written off.

The entity then reduces the carrying amount of other assets in the unit on a pro-rata basis. Hence the remaining loss of CU10 will be allocated pro-rata between the property, plant and equipment and the patent, reducing their carrying amounts to CU54 and CU36 respectively.

An annual impairment test for a cash-generating unit that goodwill has been allocated to may be carried out at any time during the period, provided that it is carried out at the same time each period.

5 Reversing an Impairment Loss

If the recoverable amount subsequently increases then in certain circumstances the impairment is reversed. A reversal of an impairment loss reflects an increase in the estimated service potential of an asset or group of assets. The increased service potential may be through use or sale.

Any reversal of an impairment loss for an asset, other than goodwill, should only be recognised to the extent that it increases the carrying amount of the asset to its original pre-impaired value less subsequent depreciation.

The reversal of any impairment is recognised consistently with the original recognition of the impairment loss. The reversal will therefore normally be recognised in the income statement. However, to the extent that the asset was revalued and the impairment loss was recognised in the revaluation reserve, as discussed above, the reversal will also be recognised as a reserves movement only. [IAS 36.117, 119]

If the reversal of the impairment is in relation to a cash-generating unit, then the reversal is recognised on a pro-rata basis with the carrying amount of the assets, excluding goodwill. [IAS 36.122]

An impairment loss recognised in respect to goodwill should not subsequently be reversed. This is because it is likely that any increase in the recoverable amount of goodwill in future periods will arise as a result of increases in internally generated goodwill rather than the reversal of an impairment. [IAS 36.124]

Illustration 6

Sometime later when the property, plant and equipment and patent have carrying amounts of CU45 and CU25 respectively, the impairment in illustration 5 reverses. The recoverable amount is now assessed as CU110.

If the original impairment had not occurred the property, plant and equipment would now have shown in the balance sheet at CU55 and the patent at CU30 – i.e. the total carrying amount of these assets would have been CU85.

The impairment on the goodwill cannot be reversed. The impairment of the other assets can only be reversed to the extent that they are restored to their pre-impairment values less any subsequent depreciation. Hence their maximum value is CU85. As the original impairment loss was taken to the income statement, the amount of the reversal is also recognised in the income statement.

6 Disclosure

The following information should be disclosed for each class of assets: [IAS 36.126]

- the amount of any impairment loss recognised or reversed in the income statement, identifying the line item where it has been included;

- the equivalent information for any impairment recognised or reversed via the revaluation reserve in the statement of changes in equity; and

- if the entity is required to comply with IAS 14 *Segment reporting*, the reportable segment(s) to which the recognition or reversal relates.

If an impairment loss recognised or reversed for an individual asset, including goodwill, or a cash-generating unit, is significant to the financial statements as a whole, additional information should be disclosed, including: [IAS 36.130]

- the events which led to the recognition/reversal;

- the amount;

- the nature of the asset or a description of the cash-generating unit and the reportable segment to which the asset belongs if appropriate; and

- whether the recoverable amount is fair value less costs to sell or value in use, with information about the basis of any fair value calculation or the discount rate applied in the value in use calculation.

Additional information is required for each cash-generating unit where the carrying amount of the goodwill or indefinite life intangibles are significant compared with the entity's total goodwill or indefinite life intangibles. [IAS 36.134]

7 Chapter Review

This chapter has been concerned with the key issues relating to how an impairment of an asset is identified, measured and disclosed in the financial statements.

This chapter has covered:

- the objectives, scope, definitions and disclosure requirements of IAS 36;

- events which might indicate an impairment has occurred;

- measuring recoverable amounts; and

- recognising and reversing impairment losses.

Chapter 14
PROVISIONS AND CONTINGENCIES

1 Business Context

Business life is full of uncertainties regarding future events and management is therefore required to make informed estimates on the outcome of such events. For example, will there be sufficient demand to sell all products held in inventories and are customer debts fully recoverable?

Assets should not be reported in the financial statement above the amount at which they are recoverable. However, due to uncertainties in assets' recoverable amounts a provision is set up which reduces asset carrying amounts to their estimated recoverable amount.

The creation of a provision has traditionally provided entities with an opportunity to smooth results. For example, in periods where performance has exceeded expectations an entity might be tempted to make what has been commonly referred to as a "rainy day" provision. The provision set up in prosperous times would be released to increase profits in periods when results were not quite up to expectations.

As a consequence an international standard was introduced to restrict an entity's ability to make large "general" provisions which can have a significant impact on the results of an entity. Guidance is provided on the type of provisions that can be made and on the general principles surrounding recognition.

2 Chapter Objectives

This chapter covers the accounting and disclosure requirements of provisions, contingent liabilities and contingent assets.

Such items require significant judgements to be made by management and have a direct effect on an entity's reported profit or loss for the period.

On completion of this chapter you should be able to:

- demonstrate a knowledge of the objectives and scope of IAS 37 *Provisions, contingent liabilities and contingent assets*;

- demonstrate a knowledge of the important terminology, definitions and key principles which relate to the recognition, measurement, presentation and disclosure of provisions, contingent liabilities and contingent assets; and

- apply knowledge and understanding of IAS 37 in particular circumstances through basic calculations.

3 Objectives, Scope and Definitions of IAS 37

The objective of IAS 37 is to ensure that provisions, contingent liabilities and contingent assets are measured, recognised and presented appropriately in the financial statements.

IAS 37 applies to all entities when accounting for provisions, contingent liabilities and contingent assets except for:

- those relating to financial instruments which are carried at fair value;

- those resulting from an executory contract. In essence, this is a contract that does not have any loss making potential, for example both parties to the contract have performed their obligations to an equal extent. An example is a service contract with an employee running for, say, three years. At the end of the first year, the employee has completed one year of service and the employer has paid for one year of services;

- those arising in respect of contracts with insurance policyholders for entities in the insurance industry, although the standard applies to other provisions relating to insurance businesses; and

- those specifically covered by another international standard, for example pension provisions covered by IAS 19 *Employee benefits.*

In its simplest form a provision is a liability where there is uncertainty over its timing or the amount at which it will be settled. [IAS 37.10]

A contingent liability is where there is significant uncertainty about a number of aspects regarding the liability. A contingent liability arises where an event that occurred in the past may lead to the entity having a liability in the future but the financial impact of the event will only be confirmed by the outcome of some future event not wholly within the entity's control. The giving of a guarantee to another entity that is in financial difficulty is likely to be a contingent liability. If the likelihood of making a payment under the guarantee is remote it is not a contingent liability. A liability that does not meet the provision recognition criteria, for example because the amount of the obligation cannot be measured reliably, is a contingent liability. [IAS 37.10]

A contingent asset is a potential asset that arises from past events but whose existence can only be confirmed by the outcome of future events not wholly within the entity's control. [IAS 37.10]

4 Recognition

4.1 Provisions

A provision should be recognised when: [IAS 37.14]

- an entity has a present obligation as a result of a past event. Such an obligation may arise from a legally binding arrangement such as a contract or from a constructive obligation. A constructive obligation is where there is an established past practice that has led to an expectation that an entity will discharge those responsibilities in the future. For example a retail store which has a long-established practice of offering a "no quibble" returns policy;

- it is probable that an outflow of resources (i.e. cash or other assets) will be required to settle the obligation. In circumstances where it is uncertain whether such an outflow will be required to settle the obligation, the entity should assess the probability of having to meet that obligation based on a more likely than not assessment; [IAS 37.15] and

- a reliable estimate can be made of the amount.

If one or more of these criteria are not met, a contingent liability may exist, but no provision should be recognised.

IAS 37 describes a "past event" as an obligating event. It is the original action causing a liability to arise. As an example, if an entity is required to operate within certain emission levels and these were breached at some point in time, the past event is when the emission levels were breached rather than when the breach was discovered. It is important to realise that an obligating event involves another party, to whom the obligation is owed. In the above example, a penalty may be payable to, say, a regulatory body.

4.1.1 Future operating losses

A provision should not be recognised in respect of future operating losses since there is no present obligation arising from a past event. However, an expectation that the entity will incur future operating losses, may indicate that there has been an impairment (a reduction in value) of assets and an impairment review should be carried out in accordance with IAS 36 *Impairment of assets*. [IAS 37.63]

4.1.2 Onerous contracts

If the future benefits under a contract are expected to be less than the unavoidable costs under it, then the contract is described as onerous. The excess unavoidable costs should be provided for at the time the contract becomes onerous. The entity has an obligation to meet these future costs as a result of signing the original contract, it will be required to pay them and they can be measured reliably. Where an onerous contract has been identified an impairment review should be carried out before a provision is recognised. [IAS 37.66]

When making a best estimate of the provision for an onerous contract the entity should take into account an estimate of any likely income that will be received under the contract.

Illustration 1

An entity entered into a 10 year lease of a building. The annual rent under the lease agreement is CU36,000. The entity has decided to relocate its head office with 5 years still to run on the original lease. The entity is permitted to sublet the building and believes that although market rentals have decreased it should be able to sublet the building for the full 5 years. The expected rental is CU24,000 per annum.

A provision should be recognised for the excess costs under the lease contract above the expected benefits to be received. The obligating event was the signing of the lease agreement and CU36,000 is required to be paid in each of the remaining 5 years.

A provision for the following amount should be recognised:

Annual outflow	CU36,000
Annual expected inflow	CU24,000
Excess annual outflow expected	CU12,000

A provision of CU60,000 (CU12,000 x 5 years) should be recognised.

Note: all other costs and the time value of money have been ignored.

4.1.3 Restructuring

A provision should only be recognised in respect of restructuring costs, for example closing a division or reducing the number of employees, where specific criteria have been met, as detailed below.

A constructive obligation to restructure an entity only arises when: [IAS 37.72]

- a detailed formal plan has been made. This should include identifying the area of the business and location that is going to be restructured, an estimate of the number of employees that will be affected, the likely cost of the restructuring and the estimated time scales involved; and

- an announcement about the restructuring plan has been made to those who will be affected. Time scales should be mentioned as part of this announcement, or the entity should have started to carry out the restructuring. Evidence that a restructuring plan has commenced might be the removal or dismantling of assets at the affected location. If an announcement has been made then commencement of the plan should be within a short period of time to reduce the likelihood of significant changes being made.

A restructuring provision should only include direct expenditure arising from the restructuring. Costs which relate to the future activities of the entity should not be provided for as part of the restructuring, for example relocating or retraining staff. [IAS 37.80]

4.2 Contingent liabilities and contingent assets

A contingent liability or asset should be disclosed in the financial statements rather than being recognised in the balance sheet. [IAS 37.27, 37.31]

A contingent liability should be disclosed unless the possible outflow of resources to meet the liability is remote. If the outflow is thought to be remote, no disclosure is required.

A contingent asset should be disclosed when the expected inflow of economic benefits is probable. An example of a contingent asset is a legal claim that the entity is pursuing, where the outcome is uncertain although it is probable that the entity will gain some financial benefit from it.

Where the outflow of resources is probable, a provision should be recognised rather than a contingent liability disclosed. However, in relation to assets a 'probable' inflow of economic benefits only results in the disclosure of a contingent asset; for an asset to be recognised, the inflow of benefits should be 'virtually certain'.

5 Measurement

5.1 Best estimate

In order to recognise a provision an entity is required to calculate its best estimate of the expenditure required to settle the present obligation at the balance sheet date. This is the amount an entity would rationally pay to settle the obligation or to transfer it to a third party. [IAS 37.36]

Management will generally be required to make a number of judgements to arrive at a best estimate for a provision. Judgements should be supplemented by experience of similar transactions and, where appropriate, by advice from independent experts. The outcome of events occurring after the balance sheet date should be taken into account in making estimates, for example if a retail business sees that the proportion of sales giving rise to refunds increase in the first few weeks of a new financial year the increased proportion should be used in estimating the amount of the provision at the end of the previous financial year. Where there are a number of possible outcomes probability weightings should be used.

If the best estimate for a single obligation is CU10,000, and there is a 55% chance of the expenditure being incurred, then the best estimate is CU10,000, not 55% of CU10,000.

When making an estimate management will need to take into account the risks and uncertainties surrounding the likely outcome.

Illustration 2

A business sells goods which carry a one-year repair warranty. If minor repairs were to be required on all goods sold in 2003, the repair cost would be CU100,000. If major repairs were needed on all goods sold, the cost would be CU500,000.

It is estimated that 80% of goods sold in 2003 will have no defects, 15% will have minor defects, and 5% will have major defects.

The provision for repairs required at 31 December 2003 is:

	CU
80% of the goods will require no repairs	–
15% will require minor repairs 15% × CU100,000	15,000
5% will require major repairs 5% × CU500,000	25,000
Best estimate of provision required	40,000

5.2 Present value

The expenditure required to settle an obligation may occur within a short period after the balance sheet date, in which case the time value of money can be ignored. However, if the outflow of resources is expected to occur a significant time after the obligation itself arose, the effect of the time value of money should be taken into account in estimating the provision. [IAS 37.45]

The discount rate used should be a pre-tax rate that reflects the current market assessments of the time value of money and the risks specific to the liability. The unwinding of the discount each period should be included as a finance cost in the income statement. [IAS 37.47]

5.3 Other measurement points

It is possible that the amount required to settle an obligation will be dependent on a number of future events. For example, where it is expected that there will be technological advances that will reduce, say, future clean up costs, the expected effect of these future events should be taken into account in assessing the provision.

Gains from the expected disposal of assets should not be taken into account in measuring a provision. IAS 37 does not override other standards, so such gains should be dealt with under the relevant standard. For plant and equipment the relevant standard is IAS 16 *Property, plant and equipment.* [IAS 37.51]

6 Reimbursement, Changes in and Uses of Provisions

In some cases, an entity may be able to look to another party, such as an insurance company or a supplier under a warranty, for reimbursement of all or part of the entity's expenditure to settle a provision. The entity generally retains the contractual obligation to settle the provision, even if the other party fails to make the reimbursement. IAS 37 requires that the reimbursement should be recognised only when it is virtually certain that the amount will be received. If it is only probable that a reimbursement will be received then the amount is considered to be a contingent asset and will be disclosed. If an asset in respect of the reimbursement can be recognised then it should be reported as a separate asset in the balance sheet and not netted against any outstanding provision. The recognition of any reimbursement asset is restricted to the amount of the related provision. [IAS 37.53]

Although the provision and reimbursement asset cannot be netted off in the balance sheet, it is appropriate to net off the two amounts in the income statement. [IAS 37.54]

Because provisions are inherently uncertain amounts, IAS 37 requires them to be reviewed at each balance sheet date and adjusted to reflect the most up to date information about the estimate. If at the balance sheet date it is assessed that a transfer of economic benefits is no longer probable, the provision should be reversed. A provision should only be utilised against the expenditure which it was originally set up for. [IAS 37.57, 37.61]

Illustration 3

An entity has received a claim for damaged goods from a customer. The entity's legal advisors believe that it is probable that a settlement will need to be made of CU10,000 in favour of the customer. However, in their opinion it is also probable that a counterclaim by the entity against their supplier for contributory negligence would successfully recover the damages.

A provision should be made for CU10,000 as the outflow of economic benefits is probable. The counterclaim asset is not recognised since it is only probable that it will be received. It can only be recognised when it is virtually certain to be received. It should be disclosed as a contingent asset.

7 Disclosure

A number of disclosures are required in relation to provisions, contingent liabilities and contingent assets.

For a provision, a full reconciliation should be presented, clearly identifying movements during the period. These might include revisions of the estimate, utilisation of the provision or a release of part of the provision. [IAS 37.84]

An explanation should be provided for each class of provision, detailing what the provision is for, the expected timing of outflows, an indication of uncertainties over timing or amount of expected outflows and whether any reimbursement has been recognised. [IAS 37.85]

For a contingent liability, assuming the expected outflow is not remote, a brief description should be provided for each class of contingent liability. This should include an estimate of the financial effect, an indication of any uncertainties and the likelihood of any reimbursements being forthcoming. [IAS 37.86]

Where a contingent asset is disclosed because the receipt of economic benefits is probable, the entity should briefly explain the nature of the contingent asset and where practicable the financial effect of such an asset. If information about a contingent liability or asset is not disclosed on practicality grounds then this fact should be disclosed. [IAS 37.89, 37.91]

If the disclosure of information surrounding a provision, contingent liability or contingent asset would be seriously prejudicial to an entity, then the general nature of the item should be disclosed with an explanation of why no additional disclosure has been made. This is expected to be extremely rare in practice, although it may be appropriate in circumstances where there are legal proceedings in progress, the outcome of which could be affected by the disclosure of the estimated settlement. [IAS 37.92]

8 Chapter Review

This chapter has been concerned with the recognition, measurement and disclosure requirements for provisions, contingent liabilities and contingent assets.

This chapter has covered:

- the objectives and scope of IAS 37;
- the critically important definition of provisions, contingent liabilities and contingent assets;
- the application of these definitions to a range of practical situations;
- the criteria for recognising provisions, contingent liabilities and contingent assets; and
- the measurement criteria and disclosure requirements in IAS 37.

Chapter 15

TAXATION

1 Business Context

Corporate income taxes are an important means of raising government revenue and therefore represents a potential major cash outflow from a business. This is particularly the case in developed countries where typically 5% to 15% of total government revenue comes from such taxes.

Taxes on business can take several different forms and these vary from country to country. Entities can incur taxes levied on a variety of bases and transactions although probably the most significant is that in relation to income generated by an entity through its normal operating activities.

Taxation is not just a means of raising revenue for government. Governments may wish to provide incentives or disincentives for entities to act in a particular way. For example, to encourage investment in a particular geographical area or carry out a certain business activity, generous tax allowances may be offered as an incentive for this type of expenditure. The implication of this is that taxes can interact with business decisions, for example in relation to business location. This is of particular significance where businesses have foreign operations in different tax jurisdictions.

2 Chapter Objectives

This chapter deals with IAS 12 *Income taxes*. It considers both the treatment of the current tax charge and liability (current taxes) and deferred tax, which is a means of accounting for the difference between the effect of the tax and accounting treatment (deferred tax) of transactions.

On completion of this chapter you should be able to:

- understand the nature and scope of IAS 12 on income taxes;

- interpret the important terminology and definitions which relate to the treatment of current tax and deferred tax in financial statements;

- understand the key principles relating to the recognition and measurement of current tax and deferred tax;

- demonstrate knowledge of the principal disclosure requirements of IAS 12; and

- apply knowledge and understanding of IAS 12 in particular circumstances through basic calculations.

3 Objectives, Scope and Definitions of IAS 12

The objective of IAS 12 is to prescribe the accounting treatment for income taxes. [IAS 12.1]

The term 'income taxes' is wide and covers all domestic and foreign taxes which are based on an entity's taxable profits, as well as other taxes such as a withholding tax which is payable when an entity pays a dividend.

IAS 12 concerns two different taxation issues:

1. *Current tax:* this is defined as the amount of income tax payable, or recoverable, by an entity in respect of its taxable profit, or loss, for a period. [IAS 12.5]

2. *Deferred tax:* this is an accounting measure rather than a tax levied by government; it represents tax payable or recoverable in future accounting periods in relation to transactions which have already taken place.

4 Current Tax

IAS 12 does not set out how current tax should be calculated since this is largely driven by the application of the taxation rules in individual jurisdictions. However, IAS 12 requires a tax liability to be recognised where an entity has unpaid current tax, whether arising from the current or prior periods. Conversely, if an entity has overpaid its tax liability then it should recognise a tax asset for the amount recoverable. [IAS 12.12]

It is sometimes possible for an entity that has made a loss in its current period to recover tax paid in previous periods by carrying the loss back to offset against profits of the earlier period. Where an entity is able to recover tax paid in a previous period, an asset should be recognised in the period in which the loss is made. [IAS 12.13]

The tax rate to be used in determining a current tax asset or liability is the rate that is expected to apply when the asset is expected to be recovered, or the liability to be paid. These rates should be based upon tax laws that have already been enacted (are already part of law) or substantively enacted (have already passed through part of the legal process) by the balance sheet date. [IAS 12.46]

4.1 Income statement

The tax expense recognised in the income statement comprises an aggregate amount of the current tax expense and the deferred tax expense based on the net profit or loss for the period. [IAS 12.5]

5 Deferred Tax

The current tax liability of an entity is based on both the accounting treatment for transactions and on a number of specific requirements set out in local tax legislation. As a result it may not be possible to calculate the tax charge for a reporting period by reference to an entity's reported profit or loss for that period. Differences may arise because the tax liability occurs in a period different to that in which the underlying transaction is reported. To ensure that the financial statements are internally consistent, an adjustment may be required to the current tax expense, so that the total tax charge is based on an entity's financial reporting profit for the period. This adjustment is referred to as 'deferred tax'. It is important to appreciate that deferred tax does not alter the tax to be paid, only the means by which it is reflected in the financial statements.

IAS 12 requires that deferred tax is calculated using what is commonly referred to as the balance sheet liability method. This method is based on an assessment of temporary differences. A temporary difference is the difference between the carrying amount of an asset or liability in the balance sheet and the amount of that item for tax purposes, which is called its tax base. [IAS 12.5]

The concept of deferred tax is best described through the use of a simple example.

Illustration 1

An entity acquires a new computer for CU1,200 in the year. The entity depreciates computer equipment over 3 years in accordance with IAS 16 *Property, plant and equipment*. Local government provides a tax incentive to businesses for investments in new computer equipment and therefore the full cost of the equipment is allowable for tax purposes in the year that it is purchased.

At the end of the year, the computer equipment has the following carrying amount and tax base:

Balance sheet carrying amount:

CU1,200 less depreciation of (CU1,200 x 1/3) CU400 = CU800

Tax base:

CU1,200 less amount deductible for tax purposes of CU1,200 = nil

A temporary difference arises of CU800, being the difference between the carrying amount in the balance sheet and the value for tax purposes.

The temporary difference reflects the fact that the entity has reduced its actual tax liability by CU1,200 multiplied by the tax rate although only CU400 is shown an expense in its income statement. This means that the current tax expense is less than what a user would expect to see based on the results reported in the entity's income statement, and in future periods the current tax expense will be more than what a user would expect.

The reason that an entity is required to recognise deferred tax is because:

- a deferred tax liability will ultimately translate itself into an actual liability by, for example having a larger tax liability in future periods;

- the matching of items recognised in an entity's financial statements is consistent with the requirements of IAS 1 *Presentation of financial statements* on the preparation of an entity's financial statements; and

- ignoring deferred tax may lead to the reported profit in a period being misinterpreted.

6 Deferred Tax: Recognition and Measurement

An entity is required to recognise a deferred tax liability where it has identified a taxable temporary difference between an asset or liability's value for accounting purposes and its value for tax purposes. A deferred tax liability arises where the carrying amount of the item for accounting purposes is greater than its tax value. [IAS 12.15]

There are two exceptions to this requirement: firstly, where a deferred tax liability arises from the initial recognition of goodwill (i.e. the excess paid for a business above the value of its net assets) and secondly, where the initial recognition of an item, that is not part of a business combination, does not affect accounting or tax profit. [IAS 12.15]

IAS 12 requires that an entity should recognise a deferred tax asset where tax is recoverable in the future, as a result of a deductible temporary difference arising on the assessment of an asset's or liability's value for accounting and tax purposes. For a deferred tax asset to be recognised the entity should assess its recoverability as being probable. [IAS 12.24]

A potential deferred tax asset arises where the carrying amount of the item for accounting purposes is less than its tax value.

As with a deferred tax liability, an entity should not recognise a deferred tax asset where it arises from a transaction that is neither a business combination nor affects accounting or tax profit at the time of recognition. [IAS 12.24]

The recognition and measurement of deferred tax balances can be determined by a number of steps which are explained in the remainder of this chapter.

6.1 Carrying amount versus tax base

An entity should determine an asset's or liability's carrying amount in its balance sheet and its value for tax purposes, i.e. its tax base. Where there is a difference between the two amounts the entity may need to recognise a deferred tax asset or liability.

The tax base of an asset is the amount that will be deductible for tax purposes against future profits generated by the asset. In simple terms the asset's tax base is the amount of the asset in the current period for tax purposes.

Illustration 2

An entity has an asset in its balance sheet representing interest receivable of CU500. Although the interest was not received until after the balance sheet date, it has been earned in the current period and therefore has been recorded as income in the income statement. The carrying amount of the asset at the balance sheet date is therefore CU500.

The interest will be chargeable to tax when the cash is received, i.e. in the following period. The interest asset has no value for tax purposes in the current period, so its tax base is nil.

The tax base of a liability is its carrying amount less any amount that will be deductible for tax purposes in future periods.

Illustration 3

An entity has recognised a current liability for expenses that it has incurred but not yet paid at its balance sheet date of CU1,000. The expenses will be fully allowable for tax purposes when they are paid in the following period.

The carrying amount of the liability at the balance sheet date is therefore CU1,000.

The tax base is nil, being the carrying amount of CU1,000 less the amount that will be deductible for tax purposes in future periods i.e. CU1,000.

6.2 Calculate the temporary difference

Temporary differences are differences between the carrying amount of an asset or liability in the balance sheet and its tax base.

Temporary differences may be either: [IAS 12.5]

(a) *taxable temporary differences,* which result in taxable amounts arising in future accounting periods, as the carrying amount of the asset or liability is recovered or settled. This is where the carrying amount of an item is greater than its tax base; or

(b) *deductible temporary differences,* which result in amounts that are deductible in future periods as the carrying amount of the asset or liability is recovered or settled. This is where the carrying amount of the item is less than its tax base.

Illustration 4

The temporary differences in illustrations 2 and 3 are:

Illustration 2: Carrying amount of the interest receivable is CU500 less its tax base of nil – temporary difference is CU500.

Illustration 3: Carrying amount of the liability is CU1,000 less its tax base of nil – temporary difference is CU1,000.

The temporary differences above are both therefore taxable temporary differences because the carrying amounts are greater than their tax bases.

6.3 Determining deferred tax

Deferred tax liabilities represent income taxes payable in future periods in respect of taxable temporary differences. A taxable temporary difference therefore creates a deferred tax liability. [IAS 12.5]

Deferred tax assets are *"amounts of income taxes recoverable in future periods in respect of deductible temporary differences"*. [IAS 12.5]

Deferred tax assets may also arise as a result of tax losses and tax credits that can be used to reduce an entity's future tax liability. An entity should only recognise a deferred tax asset in respect of tax losses and recoverables where it is probable that it will gain benefit from them, i.e. taxable profits will be made in future periods that they can be offset against. A deductible temporary difference therefore creates a potential deferred tax asset. [IAS 12.34]

A deferred tax asset or liability is calculated by multiplying the temporary difference by the relevant tax rate.

The tax rate to be used in the calculation for determining a deferred tax asset or liability is the rate that is expected to apply when the asset is realised, or the liability is settled. These rates should be based on tax laws that have already been enacted or substantively enacted by the balance sheet date. [IAS 12.47]

Illustration 5

An entity operates in Muldovia, and enters into a long-term contract to build a motorway in that country. During the year ended 31 December 2003, the entity recognises CU4million of income on this contract in its income statement although it does not expect to receive the related cash until the year ending 31 December 2005.

Under the tax rules of Muldovia tax is charged on a cash receipts basis.

The tax rate for businesses in Muldovia was 30% in the year to 31 December 2003, but their government has voted in favour of a reduction to 29% for 2004. There is currently a rumour that the rate will drop to 28% in 2005, but no announcement has been made.

The rate of tax that should be used to determine the deferred tax balance is 29%. This is the rate is that expected to apply when the asset is realised. The rate of 30% in 2003, when the temporary difference originated, is not relevant. The 28% would be used if it had been enacted, but currently it is only under discussion. The best estimate of the rate applying in 2005, based upon laws already enacted or substantively enacted, is the rate for 2004 of 29%.

Illustration 6

A machine cost CU50,000. For tax purposes, allowances of CU30,000 have already been deducted in the current and previous periods with the remaining CU20,000 deductible in future periods. Revenue generated by the entity from using the machine is taxable and any gain or loss made on its disposal will have tax implications. The carrying amount of the machine for accounting purposes is CU35,000.

The tax rate is currently 30% and is not expected to change in the foreseeable future.

The tax base of the machine is CU20,000 (CU50,000 less CU30,000).

There is a taxable temporary difference of CU15,000 (i.e. accounting carrying amount CU35,000 – tax base CU20,000). This generates a deferred tax liability of CU4,500 (i.e. CU15,000 x 30%).

The steps so far can be summarised in the following diagram.

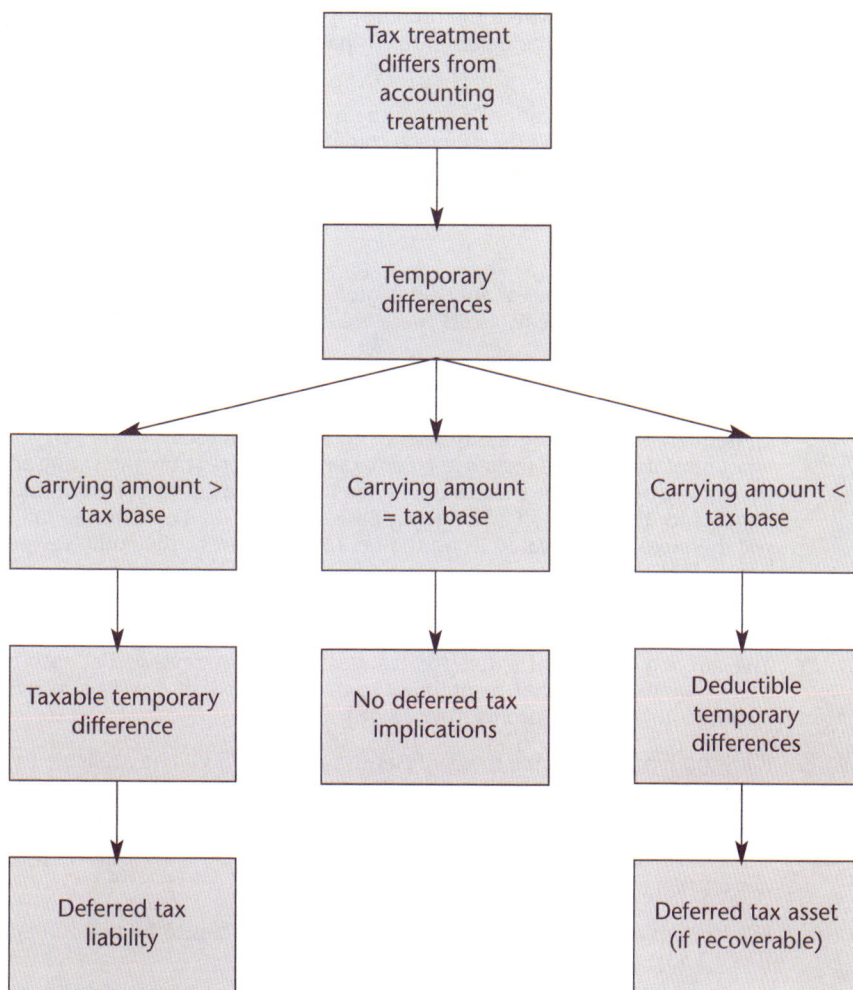

```
              ┌─────────────────┐
              │ Tax treatment   │
              │ differs from    │
              │ accounting      │
              │ treatment       │
              └────────┬────────┘
                       │
                       ▼
              ┌─────────────────┐
              │ Temporary       │
              │ differences     │
              └───┬─────┬─────┬─┘
          ┌───────┘     │     └───────┐
          ▼             ▼             ▼
┌──────────────┐ ┌──────────────┐ ┌──────────────┐
│ Carrying     │ │ Carrying     │ │ Carrying     │
│ amount >     │ │ amount       │ │ amount <     │
│ tax base     │ │ = tax base   │ │ tax base     │
└──────┬───────┘ └──────┬───────┘ └──────┬───────┘
       ▼                ▼                ▼
┌──────────────┐ ┌──────────────┐ ┌──────────────┐
│ Taxable      │ │ No deferred  │ │ Deductible   │
│ temporary    │ │ tax          │ │ temporary    │
│ difference   │ │ implications │ │ differences  │
└──────┬───────┘ └──────────────┘ └──────┬───────┘
       ▼                                 ▼
┌──────────────┐                  ┌──────────────┐
│ Deferred tax │                  │ Deferred tax │
│ liability    │                  │ asset        │
│              │                  │ (if          │
│              │                  │ recoverable) │
└──────────────┘                  └──────────────┘
```

6.4 Recognition criteria: further issues

6.4.1 Revaluations

IFRS permit certain assets to be carried at fair value or at a revalued amount.

The act of revaluing an asset will not generally result in a taxable event. However, the future recovery of the asset, either through its continuing use or through disposal, will lead to taxable amounts being generated by the entity. The amount that will be deductible for tax purposes, based on cost, will differ from that for accounting purposes, based on the revalued amount.

Consequently, the difference between the carrying amount of a revalued asset and its tax base is a temporary difference. An upward revaluation of an asset will therefore give rise to a deferred tax liability.

Most transactions creating temporary differences relate to transactions in the income statement, so the related deferred tax is also recognised in the income statement. However, where the underlying transaction, such as a revaluation, is recognised in equity, the deferred tax impact is also recognised as part of equity. [IAS 12.61]

The Standing Interpretations Committee issued SIC 21 *Income taxes – recovery of revalued non depreciable assets* which clarifies that deferred tax should be recognised, where appropriate, even when a non-current asset is not depreciated, for example land. This is because the carrying amount of the asset will ultimately be recovered on disposal rather than through the charging of depreciation.

Where the market value of an asset is greater than its carrying amount but the entity does not revalue its assets there are no deferred tax implications.

6.4.2 The expected manner of recovery of an asset

The measurement of deferred tax liabilities (and assets) should reflect the tax consequences of how an entity intends to settle (and recover) the carrying amount of its liabilities (or assets). For example, different tax rates may apply, depending on whether the entity intends to use an asset to generate future benefits for the entity on an ongoing basis or to sell it. The deferred tax amount will therefore be calculated using the tax rate relevant to the entity's expected use. [IAS 12.51]

6.4.3 Annual review

The carrying amount of a deferred tax asset should be reviewed at each balance sheet date to ensure that it continues to be probable that it will be recovered against future taxable profits. [IAS 12.56]

If it is no longer probable that sufficient taxable profit will be available to utilise the benefit of the deferred tax asset then its carrying amount should be written down accordingly. If sufficient profits later become available, then the amount written down should be reversed. [IAS 12.56]

6.4.4 Discounting

IAS 12 does not permit deferred tax assets and liabilities to be discounted. [IAS 12.53]

6.4.5 Temporary differences and investments

Temporary differences may arise from investments in subsidiaries, branches, associates and joint ventures. Such differences arise as a result of the carrying amount of investments being different from their tax base. Differences may arise, for example, due to the entities having undistributed profits or through exchange rate differences.

A deferred tax liability arising on such temporary differences should be recognised, except where two condition are met: the investor is able to control the timing of the reversal of the temporary differences and it is probable that the amounts will not reverse in the foreseeable future. [IAS 12.39]

Similarly, a deferred tax asset should be recognised in relation to deductible temporary differences where they will reverse in the foreseeable future and the entity will be able to utilise the resulting deferred tax asset. [IAS 12.44]

7 Change in Tax Status

Where are entity's tax status changes, for example following a restructuring of its equity, this may impact directly on the entity's current and deferred tax assets and liabilities. SIC 25 *Income taxes - changes in the tax status of an enterprise or its shareholders* sets out guidance on how such changes in an entity's tax status should be treated.

SIC 25 sets out that both the current and deferred tax adjustments required as a result of a change in the tax status of an entity should be included directly in the income statement as part of the entity's profit or loss for the period. If, however, the consequences of the change directly impacted equity then the tax consequences should also be recorded as part of equity.

8 Presentation and Disclosure: Current and Deferred Tax

Current and deferred tax movements should be recognised directly in the income statement as part of the net profit or loss for the period, except where the tax arises from: [IAS 12.58]

- a transaction that is accounted for directly in equity (such as a revaluation); or

- a business combination.

The tax expense or income in respect of the profit or loss from the entity's ordinary activities should be presented on the face of the income statement. [IAS 12.77]

The main components of the tax expense, or income, should be disclosed separately in the financial statements. The main components of the tax expense or income may include, for example: [IAS 12.79]

- current tax expense (income);

- adjustments recognised in the period for current tax of prior periods;

- deferred tax expense (income) relating to temporary differences;

- an adjustment to the deferred tax expense (income) relating to changes in tax rates; and

- an adjustment made in respect of amounts charged in prior periods for deferred or current tax.

IAS 12 requires a number of detailed disclosures to be made in relation to both the current and deferred tax amounts recognised in the financial statements. These disclosures include: [IAS 12.81]

- the aggregate amount of current and deferred tax that has been charged or credited to equity;

- a reconciliation of the tax expense (income) to the amount calculated as the accounting profit multiplied by the tax rate. This reconciliation may be presented by reconciling the average effective tax rate to the actual tax rate for the period;

- an explanation of any changes in the applicable tax rates, compared to the previous accounting period;

- the amount of any potential deferred tax asset which has not been recognised because of uncertainties over its recoverability;

- an analysis of deferred tax in terms of the type of temporary difference;

- the aggregate amount where a deferred tax liability for temporary differences in relation to investments in subsidiaries, associates, branches and investments in joint ventures has not been recognised;

- where an entity has discontinued operations accounted for in accordance with IFRS 5 *Non-current assets held for sale and discontinued operations* the tax expense relating to the gain or loss on discontinuance; and

- the income tax consequences of dividends that were proposed or declared after the balance sheet date and not therefore recognised as a liability at the balance sheet date.

Where an entity has recognised a deferred tax asset at the balance sheet date, it should disclose the nature of the evidence supporting its future recoverability. [IAS 12.82]

IAS 1 requires that where current and non-current assets and liabilities are separately classified on the face of the balance sheet, deferred tax assets and liabilities should not be disclosed as part of current assets and liabilities.

8.1 Offsetting

Where appropriate deferred tax assets and liabilities should be offset in the balance sheet.

However, a current tax asset and a current tax liability should only be offset by an entity where it has a legally enforceable right to set off the amounts and it intends to settle them on a net basis. If the amounts are not settled on a net basis then they should be settled simultaneously. [IAS 12.71]

Deferred tax assets and liabilities should similarly only be offset where the entity has a legally enforceable right to set off current tax assets against current tax liabilities and the deferred tax assets and liabilities have arisen on income taxes levied by the same taxation authority. In addition, the amounts should be in relation to the same taxable entity, or where they have arisen in respect of different taxable entities there should be the right to settle the amounts on a net basis or simultaneously. [IAS 12.74]

8.2 Other related disclosures

An entity should disclose any tax-related contingent liabilities and contingent assets, in accordance with IAS 37 *Provisions, contingent liabilities and contingent assets*. Contingent liabilities and contingent assets may arise from unresolved disputes with the taxation authorities.

Where changes in tax rates or tax laws are enacted or announced after the balance sheet date, an entity should disclose any significant effect of those changes on its current and deferred tax assets and liabilities.

9 Chapter Review

This chapter has been concerned with accounting for income taxes. This includes both current tax and deferred tax. The primary emphasis has been on deferred tax and included issues of recognition and measurement and the application of these criteria in determining deferred tax balances and charges.

This chapter has covered:

- the objective and scope of IAS 12;

- the nature of deferred tax and why it is necessary;

- the key principles of recognition and measurement of deferred tax relating to temporary differences and deferred tax assets and liabilities; and

- the principal presentation and disclosure requirements of IAS 12.

Chapter 16
LEASES

1 Business Context

Businesses may obtain financing from a number of different sources. Such financing arrangements may vary significantly in nature, from a simple bank overdraft to a complex sale and leaseback transaction.

Leases can be a major source of finance to a business and it is therefore important that the financial statements provide sufficient information for users to be able to understand fully the substance of such transactions. The accounting treatment for leases has caused much debate among national standard setters, with important issues such as gearing and off-balance sheet (i.e. 'hidden') financing at the centre of the debate.

IAS 17 *Leases* sets out the treatment for reporting lease transactions in the financial statements and provides a framework for investors to understand how an entity deals with the financing it accesses in the form of leases.

The debate on the accounting for lease transactions is continuing with the IASB currently having it on its agenda as a research project. The outcome of the project is expected to result in a fundamental change in the treatment of leases.

2 Chapter Objectives

On completion of this chapter you should be able to:

- explain how the concept of substance over form relates to the treatment of leases;

- identify and justify whether a lease should be treated as an operating or a finance lease;

- understand the difference between the accounting requirements for a lessee and a lessor;

- calculate the amounts to be included in the income statements and balance sheets of lessees and lessors for each type of lease; and

- describe the relevant disclosures for both types of leases.

3 Objectives, Scope and Definitions of IAS 17

IAS 17 sets out the appropriate accounting treatment and disclosures for lease transactions in the financial statements of an entity; it should be applied in accounting for all lease transactions except those that are specifically identified below. IAS 17 sets out the accounting requirements for both lessees and lessors.

IAS 17 does not apply to: [IAS 17.2]

- lease agreements set up for the exploration or use of minerals, oil, natural gas and similar non-regenerative resources; and

- licensing agreements that are entered into for items such as motion picture films, video recordings, plays, manuscripts, patents and copyrights.

In addition, the measurement basis of IAS 17 does not apply to items which due to their unique nature are specifically addressed in other international standards. Examples include:

- properties that are recognised as investment properties in accordance with IAS 40 *Investment property;* and

- biological assets that are held by a lessee under finance lease arrangements or provided by a lessor under an operating lease and accounted for in accordance with IAS 41 *Agriculture.*

A 'lease' is a transaction between two parties, a lessor and a lessee, whereby the right to use an asset is transferred to the lessee in return for a defined series of payments to the lessor. IAS 17 applies even if under the terms of the lease the lessor provides substantial services in connection with the operation or maintenance of the asset. An example of such a service would be the provision of ongoing security arrangements for the asset. [IAS 17.4]

IAS 17 identifies two types of lease transaction: [IAS 17.4]

- a finance lease which *"is a lease that transfers substantially all the risks and rewards incident to ownership of an asset. Title may or may not eventually be transferred";* and

- an operating lease which is *"a lease other than a finance lease".*

4 Substance over Form

In the *IASB Framework,* one of the key qualitative characteristics of financial statements is reliability. For information to be reliable, it should faithfully represent transactions, which should be accounted for in accordance with their commercial substance, not merely their legal form. The accounting for a lease is an example of the application of this concept, because the classification of a lease as either a finance lease or an operating lease depends on the substance of the transaction rather than the legal form of the contract.

Where a series of related transactions take place which involve the legal form of a lease, an entity should consider carefully whether the transactions are independent of each other or are, in fact, part of one transaction and should therefore be linked. An example of where it may be appropriate to link a series of transactions is a sale of an asset, which is then leased back to the original entity soon after the original transaction. In such circumstances the overall substance of the transaction may be considered to be one of financing rather than, for example, a sale where a profit was made and recognised.

The Standing Interpretations Committee published SIC 27 *Evaluating the substance of transactions involving the legal form of a lease* to help preparers identify the substance of series of transactions. SIC 27 confirms that the accounting treatment for a series of linked lease transactions should be in accordance with IAS 17 where the substance of the transactions is such that there is a right to use an asset for a specified period of time.

It is an becoming increasingly common for businesses to enter into different types of arrangements with other businesses, often in the same industry, which although not taking the legal form of a lease, include the characteristics of a lease arrangement. An example of such an arrangement is where a supplier in the telecommunications industry provides a contractual right to purchasers to use its network capacity or where a supplier provides the use of an infrastructure asset to a purchaser. The International Financial Reporting Interpretations Committee (IFRIC) issued a draft proposal IFRIC D3 *Determining whether an arrangement contains a lease* in January 2004, which provides draft guidance for determining whether such arrangements contain a lease and should therefore be treated for in accordance with IAS 17.

The illustration below shows how the substance of a finance lease may differ from its legal form.

Illustration 1

P needs to buy a new item of plant and machinery which would cost CU100,000 if bought for cash and which has a useful life of five years. P has no surplus cash available and has identified the following two financing options:

Option 1

Borrow CU100,000 from a bank. This loan is repayable in five annual instalments of CU24,000 each (each instalment including interest of CU4,000).

The cash transaction will be accounted for by recording:

a) an asset for the purchase of the new item of plant and machinery at CU100,000;

b) a liability of CU100,000 to the bank;

c) as each annual instalment is paid, a reduction in cash of CU24,000, a reduction in the liability of CU20,000 and interest of CU4,000 in the income statement; and

d) depreciation of CU20,000 per annum in the income statement.

Option 2

Ask the leasing division of the bank to purchase the plant and then lease it from that division in return for paying five annual lease instalments of CU24,000 each.

Without IAS 17 the transaction would involve recording in the income statement the annual rental instalments of CU24,000 as they become payable.

Issue

The two accounting treatments are different and have a significant impact on the 'picture' presented by the financial statements. In Option 2 no asset or debt is recognised in the balance sheet and hence there is no finance cost or depreciation in the income statement. The substance of these two options is, however, the same, since P:

- has possession and use of the asset for the whole of its five year useful life; and

- is paying a total of CU120,000 for the use of the asset - CU20,000 more than its cash price, so CU20,000 is interest

In substance, P has 'bought' the asset under both options, and the bank has provided the finance. The only real difference is that under Option 2 the entity never gets legal title.

Option 2 would allow P to avoid showing debt in the balance sheet and take advantage of a form of off-balance sheet finance.

5 Distinguishing Between Finance and Operating Leases

In the illustration above, it is clear that Option 2 is a financing arrangement and should therefore be classified as a finance lease. However, if P only leased the plant and machinery for one year, paying a total of CU24,000, it would have use of the asset for only a small proportion of its useful life and is not therefore effectively 'buying' the asset. In this scenario the arrangement would not be a financing transaction but instead a rental transaction, and should therefore be treated as an operating lease. The accounting treatment varies according to which type of lease the lessor holds.

It is sometimes difficult in practice to distinguish between the two types of lease transaction, since arrangements can be very different and often have characteristics of both financing and rental. IAS 17 therefore provides detailed guidance to assist an entity in making the correct distinction.

5.1 Risks and rewards

The classification of a lease is based on the extent to which risks and rewards associated with ownership are transferred from the lessor to the lessee. If a lease transfers substantially all the risks and rewards normally associated with the ownership of an asset it should be classified as a finance lease; otherwise, it should be classified as an operating lease. [IAS 17.8]

Examples of the key risks and rewards that arise from the ownership of an asset are shown in the following table.

Illustration 2

Risk	Reward
Losses may arise: ■ where the asset stands idle for some time due to lack of sufficient demand; ■ from a fall in the value of the asset through technical obsolescence; and ■ from meeting the costs of maintaining and repairing the asset.	Gains may arise from: ■ the generation of profits from use of the asset; ■ use of the asset for substantially the whole of its useful life; and ■ a potential gain arising on the future sale of the asset where it increases in value.

5.2 Situations indicating the existance of a finance lease

In addition to the guidance described above, IAS 17 also sets out specific situations that, individually or collectively, would normally lead to a lease being classified as a finance lease. Such situations include where:

- ownership of the asset transfers to the lessee by the end of the lease term (such arrangements are sometimes known as a hire purchase);

- although ownership of the asset does not automatically pass to the lessee at the end of the agreement, the lessee has an option to purchase the asset. The price at which the option is set is such that it is reasonably certain that the option will be exercised. In other words, the price is set significantly below the fair value expected of the asset at the date the option becomes exercisable (this is sometimes referred to as a bargain purchase option);

- although ownership of the asset is not transferred at the end of the lease term, the term of the lease is for the majority of the economic life of the asset. At the end of the lease, therefore, the asset will have virtually no further ability to generate future economic benefits;

- the asset is so specialised that only the lessee can use it without major modifications; and

- the present value of the minimum lease payments payable by the lessee under the lease is equal to substantially all of the fair value of the asset. Where this is the case, the lessee has effectively paid for the asset in full and therefore should treat the asset as if it had acquired it through a financing arrangement.

Fair value is the amount *"for which an asset could be exchanged, or a liability settled, between knowledgeable, willing parties in an arm's length transaction"*. [IAS 17.4]

The economic life of an asset is the total period over which it is expected to be able to generate economic benefits for one or more users. [IAS 17.4]

The minimum lease payments are the minimum amount that is payable by the lessee to the lessor under a lease agreement. This comprises all amounts payable under the contract, including any amounts guaranteed to the lessee by the lessor or any party related to it. In addition, in the context of a lessee, where there is an option to purchase the asset at the end of the contract and it is expected to be exercised because it has been set at a 'bargain price', then this amount should also form part of the minimum lease payments. [IAS 17.4]

As well as the circumstances described above, IAS 17 provides three additional situations that may lead to classification as a finance lease:

- losses associated with any cancellation of the lease are borne by the lessee;

- fluctuations in the fair value at the end of the lease term fall to the lessee; and

- the lessee has the option to extend the lease for a secondary period at a rate that is substantially below market rate (this is often known as a 'peppercorn rent').

To identify the characteristics of a lease over land and buildings the two elements should be separated. Land is generally considered to have an indefinite life and therefore an associated lease will normally be classified as an operating lease, unless there are other characteristics, such as title of the land transferring to the lessee, that suggest otherwise. [IAS 17.4]

6 The Accounting Treatment by Lessees

6.1 An overview

The following section provides a basic overview of the recognition requirements for the two types of lease.

Finance lease recognition

- Balance sheet

  - Recognise a non-current asset

  - Recognise a liability for the total amount of the lease obligation (i.e. the total payments outstanding including repayment instalments and finance charges accrued to date)

- Income statement

  - Recognise a charge for the depreciation of the non-current asset

  - Recognise a finance charge for the year

Operating lease recognition

- Income statement

  - Recognise the lease instalment charge for the year

The classification of a lease as finance or operating is made at the inception of the lease and should only be revisited if changes to the lease conditions are made which, if made at the outset, would have resulted in a different classification.

The 'inception' of the lease is the earlier of: [IAS 17.4]

- the date of the lease agreement; and
- the date that a commitment is made by the parties to the principal provisions under the lease agreement.

The inception date is also of particular importance for a finance lease as it is the date at which the values for the asset and liability are determined.

The 'lease term' is the non-cancellable period for which the lessee has contracted to lease the asset, plus any extension which is likely to be taken up by the lessee. This period is the useful life for a finance lease asset's depreciation charges and the period over which operating lease payments are charged to the income statement.

6.2 Finance lease recognition

6.2.1 Initial recognition

A lessee should recognise an asset and liability in its balance sheet at the commencement of the lease term. The amounts should be recorded at the fair value of the asset or, if lower, the present value of the minimum lease payments, determined at the inception of the lease. [IAS 17.20]

The present value of the minimum lease payments is calculated by establishing the minimum lease payments due under the lease, as explained above, and discounting them to take account of the time value of money. [IAS 17.20]

If the minimum lease payments under the lease (including any unguaranteed residual value, i.e. the amount that the asset could be sold for at the end of the lease term that is not guaranteed by the lessee) are discounted at the 'interest rate implicit in the lease', the result should equal the fair value of the leased asset. Any initial indirect costs incurred by the lessee are added to the asset's cost. [IAS 17.4]

Initial indirect costs are incremental costs that are directly attributable to *"negotiating and arranging a lease"*. [IAS 17.4]

6.2.2 Depreciation

Since under a finance lease a non-current asset is recognised in the lessee's balance sheet, IAS 17 also requires the asset to be depreciated in accordance with IAS 16 *Property, plant and equipment*. The asset should be depreciated over its useful life or, if there is no reasonable certainty that the lessee will obtain ownership of the asset at the end of the lease term, the period of the lease if that is shorter. The depreciation policy for leased assets should be consistent with those of legally owned assets. [IAS 17.27]

Illustration 3

On 1 January 2004 an entity enters into a finance lease for a photocopier with a fair value of CU8,000. The lease term is for 3 years, with no option to extend, and the copier will be returned to the lessor at the end of the 3 years. The present value of the minimum lease payments is CU7,600.

The copier should therefore be initially recognised at CU7,600, which is the lower of the fair value and the present value of the minimum lease payments.

The useful life of the copier is estimated to be 4 years with a nil residual value. The entity operates a straight-line method of depreciation with a full charge in the year of acquisition.

The depreciation charge on the copier in 2004 is:

$$CU7,600 / 3 \text{ years} = CU2,533$$

Because the lessee will not gain ownership at the end of the 3 year period, the copier is depreciated over a 3 year period being the shorter of the lease term and the asset's useful life,

6.2.3 Finance charge

Each instalment made under a finance lease consists of a mixture of a finance charge and the repayment of capital. [IAS 17.25]

The total finance charge over the total period of the lease is:

	CU
Total lease rentals	X
Less: initial finance lease obligation being the lower of fair value and PV of the minimum lease payments.	(X)
Total finance charges	X

The total interest cost should be charged in the income statement over the accounting periods for which the lease liability is in existence. This is from the start of the lease until the last repayment is made.

The period over which the lease liability is in existence is not necessarily the same as the term of the lease. For example, if lease rentals are paid annually in advance, the lease finance will be paid off when the final payment is made at the start of the last year, but the lease term will include the last year, even though no liability will remain.

6.2.4 Methods of allocating finance charges

IAS 17 requires the total finance charge to be allocated over accounting periods so as to produce a constant periodic rate of interest on the outstanding lease obligation. [IAS 17.25]

The two main ways of allocating the finance charge to accounting periods are the actuarial method and the sum of digits methods. The sum of digits method provides an approximation to the actuarial method. This approximation is permitted on the grounds of practicality.

6.2.4.1 Actuarial method

The actuarial method charges interest at a constant percentage on the outstanding liability and therefore matches the interest to the 'loan' balance. This is the most accurate method, but to apply it, the rate of interest implicit in the lease is required.

The interest charge for each period is the interest rate multiplied by the balance remaining immediately after a rental payment has been made.

Illustration 4

An entity entered into a five year finance lease on 1 January 2003. The fair value of the leased asset was CU11,500. Lease rentals of CU3,034 are payable annually in arrears on 31 December each year. The rate of interest implicit in the lease is 10%.

The asset is included in non-current assets at its fair value of CU11,500 and depreciated over the five year term.

The finance charge for the year to 31 December 2003 is calculated on the outstanding balance of CU11,500. The finance cost will be CU1,150.

At 31 December 2003 the lease liability of CU9,616 is calculated as the initial amount of CU11,500 plus the accrued interest of CU1,150 less the repayment of CU3,034.

6.2.4.2 Sum of digits method

The sum of digits method approximates the interest charge for each period by weighting the periods in reverse order, so that most interest is charged in earlier periods.

6.2.5 Disclosures for finance leases

IAS 17 requires a number of disclosures to be made in relation to the effect that a finance lease has had on an entity's financial statements during a period. Reference should also be made to IAS 32 *Financial instruments: disclosure and presentation*.

For each class of assets, for example land, buildings, plant and machinery, an entity should disclose the net carrying amount that relates to assets held under finance leases. An entity should present a reconciliation of the future minimum lease payments due at the balance sheet date to their present value. These minimum lease payments and their present value should also be allocated over the periods in which payments will be made, as follows: [IAS 17.31]

- within one year;

- within two-five years; and

- after more than five years.

Disclosure should be made of any contingent rents that have been recognised as an expense during the period and the amount of any payments expected to be received under non-cancellable subleases. Contingent rents are the part of the lease payments which varies by reference to a factor other than time, such as a percentage of sales generated from use of the leased asset. [IAS 17.31]

A description of an entity's significant leasing arrangements should be presented. Such information will normally include the basis on which contingent rents are determined, the existence and terms of any options to extend the lease term or purchase the asset and any restrictions that are imposed on the lease arrangements. [IAS 17.31]

6.3 Accounting treatment of operating leases

The definition of an operating lease, as detailed at the start of this chapter, is any lease other than a finance lease.

IAS 17 requires lease payments made under an operating lease to be charged as an expense directly in the income statement on a systematic basis over the lease term. A straight-line basis should be used unless another basis is more representative of the timing of the benefits obtained by the user of the asset. [IAS 17.33]

Illustration 5

An entity enters into an operating lease arrangement for the use of a piece of machinery for a period of three years. The economic life of the asset is estimated as being around 15 years. The entity will pay annual rentals of CU1,000 over the three years.

The entity expects the machinery to be used evenly over the three year period so the annual rental of CU1,000 should be recognised in each of the three years.

6.3.1 Operating lease incentives

It is not uncommon for a form of lease incentive to be provided to a lessee to encourage it to enter into a particular leasing arrangement. Incentives take various forms, such as a rent-free period and lump sum payments either on entering the lease or as a reimbursement for leasehold improvements. IAS 17 does not address such issues and therefore the Standing Interpretations Committee issued SIC 15 *Operating leases – incentives* to address the Issue.

SIC 15 requires that where a lease incentive is provided it is recognised as an integral part of the net consideration payable under the lease arrangement irrespective of the reason behind the incentive payment. The lessee should therefore treat the incentive payment as a reduction of its rental expense on a straight-line basis, unless a different basis is more appropriate.

6.3.2 Disclosures for operating leases

IAS 17 requires a number of disclosures to be made in relation to any operating leases. Reference should also be made to IAS 32.

An entity should disclose the outstanding payments under non-cancellable operating leases allocated between the following periods: [IAS 17.35]

- within one year;
- within two to five years; and
- after more than five years.

Where an entity expects to receive sub-lease rentals under an operating lease arrangement the total minimum payments should be disclosed at the balance sheet date. [IAS 17.35]

The total amount recognised in the income statement for amounts under operating leases, including subleases, should be disclosed identifying amounts representing the minimum lease payments, contingent rents and sublease amounts. [IAS 17.35]

A description of an entity's significant leasing arrangements should be presented. Such information will normally include the basis on which any contingent rents are payable, the existence and terms of any options to extend the lease term, any escalation clauses or purchase options and any restrictions that are imposed on the lease arrangements. [IAS 17.35]

Illustration 6

An entity has the following outstanding non-cancellable operating lease commitments at its balance sheet date:

- rental on buildings of CU100,000 per annum for 15 years;
- rental on plant of CU30,000 per annum for 3 years; and
- rental on cars of CU40,000 for 11 months.

The operating lease commitment note should include:

The minimum lease payments under non-cancellable operating leases are:

		CU
within 1 year	(100,000 + 30,000 + 40,000)	170,000
within 2-5 years	((100,000 x 4yrs) + (30,000 x 2yrs))	460,000
after 5 years	(100,000 x 10yrs)	1,000,000
		1,630,000

7 The Accounting Treatment by Lessors

7.1 Finance leases

Just as a lessee accounts for the substance, not form, of a finance lease, so should a lessor. Under a finance lease the lessor is entitled to a stream of leasing receipts, so it should recognise the amounts receivable as an asset, rather than the leased item as a non-current asset. The receivables should be measured at the net investment in the lease. [IAS 17.36]

The net investment in the lease is defined as being the *"gross investment in the lease discounted at the interest rate implicit in the lease"*. This gross investment is calculated as the lessee's minimum lease payments (which includes any residual value guaranteed by the lessee) plus any unguaranteed amount accruing to the lessor. [IAS 17.4]

The interest rate implicit in the lease is the same as that explained in relation to the lessee. The way the it is calculated automatically includes any initial direct costs incurred by the lessor in the amounts receivable from the lessee, so they should not be added separately.

The income receivable under a finance lease arrangement should be recognised based on *"a pattern reflecting a constant period rate of return on the lessor's net investment in the finance lease"*. [IAS 17.39]

A manufacturer or dealer lessor effectively has income arising from two sources, being:

- the profit or loss that would have arisen from an outright sale of an asset; and

- the finance income over the lease term.

The selling profit or loss should be recognised in the same period as it would have been recognised in had the asset been sold without the financing arrangements, so a consistent policy is adopted for the recognition of selling profit or losses. [IAS 17.42]

If the interest rate charged by a manufacturer or dealer lessor on the financing of the purchase of an asset is artificially low then the selling profit should be adjusted so that a market rate of interest is charged. This will result in a deferral of some of the selling profit. [IAS 17.42]

Any incremental costs incurred in negotiating a lease by a manufacturer or dealer lessor should be recognised as an expense when the selling profit is recognised.

7.1.1 Disclosure by a lessor for finance lease arrangements

A number of disclosure requirements should be presented in the financial statements of a lessor in respect of finance lease arrangements. Reference should also be made to IAS 32.

A lessor should provide a general description of its significant leasing arrangements. [IAS 17.47]

A lessor should present a reconciliation of the gross investment in finance leases to the present value of the future minimum lease receipts due under them at the balance sheet date. The gross investment in the lease and the present value of the minimum lease payments for each of the following periods should also be disclosed: [IAS 17.47]

- within one year;

- within two to five years; and

- after more than five years.

In addition, a lessor should disclose any unearned finance income, any unguaranteed residual values that accrue to the lessor (the amount that the asset will be worth at the end of its useful life) and contingent rents received during the period. [IAS 17.47]

A lessor should also identify any allowance that has been made for uncollectable lease payments receivable. [IAS 17.47]

7.2 Operating leases

A lessor should recognise assets that are leased under operating leases in its balance sheet according to the nature of the asset. Where it is the lease of a photocopier, for example, it would be presented as a non-current asset as part of property, plant and equipment. [IAS 17.49]

The lessor will recognise depreciation on depreciable non-current assets under operating lease arrangements in accordance with IAS 16. The depreciation policy for leased assets should be consistent with that for other non-current assets held by the lessor that are not subject to lease arrangements. [IAS 17.53]

Initial direct costs, as described above, should be added to the carrying amount of the asset and will therefore be recognised as an expense over the period of the useful life of the asset as it is depreciated. [IAS 17.52]

The income received under an operating lease should be recognised in the lessor's income statement based on a straight-line basis over the lease term. A different systematic basis of recognition should be used where it represents more fairly the timing of the benefits derived from the asset as the lessee uses it. [IAS 17.50]

7.2.1 Disclosure by a lessor for operating lease arrangements

A number of disclosures should be made by a lessor in its financial statements as required by IAS 17 in respect of operating lease arrangements. Reference should also be made to IAS 32.

Disclosures should include a general description of the entiy's leasing arrangements and the amount of contingent rents received in the period. [IAS 17.56]

A lessor should disclose the future minimum receipts under non-cancellable operating leases allocated between the following periods: [IAS 17.56]

- within one year;

- within two to five years; and

- after more than five years.

7.2.2 Operating lease incentives

Where a lessor has provided an incentive to a lessee as described above it should recognise the aggregate cost of the incentive as a reduction in the rental income over the period of the lease. The incentive should normally be recognised on a straight-line basis, unless a different method is more appropriate. [SIC 15]

8 Sale and Leaseback Transactions

An entity may enter into a financing arrangement to improve its liquidity through what is commonly referred to as a sale and leaseback transaction. In such circumstances, the entity sells the asset to a third party, receives proceeds for the sale and then leases the asset back and pays rentals for its use.

A sale and leaseback transaction can result in a finance or operating lease, depending on the substance of the transaction.

If the lease is identified as a finance lease, finance has been provided and the asset has been given as security for that finance. Any profit made on the sale of the asset is deferred. The excess of sale proceeds over the carrying amount of the asset at the date of the transaction is deferred in the balance sheet and amortised in the income statement over the period of the lease. [IAS 17.59]

If the lease is identified as an operating lease and the lease payments and the sale price are established at fair value, any profit made on the sale should be recognised as such in the income statement immediately. [IAS 17.61]

If, however, the sale price is below fair value then any loss arising should be deferred to the extent that future rental payments are below market value. The loss will be recognised in the income statement as the rentals are recognised. If the sale price was above fair value, the excess profit over fair value should be deferred and recognised in the period over which the asset is expected to be utilised. [IAS 17.61]

Where an operating lease results and the fair value of the asset is less than its carrying amount at the time of the sale, then this loss should be recognised immediately. A loss arising in such circumstances is essentially an impairment of the asset (i.e. a decrease in the recoverable amount of the asset). [IAS 17.63]

Illustration 7

An entity had two sale and leaseback transactions during the year ended 31 March 2004.

(1)	It sold a non-current asset with a carrying amount of CU20,000 for its fair value of CU24,000 under a finance leaseback arrangement. The lease period was for five years at an annual rental of CU7,000. The machine has a useful life of five years.
(2)	It sold a property under an operating leaseback arrangement for its fair value of CU40,000 when the property had a carrying amount of CU36,000 The annual operating leaseback payments are CU10,000 per annum for three years, which reflect market rentals.

Transaction 1

Although the machine has been sold at fair value, no profit is recognised immediately as the machine remains a non-current asset. The proceeds are recognised as a liability and the finance charge of CU11,000 ((CU7,000 x 5) less CU24,000) is allocated over the five year period.

Transaction 2

The gain on disposal of the property of CU4,000 (CU40,000 less CU36,000) is recognised immediately, because the sale price and the rentals are at fair value. The operating lease rentals are recognised as an expense in the income statement.

9 Service Concession Arrangements

A service concession is the provision of services that give the public access to major economic and social facilities, for example motorways, bridges and telecommunication networks. Within such arrangements there are two parties, a concession operator and a concession provider. The outsourcing of an entity's internal services are not service concessions, for example building maintenance and employee restaurant facilities.

A service concession will generally arise where the concession provider, which may be a public (governmental) or private sector entity, provides to the concession operator "the right to provide services that give the public access to major economic and social facilities". This may involve the use of certain assets. In return the concession operator has the obligation to provide public services.

Such arrangements have many of the characteristics of a lease contract and the acquisition of a non-current asset but also may include an executory contract. SIC 29 *Disclosure - service concession arrangements* sets out a number of additional disclosures to be presented where such arrangements exists. Disclosures include a description of the arrangement as well as the nature and extent of the use of assets and obligations undertaken as a direct consequence of entering the arrangement.

10 Chapter Review

This chapter has dealt with the treatment of finance and operating leases by lessees and lessors.

This chapter has covered:

- how leases are accounted for by reference to their substance, not necessarily their legal form;

- the objectives, scope, definitions and disclosure requirements of IAS 17;

- the difference between finance leases and operating leases and their respective accounting treatment;

- rental payments and the allocation of finance charges in a finance lease;

- the different accounting treatment for leases required by a lessee and a lessor; and

- the treatment of sale and leaseback transactions and operating lease incentives.

Chapter 17

EMPLOYEE BENEFITS

1 Business Context

One of the key business problems in recent years has concerned the funding by entities of their employee pension schemes. With falling equity values, pension funds have watched their investments significantly decrease in value, leading to many schemes having a deficit in recent years.

Although pension plans are generally operated by independent trustees, they are set up for the benefit of the employing entity's employees, with the employing entity often retaining some of the obligations under the plans. In some cases pension plans may in substance be assets and liabilities of the employing entity itself. To ensure that all pension plans are accounted for and presented in a consistent manner IAS 19 *Employee benefits* sets out the accounting requirements.

Employees generally receive a number of different benefits as part of their complete remuneration package and these are also addressed in IAS 19.

The provision of shares and share options has long been a popular remuneration tool for management but the recent dot.com boom saw the widespread use of such benefits for all employees and as payment to suppliers. Newly set-up entities with limited cash resources used the promise of share growth as a way to attract and retain high calibre individuals. Before the recent publication of IFRS 2 *Share-based payment,* the provision of, say, a share option was not recognised in the employing entity's income statement under the application of international standards. This led to significant employee benefits provided by an entity not being recognised in its financial statements.

2 Chapter Objectives

This chapter deals with the accounting and disclosure requirements for various forms of employee remuneration and post-retirement benefits.

On completion of this chapter you should be able to:

- distinguish between the different forms of remuneration that make up employee benefits;

- demonstrate a knowledge of the distinction between short and long-term benefits;

- for each of the benefit types, understand the recognition and measurement rules;

- understand the difference between a defined contribution plan and a defined benefit plan and hence the different accounting treatment that each requires; and

- understand the implications of share-based payment transactions as a form of employee benefit.

3 Objectives, Scope and Definitions of IAS 19

IAS 19 should be applied by all entities in accounting for the provision of all employee benefits, except those to which IFRS 2 applies. The standard applies regardless of whether the benefits have been provided as part of a formal contract. [IAS 19.1]

Employee benefits are all forms of consideration, for example cash bonuses, retirement benefits and private health care, given to an employee by an entity in exchange for the employee's services. [IAS 19.7]

A number of accounting issues arise due to:

- the valuation problems linked to some forms of employee benefits; and
- the timing of benefits, which may not always be provided in the same period as the one in which the employee's services are provided.

IAS 19 is structured by considering the different forms of employee benefits as follows:

- short-term employee benefits;
- post-employment benefits;
- other long-term employee benefits; and
- termination benefits.

4 Short-term Employee Benefits

4.1 All short-term benefits

Short-term employee benefits are employee benefits (other than termination benefits) that fall due within twelve months from the end of the period in which the employees provide their services. [IAS 19.7]

Short-term employee benefits include:

- wages, salaries and social security contributions;
- short-term absences where the employee continues to be paid, for example paid annual vacation, paid sick leave and paid maternity/paternity leave. To fall within the definition the absences should be expected to occur within twelve months of the end of the period in which the employee services were provided;
- profit-sharing and bonuses payable within twelve months of the end of the period; and
- non-monetary benefits, for example private medical care and company cars.

As set out in IAS 1 *Presentation of financial statements*, financial statements should be prepared by applying the accrual concept. The application of the accrual concept in relation to liabilities means that an entity should recognise a liability when it becomes payable rather than when it is actually paid. A short-term benefit should therefore be recognised as an employee provides his or her services to the entity on which the benefits are payable. The benefit will normally be treated as an expense, and a liability should be recognised for any unpaid balance at the year-end. [IAS 19.10]

4.2 Short-term compensated absences

Compensated absences are periods of absence from work for which the employee receives some form of payment, for example paid annual vacation and paid sick leave. These benefits fall into two categories:

- *accumulating absences.* These are benefits, such as paid annual vacation, that accrue over an employee's period of service and can be potentially carried forward and used in future periods; and

- *non-accumulating absences.* These are benefits that an employee is entitled to, but are not normally capable of being carried forward to the following period if they are unused during the period, for example paid sick leave.

The cost of providing compensation for accumulating absences should be recognised as an expense as the employee provides his or her services on which the entitlement to such benefits accrues. Where an employee has an unused entitlement at the end of the reporting period and the entity expects to provide the benefit, a liability should be created. [IAS 19.11, 19.14]

The cost of providing compensation for non-accumulating absences should be expensed as the absences occur. [IAS 19.11]

Illustration 1

An entity has 5 employees and each is entitled to 20 days paid vacation per year, at a rate of CU50 per day. Unused vacation is carried forward to the following year.

All 5 employees work for the entity throughout the year and are therefore entitled to their 20 days of vacation. An expense should be recognised in the income statement for:

5 employees x 20 days x CU50 = CU5,000

4 of the employees use their complete entitlement for the year and the other, having used 16 days is permitted to carry forward the remaining 4 days to the following period. A liability will be recognised at the period end for:

1 employee x 4 days x CU50 = CU200

4.3 Profit-sharing and bonus plans

An entity should recognise an expense and a corresponding liability for the cost of providing profit-sharing arrangements and bonus payments when: [IAS 19.17]

- the entity has a present legal or constructive obligation, (i.e. payment is part of an employee's employment contract, or the entity has a history of paying bonuses) to make such payments as the result of a past event; and

- a reliable estimate of the obligation can be made.

Illustration 2

An entity has a contractual agreement to pay 4% of its net profit each year as a bonus. The bonus is divided between the employees who are with the entity at its year end. The following data is relevant:

Net profit:	CU120,000
Average employees	5
Employees at start of year	6
Employees at end of year	4

An expense should be recognised in the income statement for the year in which the profits were made and therefore the employees' services were provided, for:

CU120,000 x 4% = CU4,800

Each of the 4 employees remaining with the entity at the year-end is entitled to CU1,200. A liability should be recognised if the bonuses remain unpaid at the year-end.

5 Post-Employment Benefits – Overview

Post-employment benefits are employee benefits (other than termination benefits) which are payable after the completion of employment. Such benefits include post employment benefit plans set up under formal or informal arrangements. [IAS 19.7]

Post-employment benefits include pensions and other post-employment benefits, such as continued private medical care.

There are two main types of post-employment benefit plan:

(1) *defined contribution plans*. These are post-employment plans under which payments into the plan are fixed. Subsequent payments out of the plan to retired members are based on the size of the 'pot'. The 'pot' represents contributions that have been made into the scheme and investment returns on scheme assets. The risk of the plan not providing adequate payments to retired members lies with the members; and [IAS 19.7]

(2) *defined benefit plans*. These are defined as all plans other than defined contribution plans. These plans define the amount that retired members will receive from the plans during retirement, by reference to factors such as length of service and salary levels. Contributions are paid into the scheme based on an estimate of what will have to be paid out under it. Typically, an employer retains an obligation to make up any shortfall in a plan, thereby bearing the risk of the plan under-performing. [IAS 19.7]

6 Defined Contribution Plans

6.1 Recognition and measurement

Contributions into a defined contribution plan by an employer are made in return for services provided by an employee during the period. The entity should recognise contributions payable as an expense in the period in which the employee provides his or her services for which contributions by the employer become payable. A liability should be recognised where contributions arise in relation to an employee's service, but remain unpaid at the period end. [IAS 19.44]

Where contributions are not payable during the period (or within 12 months of the end of the period) in which the employee provides his or her services on which they accrue, the amount recognised should be discounted, to reflect the time value of money. [IAS 19.45]

6.2 Disclosure

Where an entity operates a defined contribution plan during the period, it should disclose the amount that has been recognised as an expense during the period in relation to the plan. [IAS 19.46]

7 Defined Benefit Plans

The formal definition of a defined benefit plan is any post-employment benefit plan not meeting the definition of a defined contribution plan. However, it is generally a plan whereby the amount of benefits that an employee will receive on retirement is specified in some way, for example as a proportion of an employee's final salary depending on the number of year's service worked. [IAS 19.7]

As noted above, the key feature of a defined benefit plan is that the employer retains an obligation to make up any shortfall in the plan, should there be insufficient funds within it to pay out the promised benefits.

It would be inappropriate for the entity to record only the contributions paid as expenses, since in effect it is underwriting some of the risks associated in the plan.

There are many uncertainties in terms of the measurement of an employer's obligation in relation to a defined benefit plan, not least because an obligation only arises if the investments out of which the payment of benefits will be made are less than the benefits payable. In terms of the investments, the major uncertainties relate to how investments, both those already made and those to be made from future contributions, will perform in terms of investment returns and capital appreciation.

IAS 19 is based on the principle that an entity has an obligation under a defined benefit plan when an employee performs services which accrue benefits under the plan. It is therefore appropriate that an expense is recognised for an employee's services during the period in which they are performed and for which benefits will be payable under the defined benefit plan. Because of the long-term nature of a defined benefit plan and the level of uncertainty of actual obligations that will fall due under it, the specialist services of an actuary are required. An estimate of the level of the obligations payable under the plan and whether the value of the plan's assets will be sufficient to meet these estimated liabilities is made.

Due to the nature of defined benefit plans an enity is required to recognise the defined benefit liability in its balance sheet.

There are two types of defined benefit plan:

- *funded plans*: these plans are set up as separate legal entities and are managed independently, often by trustees. Contributions paid by the employer and employee are paid into the separate legal entity. The assets held within the separate legal entities are effectively ring-fenced for the payment of benefits; and

- *unfunded plans*: these plans are held within employer legal entities and are managed by the employers' management teams. Assets may be allocated towards the satisfaction of retirement benefit obligations, although these assets are not ring-fenced for the payment of benefits and remain the assets of the employer entity.

7.1 Plan assets

The contributions that are paid into a defined benefit plan are invested with the intention of enhancing the plan assets to a value that will be sufficient to meet the future obligations under the plan as they fall due. These assets are described as 'plan assets' and are legally separate from the employing entity and exist solely for the benefit of the employees that are members of the plan (within a funded plan). The consequence of this legal separation means that the entity is unable to use these assets for it own activities. Assets can only be returned to an entity if the remaining assets within the plan cover the obligations under it, or they are a refund of benefits already paid to members of the plan. [IAS 19.7]

An entity is required to value the plan assets in a defined benefit plan at fair value at each balance sheet date. Fair value is defined as *"the amount for which an asset could be exchanged or a liability settled between knowledgeable, willing parties in an arm's length transaction"*. [IAS 19.7]

The fair value of plan assets will generally be their market value. However, where market prices are not available, fair value should be estimated, for example by discounting expected future cash flows.

7.2 Defined benefit obligations

The level of benefits ultimately to be paid out of a defined benefit plan are uncertain as they depend on the outcome of such factors as life expectancy and future investment returns. The expertise of an actuary is therefore used to estimate these uncertain future events to ensure that the pension plan is adequately funded (based on the assets in the plan and the expected future contributions to be made) to meet its future obligations.

To determine a defined benefit obligation is to calculate the actuarial present value of promised retirement benefits. IAS 19 defines this as being *"the present value, without deducting any plan assets, of the expected payments required to settle the obligation resulting from employee service in the current and prior periods"*. [IAS 19.7]

IAS 19 provides considerable guidance on the method to be used and the factors to be taken into account. The relevant method is that of the 'projected unit credit method', where each period of service gives rise to an additional unit of benefit under the plan. [IAS 19.64]

7.3 Actuarial assumptions

Actuarial estimates are made of the amount of future benefits that are likely to arise from employee service. Defined benefit pension plans are dependent on employee services accumulated over time, and benefits are therefore the result of past and present service.

Future benefits are based on actuarial projections, based on assumptions. Actuarial assumptions can be split into two main areas, demographic assumptions (which consider the likely characteristics of members of the plan, such as mortality rates) and financial assumptions, such as future salary increases and investment returns.

The assumptions made by an actuary should be unbiased and compatible with each other. [IAS 19.72]

Other factors that should be taken into account in measuring the post-employment benefit obligations are the current level of benefits set out in the plan and an estimate of changes in state benefits which may have a subsequent effect on the benefits payable under the plan.

Where medical benefits are provided as part of an employee's post-employment benefits, the actuarial valuation should take into account the estimated future price changes in the cost of providing such services. This estimate should take into account both general inflationary increases and specific changes expected in medical costs. [IAS 19.88]

7.3.1 The discount rate

IAS 19 requires that the defined benefit obligation be discounted to reflect the time value of money. The discount rate used does not take into account other risks, such as investment risk or the entity's credit risk. Instead IAS 19 requires that the entity should use a rate that takes into account *"market yields at the balance sheet date on high quality corporate bonds"*. [IAS 19.78]

The effect of the time value of money should be recognised as interest in the income statement.

7.3.2 Movements during the period

An entity is required to recognise a defined benefit liability or asset at each balance sheet date. This amount should be based on the present value of the defined benefit obligation, as described above, less the fair value of the plan assets. The movement in the period between the opening and closing balances for these represent: [IAS 19.54]

- the current service cost, which is the cost associated with providing an employee with an additional year's retirement benefit as a result of a providing an additional year's service;

- the interest cost, this is the unwinding of the discount factor recognising that the retirement benefit obligation is one year nearer to payment;

- the return achieved on investing the plan assets;

- contributions paid by the employing entity; and

■   retirement pension benefits paid out.

A summary of the impact of these movements on the defined benefit obligation and plan assets each period is set out below in a table. The table also highlights the effect on the income statement. [IAS 19.61]

	Present value of defined benefit obligation	Fair value of plan assets	Impact on income statement
Current service cost	Increase liability		Expense
Interest cost	Increase liability		Interest expense
Return on plan assets		Increase asset	Recognise the expected return on assets as income
Contributions paid		Increase asset	
Retirement benefits paid	Decrease liability	Decrease asset	

7.3.3 Variations in actuarial assumptions

Because actuarial techniques involve so many estimates about the future, it is likely that revisions will have to be made to those estimates in subsequent accounting periods. Allowances made in initial estimates for employee turnover, early retirement, future salary increases, the discount rate and investment returns on plan assets all need to be revised in the light of subsequent experience. These reviews may result in an increase in the defined benefit obligation over what was previously estimated, termed an 'actuarial loss', or a decrease, termed an 'actuarial gain'. [IAS 19.7]

These differences form part of the movement between the opening and closing figures in respect of defined benefit plans in the balance sheet.

The largest difference is likely to be that between the expected investment return on the plan assets and the actual return made during the period. Expected returns will be based on the long-term estimated performance of the investments.

IAS 19 requires expected returns on the assets to be reported in the income statement each period rather than actual returns, to avoid potential volatility that might otherwise result.

Actuarial gains and losses may be deferred in the balance sheet of an entity each period. A proposed amendment to IAS 19 was made in April 2004 that proposes to permit an entity a further alternative to immediate recognition in the income statement of actuarial gains and losses, or deferral in the balance sheet, which is the immediate recognition of such amounts outside of the income statement.

IAS 19 requires that an entity should reduce any balance for deferred actuarial gains and losses where the deferred figure reaches a certain level. The reduction is shown as an expense or income in the income statement spread over the average remaining working lives of the employees who are members of the plan. [IAS 19.92]

The reduction is calculated by carrying out the following steps:

- assess which is greater, the opening figure for the present value of the retirement benefit obligation or the opening figure for the fair value of the plan assets;

- whichever amount is greater, multiply by 10%. This is known as the 'corridor';

- compare this amount with the amount of actuarial gains and losses that the entity has deferred in its balance sheet;

- if the deferred balance is less than the 'corridor', the entity does not need to do anything;

- if the deferred balance is more than the 'corridor', the entity needs to release the excess to the income statement; and

- the minimum amount that should be released each period is the excess divided by the expected remaining working lives of the employees who are members of the plan.

Illustration 3

An entity set up a defined benefit pension plan for the benefit of its employees during the year.

The fair value of the scheme assets at the end of the year is CU23,000 and the present value of the scheme liabilities is CU15,000. An actuary has provided the following analysis in the movement of the net pension asset:

	CU
Net pension asset at start of year	-
Contributions paid to plan	20,000
Expected return on pension assets	2,000
Interest on scheme liabilities	(1,000)
Current service cost	(16,000)
Unrecognised actuarial gain	3,000
Net pension asset at end of year (CU23,000 less CU15,000)	8,000

The contributions paid are included in the cash flow statement

The unrecognised actuarial gain is deferred in the balance sheet so the amount presented as the net pension asset in the financial statements is CU5,000 (CU8,000 less deferred gain of CU3,000).

The net amount recognised in the income statement for the year will be CU15,000 (CU16,000 plus CU1,000 less CU2,000).

The corridor is CU2,300 (being 10% of CU23,000). As the unrecognised actuarial gain is greater than the corridor it will be released from the following year. If the remaining working lives of the employees is 14 years the minimum amount recognised in the income statement in the forthcoming year is CU50 ((CU3,000 less CU2,300)/14)

7.4 Sundry considerations

For practical reasons a full actuarial calculation is not required unless it would lead to a significant difference at the balance sheet date. The latest information should however be updated each period. [IAS 19.56]

If the balance sheet calculation results in a defined benefit asset being reported this should be restricted where the entity cannot fully recover the surplus through a refund or reduced contributions in future periods. [IAS 19.58, 19.58A]

7.4.1 Past service costs

An entity may change the benefits payable under a defined benefit plan, for example increase the percentage of final salary that is used in the calculation of an employee's retirement benefits. Where such a change is made, it may impact the cost that has been charged to the income statement in relation to an employee's services already performed. An amount should therefore be charged to the income statement on a straight-line basis over the average period remaining before the benefits vest, for the additional amount in relation to the services already performed. If any benefits have already vested (i.e. they are not conditional on an employee's continuing employment) then the additional expense should be recognised immediately. [IAS 19.96]

7.4.2 Curtailments and settlements

A curtailment in a defined benefit plan occurs when there is a significant reduction in the number of employees who are members of the plan or where employees future services will not substantially increase the benefits payable under the plan. Where such changes arise the effect of the curtailment should be reported when it occurs. [IAS 19.109]

A settlement occurs when an entity enters into a transaction that removes all future obligations under part of the defined benefit plan. An example of a settlement is where a lump sum is provided to the members of the plan but no further benefits will be received under it. Where a settlement is made it should be accounted for as it takes place. [IAS 19.109]

An entity should remeasure the defined benefit obligation immediately before the effect of a curtailment or settlement is calculated. [IAS 19.110]

The gain or loss arising on a settlement or curtailment should be calculated by assessing the impact on the present value of the defined benefit obligations, the impact on plan assets and the effect on any deferred amounts in relation to the plan. [IAS 19.109]

7.5 Disclosure and presentation of defined benefit plans

A number of detailed disclosures should be presented where an entity has a defined benefit plan, including a general description of the plan and the entity's accounting policy for recognising actuarial gains and losses. [IAS 19.120]

A reconciliation of assets and liabilities recognised in the balance sheet in relation to a defined benefit plan should be presented. The reconciliation should include the present value of the defined benefit obligation split between schemes funded and unfunded, the fair value of the plan assets, the net actuarial gains and losses and past service costs not yet recognised, any scheme surplus that has not been recognised and any separately classified reimbursement assets recognised. [IAS 19.120]

Disclosure of the fair value of the plan assets which comprise an entity's own financial instruments should be presented and property or other assets used by the entity should be identified. [IAS 19.120]

A reconciliation of the movement in the net defined benefit asset or liability recognised in the balance sheet should be disclosed and the amounts reflected in the income statement should be presented separately for:

- *"current service costs;*
- *interest cost;*
- *expected return on assets;*
- *expected return on reimbursement rights recognised;*
- *actuarial gains and losses;*
- *past service costs; and*
- *the effect of any curtailments or settlements".*

The entity should also disclose the actual return on plan assets and where the entity has separately identified reimbursements the return on these should also be disclosed. [IAS 19.120]

The principal actuarial assumptions should be clearly identified and explained, this should include the discount rate, the expected return on plan assets (including separate reimbursement assets), expected salary increases, expected increases in medical costs and any other significant assumptions made. [IAS 19.120]

8 Sundry Matters Involving Long-term Employment Benefits

8.1 Multi-employer plans

A multi-employer plan is where several entities pool contributed assets and use that pool to provide for future retirement obligations of the employees of all the pooling entities. The general requirement is that an entity should recognise a multi-employer plan in accordance with the nature of the plan. [IAS 19.7]

If the multi-employer plan is a defined benefit plan, then each entity should recognise its share of the plan's assets, liabilities and expenses and make the full disclosures required for such a plan. [IAS 19.29]

If it is not possible to split the assets, liabilities and costs in a multi-employer defined benefit plan between the participating entities then an entity should account for its contributions into the plan as if it were a defined contribution plan. An entity should clearly explain this fact. [IAS 19.30]

The identification of a multi-employer scheme and the use of the "get-out" for using defined benefit accounting caused the IASB some concern. As a result the IFRIC issued a proposed interpretation D6 *Multi-employer plans* to assist preparers in this area.

8.2 State plans

IAS 19 currently sets out that a state plan operated by national or local government should be accounted for as if it is a multi-employer plan. However, the proposed IFRIC interpretation D6 mentioned above proposes to amend this so that such plans should be accounted for as if they are defined contribution plans. [IAS 19.36]

9 Other Long-term Employee Benefits

Other long-term employee benefits are defined as *"employee benefits (other than post retirement benefit plans and termination benefits) which do not fall due wholly within twelve months after the end of the period in which the employees render the service".* [IAS 19.7]

Examples of other long-term employee benefits include long-term disability benefits and paid sabbatical leave.

Although such long-term benefits have many of the attributes of a defined benefit pension plan, they are not subject to the same level of uncertainty. As a consequence, the accounting treatment adopted is a simplified version of that for a defined benefit plan. For example, actuarial gains and losses are recognised immediately, as are any past service costs. [IAS 19.128, 19.129]

10 Termination Benefits

Termination benefits are employee benefits payable on the termination of employment, through voluntary redundancy or as a result of a decision made by the employer to terminate employment before the normal retirement date. Where voluntary redundancy has been offered, the entity should measure the benefits based on an expected level of take-up. If, however, there is uncertainty about the number of employees who will accept the offer, then there may be a contingent liability, requiring disclosure under IAS 37 *Provisions, contingent liabilities and contingent assets.* [IAS 19.7, 19.140]

An entity should recognise a termination benefit when it has made some form of commitment to end the employment. [IAS 19.133]

Such a commitment will exist where, for example, the entity has a detailed formal plan for the termination and it cannot realistically withdraw from that commitment. [1AS 19.134]

Illustration 4

The directors of an entity met on 23 July 2003 to discuss the need to decrease costs by reducing the number of employees. On 17 August 2003 they met again to agree a plan. On 6 September 2003 other members of the management team were informed of the plan. On 7 October 2003 the plan was announced to the employees affected and implementation of the formalised plan began.

The entity should only recognise the liability for the termination benefits when it is demonstrably committed to terminate the employment of those affected. This occurred on 7 October 2003 when the formal plan was announced such that there is no realistic chance of withdrawal.

11 Share-based Payment Transactions

11.1 Objectives, scope and definitions of IFRS 2

IFRS 2 *Share-based payment* sets out how share-based payment transactions should be recognised and measured in an entity's financial statements. A share-based payment transaction is one in which the entity transfers equity instruments (such as shares or share options) in exchange for goods and services supplied by employees or third parties.

IFRS 2 applies to all types of share-based payment transactions, except where another international standard deals more specifically with the transaction. For example, equity instruments that are issued by an entity in exchange for control of a business are not within the scope of IFRS 2 and should instead be accounted for in accordance with IFRS 3 *Business combinations.*

Three specific types of transaction are covered in IFRS 2, these are: [IFRS 2, Appendix A]

- *share-based payment transactions:* this is where the entity has the choice of the form the payment for goods and services received should take, i.e. either cash to be paid to a value based on the entity's share price or shares in the entity to be issued;

- *equity-settled share-based payment transactions:* this is where the entity issues, for example, shares, in exchange for the receipt of goods or services; and

- *cash-settled share-based payment transactions:* this is where the entity pays, for example, cash to a value based on the entity's share price, in exchange for the receipt of goods or services.

The rest of this chapter deals specifically with share-based payment transactions that have been entered into as a form of employee benefit.

11.2 Recognition and measurement

The overall principle of IFRS 2 is that an expense should be recognised in the income statement as part of the profit or loss for the period in which an entity enters into a share-based payment transaction. [IFRS 2.8]

The amount recognised for, say, share options granted in return for employee services received, is based on the number of options that the employee will eventually be entitled to. This is known as the number of options that vest.

An initial estimate of the number of share options that will vest is made and is then revised annually for subsequent information. An entity will make a final adjustment to this estimate on the date that the options finally vest, so that the total number of share options recognised in the financial statements equals the number that actually vest.

11.2.1 Equity-settled share-based payment transactions

The primary objective for equity-settled share-based payment transactions is to account for the employee services received as payment for the issue of equity instruments, such as shares or options. Such transactions should be treated consistently with other issues of equity instruments, by recognising the value of the services received as an increase in equity. [IFRS 2.10]

It is not generally possible to value the specific services received from an employee in return for, say, the grant of a share option, and therefore the fair value of the share option granted should be used. The granting of a share option is the giving of a right to a share option. The fair value of the share option should be measured at the 'grant date'; this is the date that the employee and the employer enter into the share-based payment arrangement. The right to the share option is provided at grant date, provided that the employee provides his or her services for the specified period of time, or other conditions are met.

11.2.2 Cash-settled share-based payment transactions

A cash-settled share-based payment transaction is one where, for example an employee is promised a cash reward based on the future movement of the entity's share price. For such transactions, the employee's services received by the entity and the corresponding liability incurred should be measured at the fair value of the liability. The entity should remeasure the liability at each reporting date and at the date the liability is settled. [IFRS 2.30]

Changes in the liability should be recognised directly in the income statement. The services received by the entity and the liability to pay for those services are recognised as the employee's services are provided. [IFRS 2.30]

11.2.3 Share-based payment transactions – cash-settled or equity-settled

Where an entity has a choice of issuing shares or paying cash in return for the provision of the employees' services the entity shall recognise a liability if it determines that it has an obligation to settle the liability in cash. If on settlement the entity issues shares rather than by paying in cash then the value of the liability should be transferred to equity. [IFRS 2.34]

11.3 Disclosure requirements

An entity is required to make a number of disclosures in relation to share-based payment transactions that it has entered into in the period, to provide users of the financial statements with sufficient information to be able to understand the impact of such transactions on the financial statements. The disclosure requirements are split into three main areas:

- the nature and extent of any share-based payment arrangements that existed during the period. This information should include, for example, a description of each arrangement and details as to the number of share options that have been granted, expired, are still outstanding and have been exercised, i.e. converted into shares; [IFRS 2.44]

- how the fair value of goods and services has been determined with reference to the fair value of the equity instrument granted; [IFRS 2.46] and

- the effect of share-based payment transactions on the entity's profit or loss for the period and on its financial position, for example the liabilities recognised in respect of such transactions. [IFRS 2.50]

12 Chapter Review

There are many forms of employee benefits that an entity can provide its employees. The accounting requirements for such transactions have been explained in this chapter. The accounting for some employee benefits, for example defined benefit plans, can be complex. Nonetheless, both IAS 19 and IFRS 2 offer a consistent, fair-value approach to the measurement and recognition of employee benefits.

In particular this chapter has dealt with the:

- various forms of employee benefits;

- important distinctions between short and long-term benefits;

- the distinction between a defined contribution and a defined benefit plan and how each is accounted for; and

- the accounting and disclosure requirements for share-based payment transactions as set out in IFRS 2.

Chapter 18
EVENTS AFTER THE BALANCE SHEET DATE

1 Business Context

In assessing business performance, pertinent information sometimes arises following the cut-off date for which financial statements are prepared that may have important implications on the financial position and performance in the year just ended. The balance sheet date is a cut-off date and events that happen after this point in time should not generally be recognised in the financial statements of the period just ended. However, information that comes to light after the balance sheet date may provide additional information about events that actually occurred before the balance sheet date and it is then appropriate to take it into account.

Financial statements should reflect the most up to date facts about events that existed at the balance sheet date. It is sometimes difficult to establish whether an event happening after the balance sheet date is new information about an existing event or a new event.

Users should be informed of significant events occurring after the year end such as acquisitions. The provision of such information will help users to understand the impact on future results.

2 Chapter Objectives

This chapter deals with the treatment of events that occur between the balance sheet date and the date when the financial statements are authorised for issue.

On completion of this chapter you should be able to:

- understand the objectives and scope of IAS 10 *Events after the balance sheet date*;

- demonstrate a knowledge of the important terminology and definitions which relate to the treatment of events after the balance sheet date;

- distinguish between adjusting and non-adjusting events after the balance sheet date;

- demonstrate a knowledge of the principal disclosure requirements of IAS 10; and

- apply knowledge and understanding of IAS 10 in particular circumstances through basic calculations.

3 Objectives, Scope and Definitions of IAS 10

The objective of IAS 10 is to provide guidance as to how to deal with events that occur after the balance sheet date but before the date on which the financial statements are authorised for issue by the directors. These are described as "events after the balance sheet date". IAS 10 makes a distinction between events that occur during this period which should be adjusted for in the financial statements and those that should instead only be disclosed.

The process of authorising financial statements for issue is not defined as this will depend on the management structure of the entity and the legal requirements of the jurisdiction in which it operates.

Adjusting events are those that provide evidence of conditions that existed at the balance sheet date, whereas non-adjusting events are those that are indicative of conditions that arose after the balance sheet date. [IAS 10.3]

When applying IAS 10, it is critical to realise that there are two key questions that need to be answered.

The first is: did the event occur before the financial statements were authorised for issue? If the event occurred after this date, then it is outside the scope of IAS 10.

The second is: did the issue to which the event relates exist at the balance sheet date? For example, if an entity with a year end of 31 December discovers in the following February that a customer has gone into liquidation, this provides additional evidence regarding the recoverability of an asset recognised at 31 December.

4 Overview of IAS 10

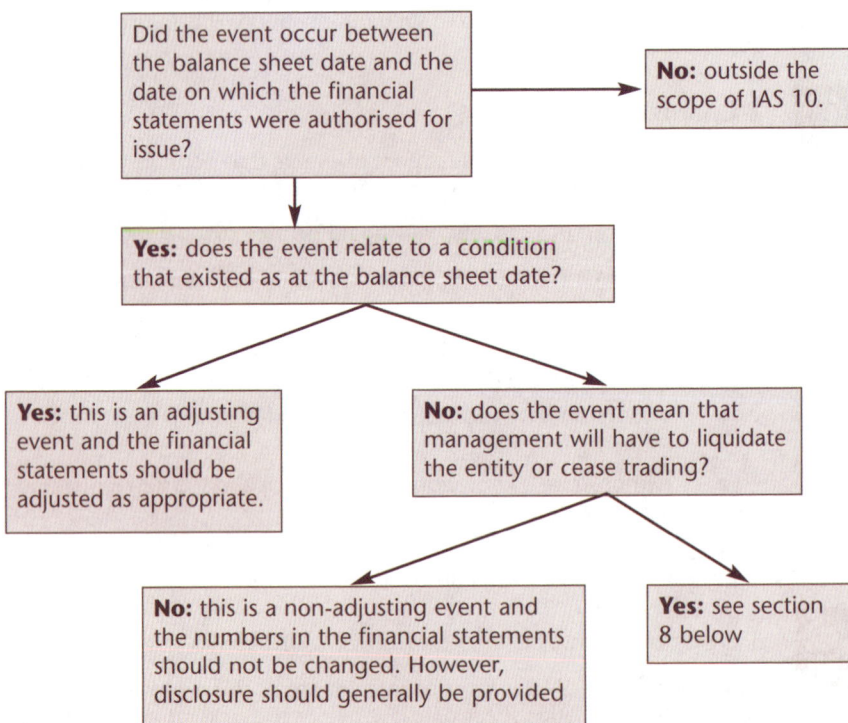

```
┌────────────────────────────┐
│ Did the event occur between │         ┌──────────────────┐
│ the balance sheet date and  │────────▶│ No: outside the  │
│ the date on which the       │         │ scope of IAS 10. │
│ financial statements were   │         └──────────────────┘
│ authorised for issue?       │
└────────────────────────────┘
               │
               ▼
┌────────────────────────────────────┐
│ Yes: does the event relate to a     │
│ condition that existed as at the    │
│ balance sheet date?                 │
└────────────────────────────────────┘
         ┌──────────────┴──────────────┐
         ▼                             ▼
┌──────────────────────┐   ┌────────────────────────────┐
│ Yes: this is an      │   │ No: does the event mean that │
│ adjusting event and  │   │ management will have to      │
│ the financial        │   │ liquidate the entity or      │
│ statements should be │   │ cease trading?               │
│ adjusted as          │   └────────────────────────────┘
│ appropriate.         │       ┌──────────┴──────────┐
└──────────────────────┘       ▼                     ▼
                    ┌────────────────────────┐  ┌──────────────┐
                    │ No: this is a          │  │ Yes: see     │
                    │ non-adjusting event    │  │ section 8    │
                    │ and the numbers in the │  │ below        │
                    │ financial statements   │  └──────────────┘
                    │ should not be changed. │
                    │ However, disclosure    │
                    │ should generally be    │
                    │ provided               │
                    └────────────────────────┘
```

5 Adjusting Events

An entity should adjust the amounts recognised in the financial statements to reflect any adjusting events that have been identified. [IAS 10.8]

IAS 10 provides a number of specific examples of adjusting events. Such examples include:

- the settlement of an outstanding court case that was provided for, or disclosed as a contingent liability at the year end. The provision at the balance sheet date should be amended to reflect the actual settlement figure, as this provides additional evidence as to the amount of the provision as required by IAS 37 *Provisions, contingent liabilities and contingent assets*. If a contingent liability was initially disclosed at the balance sheet date, a provision should now be recognised, since the settlement provides information that a present obligation which can be reliably measured existed at the balance sheet date;

- information received after the balance sheet date about the value or recoverability of an asset recognised at the year end. This might be evidence that the net realisable value for inventories was lower than estimated, in which case the inventories figure should be written down accordingly;

- the finalisation of bonuses that were payable at the year end in accordance with IAS 19 *Employee benefits*; and

- the discovery of fraud or errors which show that amounts recognised or information disclosed at the balance sheet date were incorrect.

6 Non-adjusting Events

An entity should not adjust amounts recognised in the financial statements which reflect non-adjusting events that have occurred after the balance sheet date. [IAS 10.10]

Non-adjusting events should instead be disclosed where the outcome of such events would influence the economic decisions made by users of the financial statements. Where the disclosure of such an event is required, the entity should provide details of the nature of the event and an estimate of its financial effect, or state that such an estimate cannot be made.

IAS 10 provides a number of examples of non-adjusting events that would normally require disclosure, including:

- the major purchase or disposal of assets such as property, plant and equipment or a subsidiary;

- the destruction of assets caused by a fire occurring after the balance sheet date;

- the announcement of a major restructuring plan;

- a significant fluctuation in foreign exchange rates that would affect amounts reflected in the financial statements;

- significant changes in the number of ordinary shares of the entity, perhaps from a bonus issue or share split;

- changes in tax rates that will have a significant effect on amounts reported for current and deferred tax in accordance with IAS 12 *Income taxes*;

- entering into major commitments or providing a significant guarantee; and

- the commencement of litigation following an event that happened after the balance sheet date. This is not recognised as a provision since the entity did not have an obligation at the year end.

Illustration 1

An entity's draft financial statements for the year ended 31 December 2003 were completed on 30 May 2004, approved by the finance director on 7 June 2004, authorised for issue on 20 June 2004 and approved by the shareholders on 5 July 2004.

The following events occurred after the balance sheet date (assume all amounts are significant to the entity):

1) Notification on 18 Feb 2004 that a customer owing CU100,000 as at 31 December 2003 has gone into liquidation. The financial statements already include a specific provision of CU20,000 for this customer and the entity does not make general provisions.

This is an adjusting event as it provides more up to date information about a provision that was recognised at the balance sheet date. The provision should be increased to CU100,000.

2) A rights issue on 6 April 2004 to raise CU1,500,000 for an acquisition.

This is a disclosable non-adjusting event. The rights issue occurred after the balance sheet date, but is considered to be of significant importance and should be disclosed in the financial statements.

3) Confirmation on 28 May 2004 from the entity's insurer that they will pay CU500,000 for inventories that were destroyed in a fire on 24 December 2003. The entity had claimed CU650,000 and included this as a receivable in the financial statements.

This is an adjusting event since it is in relation to an asset that was recognised at the balance sheet date. The receivable should be reduced to CU500,000.

7 Dividends

If dividends on equity shares have been proposed or declared after the balance sheet date they do not meet the definition of a liability and therefore cannot be recognised as a liability at the balance sheet date. To be recognised as a liability the entity should have an obligation at the balance sheet date. The obligation to pay the dividend only arises when it has been declared, so it is at this date, i.e. date of declaration, that a liability should be recognised. Where dividends have been proposed or declared after the balance sheet date, this should be disclosed in the notes to the financial statements. [IAS 10.12]

Illustration 2

The recent financial calendar of an entity with a 31 December year end, has included the following:

	Authorised by directors for issue	Approved in annual general meeting
Financial statements for 2002	28 February 2003	3 May 2003
Financial statements for 2003	28 February 2004	4 May 2004

Dividends on ordinary shares	proposed by directors	declared by directors	approved in annual general meeting
2002 final	28 Feb 2003	no	yes
2003 interim	31 Aug 2003	yes	no
2003 final	28 Feb 2004	no	yes

These dividends will be dealt with in the entity's financial statements for 2002, 2003 and 2004 as follows:

Financial statements for:	2002	2003	2004
2002 final dividend	disclosed in the notes	charged to statement of changes in equity	—
2003 interim dividend	—	charged to statement of changes in equity	—
2003 final dividend	—	disclosed in the notes	charged to statement of changes in equity

8 Going Concern

Financial statements are usually prepared on what is described as the "going concern" basis; this assumes that the entity will continue to operate for the foreseeable future. If, however, management determines after the balance sheet date that it intends to, or has no realistic alternative but to, liquidate the entity or to cease trading then the financial statements should not be prepared on the going concern basis. [IAS 10.14]

The entity should instead adopt a basis of preparation that is considered more appropriate in the circumstances, although no specific guidance is provided in IAS 10. Disclosure of the change in the basis of preparation should be provided in accordance with IAS 1 *Preparation of financial statements*.

9 Additional Disclosure Requirements

In addition to disclosures that may arise from information on non-adjusting events or where dividends have been declared after the balance sheet date an entity should also disclose the date when the financial statements were authorised for issue and who provided that authorisation. This date is important because events that occurred after it are not recognised or disclosed in the financial statements. [IAS 10.17]

If subsequent information comes to light after the balance sheet date about conditions that existed at the balance sheet date, the original disclosures should be updated to reflect this new information. [IAS 10.19]

10 Chapter Review

This chapter has dealt with the treatment of events that occur after the balance sheet date.

This chapter has covered:

- the objectives, scope, definitions and disclosure requirements of IAS 10;
- an overview of IAS 10;
- adjusting and non-adjusting events;
- the recognition of dividends; and
- the going concern basis of preparation.

Chapter 19
FOREIGN EXCHANGE

1 Business Context

Business is becoming increasingly international in terms of trading goods and services and in the operation of capital markets. One measure of the significance of globalisation is that most developed countries have external trade in the range of 15% to 30% of their gross domestic product.

International activity can vary enormously from relatively straightforward import and export transactions through to financing arrangements in multiple currencies or maintaining operations overseas, for example, in the form of a subsidiary or branch.

Operating in multi-currency locations presents a number of accounting challenges, including:

- *conversion* – accounting for transactions where one currency has been physically changed into another currency;

- *translation* – restating assets and liabilities initially recognised in more than one currency into a common currency; and

- *exchange gains and losses* – where relative currency values change and gains and losses arise which need to be appropriately measured and recognised.

2 Chapter Objectives

This chapter deals with accounting for foreign currency transactions in accordance with IAS 21 *The effects of changes in foreign exchange rates*. A key aspect of the standard is to determine the main operating currency of each individual entity and how an entity, or group, should translate its financial statements where it presents those statements in a different currency.

On completion of this chapter you should be able to:

- understand the scope and objectives of IAS 21 in respect of the effects of changes in foreign exchange rates;

- identify the important terminology and definitions which relate to foreign exchange activities;

- understand and demonstrate knowledge of the key principles concerning recognition and measurement in terms of different currencies;

- demonstrate knowledge of the principal disclosure requirements of IAS 21; and

- apply knowledge and understanding of foreign exchange transactions through basic calculations.

3 Objectives, Scope and Definitions of IAS 21

An entity may carry on foreign activities either by conducting transactions in foreign currencies, for example purchasing a non-current asset from an overseas supplier, exporting goods to an overseas customer or arranging a loan in a foreign currency, or by having foreign operations, for example a subsidiary or branch located overseas.

In addition, an entity may choose to present its financial statements in a foreign currency.

The objective of IAS 21 is to prescribe how to include foreign currency transactions and foreign operations in the financial statements of an entity and how to translate financial statements into a different currency for presentation purposes.

IAS 21 applies to: [IAS 21.3]

- accounting for transactions that the entity enters into which are in a foreign currency and any resulting balances (note that items that fall within the scope of IAS 39 *Financial instruments: recognition and measurement* are dealt with by that standard);

- translating the financial statements of foreign operations that are included in the financial statements of another entity, for example, on consolidation of subsidiaries or the inclusion of associates by the equity accounting method; and

- translating an entity's results and financial position into a different currency for the presentation of its financial statements.

4 Key Issues

4.1 The functional currency

The overall approach required by IAS 21 is for an entity to translate foreign currency items and transactions into its functional currency.

A functional currency *"is the currency of the primary economic environment in which the entity operates"* and the primary economic environment *"is normally the one in which it primarily generates and expends cash"*. [IAS 21.8]

In a group, each entity, for example the parent, each subsidiary and associate, needs to determine its own functional currency rather than adopting a single one which is common across the whole group.

An entity cannot choose its functional currency, instead management needs to make an informed assessment of the facts. IAS 21 includes a number of practical indicators to assist entities in identifying their functional currency, for example:

- the currency that mainly influences the price at which goods and services are sold;

- the country whose competitive forces and regulations mainly influence the pricing structure for the supply of goods and services;

- the currency in which financing is generated; and

- the currency in which cash generated from an entity's operating activities is usually retained.

Additional factors should be considered to determine whether the functional currency of a foreign operation is the same as that of the reporting entity (the group). It should not be assumed that this is the case. The overriding factor is whether the foreign operation operates independently of the reporting entity or is merely an extension of that entity. Factors might include, for example, whether the foreign operations require additional funding from its parent in order to continue in operation and whether transactions with the reporting entity are a high proportion of its total operating activities.

Where an entity, for example a subsidiary, is not deemed to be autonomous of the parent (the reporting entity), it will have the same functional currency as the parent.

As a functional currency is based on an entity's underlying economic activity, it cannot be changed unless its underlying economic activity changes.

4.2 The presentation currency

Although the overall approach required by IAS 21 is for an entity to translate foreign currency items and transactions into its functional currency it is not required to present its financial statements using this currency. An entity has a completely free choice of the currency in which its financial statements are presented. This is referred to as the presentation currency. [IAS 21.8]

The approach that is required to translate the financial statements of an entity, or a group of entities, into a different presentation currency is discussed below.

4.3 Monetary and non-monetary items

IAS 21 distinguishes between monetary and non-monetary items.

Monetary items are units of currency held, and assets and liabilities to be received or paid in a fixed or determinable number of units of currency, for example cash, receivables, payables and loans. [IAS 21.8]

Non-monetary items are therefore those which do not give rise to a right to receive (or an obligation to deliver) a fixed or determinable amount of money, for example property, plant and equipment, goodwill, inventories and intangible assets.

4.4 Summary of the approach of IAS 21

For a group of entities, IAS 21 requires a two stage process:

(1)   *individual entity level:* treatment of foreign exchange transactions *(functional currency)*; and

(2)   *consolidation level:* translation of the financial statements of entities, for example subsidiaries, associates and branches, into a common currency for consolidated financial statements purposes *(presentation currency)*.

Illustration 1

A parent entity, P, operates in Cornu (where the currency is the CU). It has two wholly-owned subsidiaries, N which operates in Narnia (using N$), and A which operates in Aslan (using A$).

All three entities in the group import and export goods around the world.

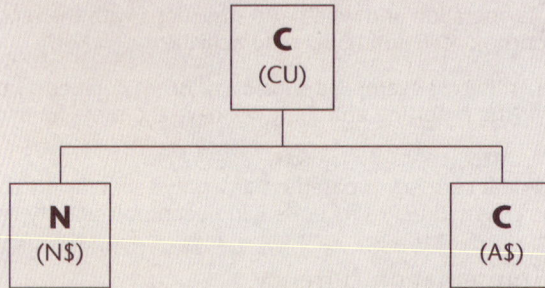

```
        ┌──────────┐
        │    C     │
        │   (CU)   │
        └────┬─────┘
      ┌──────┴───────────────┐
  ┌───┴───┐              ┌────┴────┐
  │   N   │              │    C    │
  │ (N$)  │              │  (A$)   │
  └───────┘              └─────────┘
```

Step 1: Determine the *functional currency* of each of the three entities. This is a question of fact based upon the criteria in IAS 21 outlined above. It has been assumed here that the functional currency is that of the country in which each entity operates (i.e. CU, N$, A$).

Step 2: Each entity translates foreign currency transactions arising from its import and export activities into its functional currency and reports the effects of such translation.

Step 3: In preparing the consolidated financial statements of the group, it is necessary to choose a presentation currency. IAS 21 permits the presentation currency of a reporting entity to be any currency. In this scenario the presentation currency is likely to be CU, the currency of the parent entity.

Step 4: The results and financial position of each individual entity within the group whose functional currency differs from the presentation currency (in this case N and A if CU is selected as the presentation currency) are translated for the purposes of preparing consolidated financial statements.

5 Transactions in the Functional Currency

5.1 Initial recognition

An entity should record foreign currency transactions, for example the buying or selling of goods or services whose price is denominated in a foreign currency, in a consistent manner. IAS 21 requires that an entity does this by recognising each transaction at the spot exchange rate on the date that the transaction took place. [IAS 21.21]

Thus, if an entity whose functional currency is CU buys a non-current asset for N$1 million when the spot exchange rate is CU1: N$2, then the transaction will initially be recorded at CU500,000.

Where there are high volumes of such transactions, for practical reasons an average exchange rate over the relevant period may be used as an approximation. However, if exchange rates fluctuate significantly over short periods of time it is not appropriate to use an average rate since it would not be a fair approximation for actual rates.

5.2 Reporting at subsequent balance sheet dates

At each balance sheet date the following translations of foreign currency should be carried out. [IAS 21.23]

Item	Exchange rate
Monetary items	Closing rate (i.e. the spot exchange rate at the balance sheet date)
Non-monetary items measured at historic cost	Rate of exchange at the date of the original transaction (i.e. the date of purchase of the non-current asset)
Non-monetary items measured at fair value	Exchange rate at the date when fair value was determined

5.3 Recognition of exchange differences

The difference that arises from translating the same amounts at different exchange rates is referred to as an exchange difference. Such amounts will generally arise in the preparation of a set of financial statements from the settlement of monetary amounts payable or receivable in a foreign currency and the retranslation at the entity's period end.

Exchange differences should normally be recognised directly in the income statement as part of the profit or loss for the period. However, where gains and losses on a non-monetary item are recognised directly in equity, for example a gain on the revaluation of a property in accordance with IAS 16 *Property, plant and equipment*, any exchange difference resulting from retranslation of the revalued asset is also reported as part of equity rather than in the income statement. [IAS 21.28, 21.30]

An entity may have a monetary amount receivable from, or payable to, a foreign entity (for example an overseas subsidiary) that is not intended to be settled in the foreseeable future. For a receivable this amount essentially forms part of the overall investment in the foreign entity. At the year-end monetary amounts such as this are retranslated and any differences recognised in the income statement of the appropriate entity. But IAS 21 operates on the basis that as such differences are part of the overall investment in the foreign entity, they should only be recognised in profit or loss when the foreign entity is disposed of. So in the preparation of the consolidated financial statements of the group the exchange difference should be reported as a separate component of equity not in the consolidated profit or loss for the period. If the foreign entity is subsequently sold any such exchange differences will form part of the reported profit or loss on disposal recorded in the income statement. [IAS 21.32]

It is only differences relating to the overall investment in the foreign entity which are taken directly to equity; differences on intra-group trading balances which will be settled in the short term remain in the profit or loss of the period.

5.3.1 Transactions settled within the period

When a foreign currency transaction is settled within the same accounting period as that in which it was originally recorded, any exchange differences arising are recognised in the profit or loss of that period.

5.3.2 Transaction balance is outstanding at the balance sheet date

When a foreign currency transaction is settled in a different accounting period to the one in which the transaction originated, the exchange difference recognised in the income statement for each period, up to the date of settlement, is determined by the change in exchange rates during each period.

Illustration 2

Aston has a year end of 31 December 2003 and uses the CU as its functional currency. On 25 October 2003 Aston buys goods from an overseas supplier for N$286,000. The goods are still held by Aston as part of inventory at the year end.

Exchange rates:

25 October 2003	CU1 = N$11.16
16 November 2003	CU1 = N$10.87
31 December 2003	CU1 = N$11.25

(a) If, on 16 November 2003, Aston pays the overseas supplier in full the following entries should be recognised:

25 October 2003. The initial transaction is recorded as a purchase and a liability at the exchange rate at the date that the transaction took place (N$286,000 / 11.16 = CU25,627).

16 November 2003. The actual cost of settling the liability on the date of settlement is calculated (N$286,000 / 10.87 = CU26,311). The exchange difference between the originally recorded liability and the actual amount required to settle it (CU26,311 less CU25,627 = CU684) is recorded as an exchange loss in the income statement. Inventories at the year end are non-monetary items and will be carried at their orignal value i.e. CU25,627.

(b) If the creditor had remained unpaid at the year-end, the following transactions would have been recognised:

25 October 2003. The initial transaction is recorded as above at CU25,627.

31 December 2003. The year-end balance is retranslated at the year-end exchange rate as it is a monetary liability. (N$286,000 / 11.25 = CU25,422) The difference should be reported directly in the income statement as part of the profit or loss for the period. The exchange gain in the income statement will be CU205 (CU25,422 less CU25,627 = -CU205). The value of inventories at the year end will be CU25,627 (as recorded above).

Illustration 3

Warrilow has a year-end of 31 December 2003 and uses the CU as its functional currency.

On 29 November 2003, Warrilow received a loan from a foreign bank for N$1,520,000.

The proceeds were used to finance, in part, the purchase of a new office block. The loan remained unsettled at the year-end.

Exchange rates:

29 November 2003	CU1 = N$1.52
31 December 2003	CU1 = N$1.66

The following amounts should be recorded by Warrilow, ignoring interest payable on the loan.

29 November 2003

The cash advance from the bank is translated at the rate on the date that it was received (N$1,520,000 / 1.52 = CU1,000,000) and a liability recorded for the same amount.

31 December 2003

As the loan was still outstanding at the end of the period and it is a monetary item, it should be retranslated at the exchange rate at the balance sheet date (N$1,520,000 / 1.66 = CU915,663). The exchange difference should be recognised as a gain in the income statement for the period. (CU1,000,000 less CU915,663 = CU84,337).

5.4 Change in functional currency

If the underlying economic activities change in such a way that there is a change in the functional currency of an entity, the new functional currency should be applied from the date of the change in circumstances. The entity should not restate amounts previously recorded as these reflected the economic reality at that time. [IAS 21.35]

All amounts should be retranslated into the new functional currency at the date of the change.

6 Translation into Presentation Currency

6.1 Procedures for translation into presentation currency

This section sets out how an entity should retranslate amounts from its functional currency into a different presentational currency. As mentioned above, an entity has a completely free choice over its presentation currency, assuming this is permitted by the jurisdiction in which the entity prepares its financial statements.

The translation into a presentation currency can be undertaken by an individual entity, if it decides to present its financial statements in a currency different to its functional currency. Much more commonly, it is undertaken when a number of entities within a group each have different functional currencies. For the preparation of the group's consolidated financial statements each individual entity within the group will need to retranslate its financial statements into the presentation currency being used.

The steps to translate financial statements into a different presentation currency are: [IAS 21.39]

- retranslate the assets and liabilities for each balance sheet presented (i.e. the current period end and the comparative period) at the closing rate at the date of each balance sheet;

- retranslate income and expenditure recorded in each income statement presented (i.e. the current period and the comparative period) at the exchange rates at the dates of the transactions; for practical reasons an average rate may be used assuming that the exchange rate does not fluctuate significantly during the period; and

- recognise all resulting exchange differences as a separate component of equity.

Where exchange differences relate to a foreign operation that is not wholly owned, accumulated exchange differences attributable to the minority shareholders should be allocated to minority interests in the consolidated balance sheet.

6.2 Hyperinflationary economies

Where an entity has a functional currency that is the currency of a hyperinflationary economy it is required to restate its functional currency financial statements in accordance with IAS 29 *Financial reporting in hyperinflationary economies*. [IAS 21.43]

If, however, such an entity chooses to use a different presentation currency, the requirements in IAS 21 for the retranslation of the financial statements into the presentation currency should be applied. [IAS 21.42]

6.3 Translation of a foreign operation

The group's consolidated financial statements should be prepared in accordance with IAS 27 *Consolidated and separate financial statements*. As a result intra-group balances will be eliminated in the normal way. Where a group entity such as a subsidiary, associate or joint venture is a foreign entity, exchange differences arising from intra-group monetary assets or liabilities should not be eliminated. The effect of such translation differences should continue to be reported in the consolidated financial statements to reflect the fact that there is a foreign currency risk within the group.

Such exchange differences will generally be reported in the consolidated income statement of the period. However, if the amount on which the exchange differences arise has been identified as being part of the net investment in the foreign entity, as discussed above, then the exchange differences should be reported separately as part of equity.

In the consolidated financial statements any goodwill arising on the acquisition of a foreign operation should be treated as an asset of the foreign operation. The goodwill should therefore be expressed in the functional currency of the foreign operation and translated at the closing rate at each balance sheet date. The same treatment is required of any fair value adjustments to the carrying amounts of assets and liabilities arising on the acquisition of a foreign operation. In both cases exchange differences are recognised in equity, rather than as part of the profit or loss for the period. [IAS 21.47]

Illustration 4

An entity acquires a foreign subsidiary on 15 August 2003. The goodwill arising on the acquisition is R$400,000. At the date of acquisition the exchange rate into the parent's functional currency is R$4:CU1. At the parent entity's year-end the exchange rate is R$5:CU1.

The goodwill at the date of acquisition is CU100,000 (R$400,000/4). At the year-end it is retranslated to CU80,000 (R$400,000/5). The difference of CU20,000 is recorded as an exchange loss and reported in equity.

6.4 Disposal of a foreign operation

Where a foreign entity is disposed of, any exchange differences that have been deferred as part of equity are required to form part of the profit or loss on disposal. Such amounts will therefore be eliminated from equity and recognised in the income statement in the period in which the disposal takes place as part of the profit or loss on disposal. [IAS 21.48]

7 Disclosure

A number of disclosures are required by IAS 21 to ensure that users of the financial statements are fully informed as to the effect that exchange differences have had on the financial statements of an entity or group. The disclosures include the separate identification of the total amount of exchange differences recognised in the income statement for the period and of the net amount of exchange differences recognised directly as a separate component of equity. A reconciliation between exchange differences at the start of the period and those at the end is also required to highlight the movements in the amounts expressed as a separate component of equity. [IAS 21.52]

If an entity's presentation currency is different from its functional currency, this should be clearly stated. The entity should also disclose its functional currency and the reason why a different presentation currency has been used. [IAS 21.53]

If a presentation currency has been used that is different from the functional currency and the translation has not been accounted for in accordance with IAS 21 then the entity has not fully complied with IFRS. [IAS 21.55]

If the translation to presentation currency is not in accordance with IFRS, then this information should be presented separately to distinguish it from that which does comply with IFRS. The currency that the supplementary information is presented in should be clearly identified and the entity should explain the method of translation applied. [IAS 21.57]

If there has been a change in the functional currency of the reporting entity or of a significant foreign operation, then the entity is required to disclose this fact along with the reason for the change, i.e. because of a change in the underlying economic activity of the entity. [IAS 21.54]

8 Introduction of the Euro

Since 1 January 1999, when the Economic and Monetary Union (EMU) came into being, the Euro has been a currency in its own right. At that date participating member states had their local currencies fixed to the Euro and therefore the risk of currency differences between them was eliminated.

The introduction of the Euro is not specifically addressed in IAS 21 and therefore further interpretation was required to assist preparers of financial statements in adopting the Euro. As a result the Standing Interpretations Committee issued SIC 7 *Introduction of the Euro.*

SIC 7 sets out that the requirements of IAS 21 should be applied on the adoption of the Euro, at whatever date the country joins the EMU. The SIC concluded that it was not important that the closing exchange rate could not fluctuate after the balance sheet date.

Therefore, foreign currency monetary assets and liabilities should be translated at the closing rate at the balance sheet date and exchange differences on the translation of foreign operations should continue to be reported as part of equity until the entity is sold.

9 Chapter Review

This chapter has been concerned with accounting for the effects of changes in foreign exchange rates. A number of key issues have been addressed in this chapter, in particular how to identify a functional currency and how to deal with the translation into the presentation currency for the preparation of consolidated financial statements.

Other issues have included the treatment of exchange gains and losses and the selection of appropriate exchange rates.

This chapter has covered:

- the scope and objectives of IAS 21;

- the important terminology and definitions which relate to foreign exchange activities;

- the key principles concerning recognition and measurement of foreign currency transactions;

- the treatment of functional currencies and foreign exchange transactions at the level of the individual entity;

- the translation into the presentation currency at the consolidated financial statements level; and

- the principal disclosure requirements of IAS 21.

Chapter 20
FINANCIAL INSTRUMENTS

1 Business Context

With the increasing diversity of businesses and their rapid geographical expansion, entities are entering into complex financial transactions to reduce their exposure to risks. The nature of such complex financial transactions has led to entities adopting different accounting practices, with increased use of fair values and extensive application of hedge accounting techniques (i.e. offsetting).

As a result of the widespread use of financial assets and financial liabilities as part of an entity's ordinary activities two standards have been published - IAS 32 *Financial instruments: presentation and disclosure* and IAS 39 *Financial instruments: recognition and measurement.* These standards complement each other and provide comprehensive guidance on the accounting and presentation of financial instruments.

2 Chapter Objectives

This chapter deals with the definition, recognition and measurement of financial instruments and the management of risk in relation to such instruments. It also considers the presentation and disclosure requirements.

On completion of this chapter you should be able to:

- demonstrate a knowledge of what is meant by the term financial instruments;

- understand the main components of the disclosure requirements for financial instruments under IAS 32;

- show how the main classifications of financial instruments are presented;

- understand how financial instruments are recognised and measured in accordance with IAS 39; and

- demonstrate a basic knowledge of the implications of hedging financial instruments.

3 What is a Financial Instrument?

A financial instrument is *"any contract that gives rise to a financial asset of one entity and a financial liability or equity instrument of another entity"*. [IAS 32.11]

A financial asset is cash, a contractual right to receive cash or another financial asset, a contractual right to exchange financial assets or liabilities with another entity on potentially favourable terms, or an equity instrument, for example shares, of another entity. Examples of financial assets are cash, a receivable and equity investments. [IAS 32.11]

Assets that have physical substance, such as property and machinery are not financial assets and neither are intangible assets, such as patents and brands.

These assets generate future economic benefits for an entity although there is no contractual right to receive cash or another financial asset.

A financial liability is either a contractual obligation to deliver cash or another financial asset, or a contractual obligation to exchange financial assets or liabilities with another entity on potentially unfavourable terms. Examples of financial liabilities are payables, loans and an entity's obligations, for example a lease. [IAS 32.11]

In addition, a financial asset (or liability) arises where a contract may be settled in the entity's own equity instruments, for which the entity will receive (or deliver) either a variable number of its own equity instruments, or a derivative that may be settled other than by the exchange of a fixed amount of cash or another financial asset for a fixed number of its own equity instruments. [IAS 32.11]

A derivative is a type of financial instrument that has specific characteristics, as set out below: [IAS 39.9]

- *"its value changes in response to the change in a specified interest rate, financial instrument price, commodity price, foreign exchange rate, index of prices or rates, credit rating or credit index, or other variable;*
- *it requires no initial net investment or an initial net investment that is smaller than would be required for other types of contracts that would be expected to have a similar response to changes in market factors; and*
- *it is settled at a future date".*

Examples of derivatives are financial options, forward contracts and interest rate swaps.

An equity instrument is a contract where an entity has an interest in the net assets (assets less liabilities) of another entity. [IAS 32.11]

4 Objectives and Scope of IAS 32

The objective of IAS 32 is to enhance a user's understanding of the way in which financial instruments affect an entity's financial performance, financial position and cash flows. IAS 32 sets out presentation requirements and related disclosures.

The principles that underlie the standard are consistent with, and complement, those in IAS 39, which addresses recognition and measurement criteria.

IAS 32 applies to all entities and to all types of financial instruments, except where another standard is more specific. Exceptions include subsidiaries accounted for under IAS 27 *Consolidated and separate financial statements,* associates accounted for under IAS 28 *Investments in associates,* joint ventures accounted for under IAS 31 *Interests in joint ventures,* employers' rights and obligations under employee benefit plans accounted for under IAS 19 *Employee benefits,* and contingent consideration relating to a business combination accounted for under IFRS 3 *Business combinations.* In addition, IAS 32 excludes insurance contracts and contracts that require a payment based on physical variables, such as climate. [IAS 32.4]

5 Presentation of Liabilities and Equity

When an entity issues a financial instrument, it should classify it according to the substance of the contract under which it has been issued. Classification will be as a financial asset, a financial liability or an equity instrument. [IAS 32.15]

The characteristics of the financial instrument should be considered to ensure that it is appropriately classified. If a financial instrument meets any of the criteria set out in the definition of a financial liability then it should be classified as such and not as an equity instrument.

As set out in the definition of a financial liability, a critical feature is that there is a contractual obligation to deliver cash (or another financial instrument) or to exchange financial assets or liabilities in unfavourable conditions. Where an entity issues a share to another party, that entity is not obliged to deliver cash (or another financial instrument) to the shareholder; the payment of dividends is at the discretion of the entity.

It is important that the substance of a financial instrument is considered, rather than its legal form. Some forms of financial instruments are legally classified as equity but have the characteristics of financial liabilities and should therefore be classified as such. For example, a preference share that is required under the terms of its issue, to be redeemed at a specified date for a specified amount is a financial liability.

Where an entity has the right to settle a financial instrument either by cash (or another financial asset), or by issuing its own shares to a determined value that greatly exceeds the cash alternative, the financial instrument is a financial liability. Although the financial instrument does not explicitly set out the obligation to deliver cash (or another financial instrument), its contractual terms and conditions are such that it will settle in cash (shares would be too expensive), so effectively an obligation exists.

The right to deliver an entity's own shares is not necessarily an equity instrument. If the contract is structured in a way that a variable number of shares may be issued to satisfy a fixed monetary amount then this is a financial liability.

Illustration 1

In 2002 an entity enters into a contract that requires it to issue shares to the value of CU10,000 on 1 January 2005.

This is a financial liability since the entity is required to settle the contract by issuing a variable number of shares based on a fixed monetary amount.

5.1 Settlement options

Where a derivative financial instrument, for example a share option, can be settled at the choice of either party by issuing cash or by exchanging shares, then it should be classified as a financial asset or financial liability as appropriate. Where such a choice exists, the financial instrument may only be classified as an equity instrument where all settlement options under the contract would result in issuing an equity instrument. [IAS 32.26]

5.2 Compound financial instruments

A compound financial instrument is one that contains both a liability component and an equity component. Such components should be classified separately according to their substance. [IAS 32.28]

A compound instrument should be split into its component parts at the date that it is issued. The split should not be revised for subsequent changes in market interest rates, share prices, or other events that change the likelihood that the conversion option will be exercised.

A convertible bond is an example of a compound instrument, since it has a debt element and a potential equity element (on conversion). The economic effect of issuing the convertible bond is the same as issuing a non-convertible bond and an option to purchase shares. The value of the convertible bond should therefore be split into its component parts to reflect the substance of the instrument. An entity should estimate the fair value of the component parts.

The fair value of a similar financial liability that does not have an equity element is used as an estimate of the carrying amount of the liability element, with the equity instrument being the difference between this and the fair value of the compound instrument as a whole.

Fair value is the *"amount for which an asset could be exchanged, or a liability settled, between knowledgeable, willing parties in an arm's length transaction."* [IAS 32.11]

If the compound financial instrument is converted, the carrying amount of the financial liability element should be reclassified as part of equity, with the original equity amount also remaining as part of equity. No gain or loss is recognised on conversion of the instrument at its maturity.

Illustration 2

An entity issues 3,000 convertible, 10-year bonds at CU100 each, with a nominal interest rate of 5%.

The fair value of similar 10 year bonds with no convertible element is CU250,000.

The conversion details are 100 shares for each bond to be exercised after 5 years but before the redemption date in 10 years time.

At the date of issuance of the financial instrument, the following amounts should be recognised:

Proceeds of bond issue	(3,000 x CU100)	CU300,000
Fair value of liability component		CU250,000
Equity component	(CU300,000 less CU250,000)	CU50,000

6 Treasury Shares

If an entity acquires its own shares, they are deducted from equity. Such shares are known as treasury shares. [IAS 32.33]

An entity should not recognise any gain or loss made from a transaction involving treasury shares and any consideration paid or received should be recognised directly in equity. [IAS 32.33]

The amount of treasury shares held should be disclosed either on the face of the balance sheet or in the notes to the financial statements in accordance with IAS 1 *Presentation of financial statements*.

7 Interest, Dividends, Losses and Gains

Where interest, dividends, losses or gains arise in relation to a financial instrument that is classified as a financial liability, they should be recognised as income or expense directly in the income statement to form part of the profit or loss for the period. [IAS 32.35]

Dividends payable in respect of a financial instrument that is classified as a financial liability are classified as an expense. For example, dividends payable in respect of redeemable preference shares are presented as finance costs in the income statement. They may either be reported as part of interest in the income statement or presented as a separate line item.

Distributions, such as dividends, paid to holders of a financial instrument classified as equity should be charged directly against equity. [IAS 32.35]

When equity shares are issued, the transaction costs should be deducted from equity, net of any related income tax benefit. The transaction costs to be deducted are only the incremental costs directly attributable to the transaction that would have been otherwise avoided. [IAS 32.25]

Illustration 3

An entity issues 100,000 new CU1 ordinary shares which have a fair value of CU2.50 per share.

Professional fees in respect of the share issue are CU50,000. The costs are deductible in arriving at the entity's income tax liability. The corporate rate of tax is 40%. The management of the entity estimates that costs incurred internally for time incurred working on the share issue are CU25,000.

The internal costs should be included in the income statement. The professional fees are directly attributable to the transaction and CU30,000 should be deducted from equity (CU50,000 net of 40% tax).

Equity will increase by CU220,000 ((100,000 x CU2.50) - CU30,000).

8 Offsetting

Financial assets and financial liabilities should generally be presented as separate items in the balance sheet. However, it is possible to report financial assets and liabilities net where the entity has a legally enforceable right to offset the amounts and the entity intends to settle on a net basis. If the amounts are not settled them on a net basis, then they may still be offset if the entity intends to realise the asset and settle the liability simultaneously. [IAS 32.42]

9 Objectives and Scope of IAS 39

The objective of IAS 39 is to establish principles for recognising and measuring financial assets and financial liabilities.

The scope of IAS 39 is consistent with IAS 32; however there are a number of additional exceptions to its application. These include rights and obligations under a leasing arrangement as accounted for in accordance with IAS 17 *Leases*. However, certain elements of a lease are within the scope of IAS 39. For example a lease receivable recognised by a lessor is subject to the derecognition and impairment principles, a finance lease obligation of a lessee is subject to the derecognition criteria and IAS 39 applies where a lease contains what is called an embedded derivative. [IAS 39.2]

An equity instrument that meets the definition of a financial instrument but is in relation to an investment in an associate, subsidiary or joint venture is not subject to the requirements of IAS 39, nor are certain financial guarantees that are in relation to non-payment by a specified debtor. A loan commitment that cannot be settled by the payment of cash or another financial instrument is also outside of the scope of IAS 39. [IAS 39.2]

A loan commitment designated as a financial liability at fair value with the changes in fair value reported directly in the income statement is specifically identified as being within the scope of IAS 39. [IAS 39.4]

IAS 39 also applies to a contract to buy and sell non-financial items that can be settled by exchanging cash or another financial instrument (such as a commodities contract), provided the contract is not in accordance with the entity's expected purchase, sale or usage requirements (i.e. the contract is of an investment nature). [IAS 39.5]

10 Measurement of Financial Instruments

A financial asset or financial liability should be recognised when an entity enters into the contractual provisions of the financial instrument. [IAS 39.14]

The value at which a financial asset or financial liability should originally be measured is its fair value plus, in certain circumstances, any directly attributable transaction costs, such as fees and commissions paid to brokers and advisors. [IAS 39.43]

For subsequent measurement of financial assets, the treatment depends on the categorisation of the financial asset, as explained below.

Where an entity holds investments in equity instruments that do not have a quoted price in an active market and it is not possible to calculate their fair values reliably, they should be measured at cost. Derivatives that are linked to such investments, or require the delivery of such an investment, should also be measured at cost. [IAS 39.46]

An entity is required to consider whether financial assets are impaired (held at more than their recoverable amount) at each balance sheet date. Impairment is where an event has occurred after the initial recognition of a financial asset and that event results in a detrimental effect on the cash flows expected in relation to the item. No account is taken of losses that are expected to arise as a result of future events. [IAS 39.58]

10.1 Financial assets

IAS 39 defines four categories of financial instrument:

- a financial asset (or liability) at fair value through profit and loss;
- held-to-maturity investments;
- loans and receivables; and
- available-for-sale financial assets.

10.1.1 Financial asset/liability at fair value through profit or loss

This measurement basis results in the financial asset or liability being remeasured at fair value at each balance sheet date, with changes in fair value being recognised in the income statement as part of the profit or loss for the period. This treatment is required for financial assets classified as held for trading. [IAS 39.9]

To be classified as held for trading the financial asset should have been acquired for the purpose of selling or repurchasing it in the short-term. Alternatively, the financial asset should be part of a portfolio of identified financial instruments that are managed together. In this case there should also be evidence that the entity has made profits from the turnover of such items in the short-term. [IAS 39.9]

A derivative (as defined above) is generally classified as a financial instrument held for trading. [IAS 39.9]

A financial instrument may also be recognised at fair value with changes recognised directly in the income statement where an entity chooses (i.e. designates) this treatment when the financial instrument is first recognised. This fair value treatment may not be chosen for equity instruments that do not have a quoted market price in an active market or where their value cannot be measured reliably. [IAS 39.9]

Financial assets that are classified as held for trading, or where the entity has chosen the fair value measurement option, should be remeasured at fair value at each balance sheet date. No deduction is made for the transaction costs that may be incurred on the disposal of the financial asset. All movements in fair value are recognised directly in the income statement as part of the profit or loss for the period. [IAS 39.46, 39.55]

Following the publication of the 'improved' version of IAS 39 in December 2003, the IASB subsequently issued, in April 2004, an Exposure Draft proposing an amendment to IAS 39. The proposed amendment, if finalised, will limit the use of the fair value option.

10.1.2 Held-to-maturity investments

A financial asset (that is a non-derivative) that has fixed, or determinable, payments and a fixed maturity date is classified as a held-to-maturity investment, provided the entity intends to hold it until its maturity. [IAS 39.9]

Financial assets that meet the definition of a held-to-maturity investment may be classified as held at fair value, as discussed above, or as an available-for-sale financial asset. A financial asset will not meet the definition of a held-to-maturity investment where it meets the definition of a loan or receivable. [IAS 39.9]

An entity is prohibited from classifying financial assets as held-to-maturity if, in the recent past (i.e. within the current or two preceding years) it has sold or reclassified, more than an insignificant amount of such investments, before their maturity dates. This prohibition is not applicable where the sale of a held-to-maturity investment was so close to its maturity date that the difference in fair value was minimal, or where the sale is after the entity has received substantially all the principal amount of the financial asset. Also, if the sale was a one-off unanticipated event beyond the entity's control, then the prohibition does not apply. [IAS 39.9]

A financial asset classified as a held-to-maturity investment should be measured at "*amortised cost using the effective interest method*" following initial recognition at fair value. [IAS 39.46]

The amortised cost of a financial asset is the initial amount recognised in respect of the financial asset, less any repayments of the principal sum (not payments of interest or other financing costs) and plus or minus any amortisation. The amortisation of the financial asset is calculated by applying the effective interest method to spread the financing cost over the period to maturity (i.e. the difference between the initial amount recognised for the financial asset and the amount receivable at maturity). [IAS 39.9]

The effective interest rate is the rate that exactly discounts the scheduled cash flows payable or receivable across the expected life of the financial instrument. [IAS 39.9]

Amortisation, and write downs where the value of the financial asset is impaired (i.e. below its recoverable amount), should be reported directly in the income statement. Any profit or loss on disposal of the financial asset should also be recognised directly in the income statement. [IAS 39.56]

An impairment loss should be calculated as being the difference between the asset's carrying amount (the amount reported in its balance sheet) and the present value of the future cash flows expected to arise from the financial asset. The present value should be calculated by discounting the cash flows at the original effective interest rate used for amortisation purposes. [IAS 39.63]

A reversal of a previously recognised impairment should be recognised as a reversal of the original impairment. The financial asset's carrying amount should not exceed the value of its amortised cost, had the original impairment not arisen. [IAS 39.65]

10.1.3 Loans and receivables

A non-derivative financial asset that has fixed, or determinable, payments (but no fixed maturity date) and is not quoted in an active market, is classified as a loan or receivable. Exceptions to this general classification are where it is classified as held for trading because the entity intends to sell it in the short-term, or where the entity may not substantially recover the initial investment. [IAS 39.9]

An entity may still choose to classify a financial asset as available-for-sale or at fair value with changes being recognised directly in the income statement even where it meets the definition of a loan or receivable. [IAS 39.9]

A financial asset classified as a loan or receivable should be measured at "amortised cost using the effective interest method" following initial recognition at fair value, i.e. on the same measurement basis as that used for held-to-maturity investments. [IAS 39.46]

Amortisation, and write downs where the value of the financial asset is impaired, should be reported directly in the income statement. Any profit or loss on disposal of the financial asset should also be recognised directly in the income statement. [IAS 39.56]

An impairment loss should be calculated and treated in the same way as that for a held-to-maturity investment, as discussed above.

10.1.4 Available-for-sale financial assets

An available-for-sale financial asset is one that has been designated as such or has not been classified under the above three categories. [IAS 39.9]

Available-for-sale financial assets should be measured at their fair value at each balance sheet date. [IAS 39.46]

The gain or loss arising from fair valuing the financial asset at each balance sheet date should be recognised in equity and reported in the statement of changes in equity. On disposal the cumulative gains and losses recognised in equity will form part of the profit or loss on disposal reported in the income statement. [IAS 39.55]

Illustration 4

An entity classifies a financial asset with a carrying amount of CU200 as available-for-sale. The cumulative gains recognised in equity relating to the financial asset are CU50.

If the entity disposes of the asset for CU320, the gain recognised in the income statement will be CU170, being:

- the difference between the proceeds on disposal and the carrying amount of CU120 (CU320 – CU200); plus
- the gain of CU50 previously recognised directly in equity.

Where a reduction in the value of an available-for-sale financial asset has been recognised directly in equity but there is now evidence that the asset is impaired, the cumulative loss that was previously recognised in equity should be charged to the income statement. The amount of the loss transferred to the income statement from equity should be the difference between the carrying amount of the asset and its current fair value, less any previously recognised impairment losses. [IAS 39.67, 39.68]

The amount of an impairment on an equity instrument charged to the income statement should not be reversed in the income statement in future periods.

However, if an impairment related to a debt instrument subsequently reverses this reversal should be recognised in the income statement. [IAS 39.69, 39.70]

10.1.5 Summary of treatment of financial assets

The table below summaries the accounting treatment for financial assets, as discussed above.

Asset	Sub-category	Description	Measurement	Recording of changes
Financial assets at fair value through, profit or loss	Designated	Any financial asset designated on initial recognition as one to be held at fair value through profit or loss	Fair value	Income statement
	Held for trading	Financial assets held for the purpose of selling in the short term. This will include most derivatives		
Available-for-sale financial assets	None	Non-derivative financial assets designated by an entity as available-for-sale, or not falling under the other three classifications		Directly to equity, except for impairment losses
Loans and receivables	None	Non-derivative financial assets with fixed or determinable payments, other than those quoted in a market and those designated as held for trading or available-for-sale	Amortised cost	Income statement
Held-to-maturity investments	None	Non-derivative financial assets with fixed or determinable payments and fixed maturity dates, where the entity has the intention to hold them long term and are not classified as any of the above		

10.2 Financial liabilities

Following initial recognition, financial liabilities are generally measured at *"amortised cost using the effective interest method"*. The principles for amortised cost and the use of the effective interest method are discussed above in relation to financial assets. [IAS 39.47]

However, an entity is permitted to choose to value financial liabilities at fair value with the changes being recognised directly in the income statement for the period. [IAS 39.47]

Where a derivative liability is linked to, or to be settled by, the transfer of an unquoted equity instrument whose fair value cannot be measured reliably, it should be measured at cost. [IAS 39.47]

If a financial asset is transferred but cannot be derecognised because the entity continues to have some involvement in it, any financial liability associated with it should be measured under special rules (as explained below). [IAS 39.47]

10.3 Determining fair value

As defined above, fair value is the value that an asset or liability can be exchanged for in an arm's length purchase or sale.

There is a presumption in the definition of fair value that an entity will continue into the foreseeable future, i.e. it is a going concern (as set out in the *IASB Framework* and IAS 1 *Presentation of financial statements*).

Where a quoted market price exists for a financial asset or liability, this will be its fair value, representing the price which an entity could obtain for the asset, or at which it could settle the liability, at the balance sheet date.

The appropriate market price is usually the current bid price for an asset held and financial liability to be issued, and the asking price for a liability held and an asset to be acquired. The bid price for an asset is the price at which a third party is willing to pay to acquire it, while the asking price for an asset is the lowest price at which a third party will sell an it.

Where bid and asking prices are not available, the price to be used is that at which the latest transaction occurred, assuming that there has not been a significant change in the fair value of the financial instrument since that date.

If there is no active market for a financial instrument, then its fair value should be estimated by using valuation techniques. In using such techniques, a more reliable estimate should be achievable by using as many market inputs as possible and hence as little reliance as possible is placed on entity specific inputs. Valuation techniques should also take into account any recent transactions that have taken place between willing parties, and the fair value of similar financial instruments.

11 Reclassifications

Once a financial asset or liability is classified within a category it should only be reclassified if certain conditions are met.

A financial asset or liability should not be reclassified into, or out of, the fair value profit or loss classification. [IAS 39.50]

Where the circumstances regarding a held-to-maturity financial asset change and it is no longer appropriate for it to be classified as such, it should be reclassified as available-for-sale. Such a situation arises where an entity changes its intentions, by deciding to sell the asset immediately, rather than hold it to maturity. On reclassification, the financial asset should be measured at fair value, with the gain or loss arising on reclassification being recognised in equity. [IAS 39.51, 39.55]

If an amount of a held-to-maturity asset is left over once other parts of such an item have been sold before their maturity date, the remaining balance should be reclassified as available-for-sale. [IAS 39.52]

If a financial asset or liability was not measured at fair value solely because a reliable measure was not available, and such a reliable measure subsequently becomes available, it should be measured at fair value. The gain or loss on measuring the financial instrument at fair value should be recognised in the income statement, or as part of equity where it arises on an available-for-sale financial asset. [IAS 39.53, 39.55]

If circumstances change such that it is no longer appropriate to continue to carry a financial asset or liability at fair value, then the carrying amount of the item at the date of change in measurement should be considered to be its new cost, or amortised cost as appropriate. Such circumstances may arise from a change in intention or where fair value can no longer be measured reliably, although this is rare in practice. [IAS 39.54]

Where the measurement of financial assets or liabilities has changed from one of fair value to one of cost, or amortised cost, any gain or loss that was previously recorded in equity should be treated in the following way: [IAS 39.54]

- in the case of a financial asset classified as held-to-maturity, any gain or loss previously recognised as part of equity should be amortised in the income statement over the remaining period to maturity based on the effective interest method; or

- where the financial asset does not have a fixed maturity date, then the gain or loss should remain in equity until the financial asset is sold, at which point the gain or loss becomes part of the ultimate profit or loss on disposal recognised in the income statement.

12 Derecognition

12.1 Financial assets

IAS 39 includes extensive guidance on when a financial instrument should be derecognised, i.e. removed from an entity's financial statements. A financial asset will generally be derecognised in its entirety. But there are circumstances where it is appropriate only to derecognise part of it, for example where it has been transferred but the entity retains some of the risks and rewards of ownership. [IAS 39.16]

A financial asset should not be derecognised where the entity continues to retain the risks and rewards of ownership. This assessment should be carried out by comparing the risks and rewards held by the entity before and after the transfer. The ability to control a financial asset ultimately lies with the party that has the right to sell the asset. [IAS 39.20]

An entity should derecognise a financial asset where the contractual rights to the future cash flows in relation to the instrument expire, or where the financial asset has been transferred and the transfer meets the criteria for derecognition. [IAS 39.17]

A financial asset that has been transferred should be derecognised if the entity has transferred all the contractual rights to the future cash flows relating to the asset through a sale, for example, or if, while retaining the contractual rights under the asset, the entity has an obligation to the pay out those future cash flows to a third party. [IAS 39.18]

Where an entity has such an obligation (to pay out the future cash flows relating to the asset to a third party), the asset should only be derecognised if: [IAS 39.19]

- the entity is only required to pay out the cash flows to the third party if it receives the original cash inflows in relation to the specific financial asset;

- the entity is not permitted to use the financial asset as security, other than on the payment of the cash flows in relation to the specific financial asset to the third party;

- the entity is not permitted to sell the financial asset; and

- the entity is required to pass on the cash flows received in relation to the financial asset without any significant delay to the third party.

12.1.1 Derecognition in its entirety

If a financial asset qualifies for derecognition in its entirety, the entity should recognise any profit or loss made on its derecognition directly in the income statement. The profit or loss is calculated by comparing the asset's carrying amount in the balance sheet with the aggregate of any payment received and gains or losses reported in equity in relation to the financial asset. [IAS 39.26]

If the financial asset meets the criteria to be derecognised but the entity retains some future rights to cash flows in relation to the asset, for example by servicing the asset for a fee, then the treatment above should still be applied and a separate asset or liability should be recognised at fair value for the rights retained. [IAS 39.24, 39.25]

If the financial asset qualifying for derecognition is part of a larger financial asset, then derecognition should be based on an appropriate apportionment of fair values of the larger asset, compared with the part transferred. [IAS 39.27]

12.1.2 Continuing involvement after a transfer

Where an entity retains some of the risks and rewards of ownership but retains control of the financial asset, the entity should continue to recognise the asset to the extent of its continuing involvement. The level of continuing involvement is based on the entity's exposure to changes in the fair value of the transferred asset. In these circumstances, the entity should also recognise an associated liability. The liability is measured so that the net of the asset and liability is the fair value of the amount retained. The net amount is measured by reference to the basis appropriate to the asset, i.e. either amortised cost or fair value. The asset and liability should be presented separately and not offset against each other. [IAS 39.30, 39.31, 39.36]

An entity should continue to recognise any income from the partially transferred financial asset to the extent of its retained involvement. [IAS 39.32]

Subsequent remeasurements in the financial asset and liability should be treated consistently with the general requirements of IAS 39, and the respective gains and losses should be reported separately (i.e. not offset against one another). [IAS 39.33]

12.2 Financial liabilities

A financial liability should be derecognised when an entity discharges the obligations specified in the contract, or they expire. [IAS 39.39]

Where a financial liability is exchanged with a third party for another financial liability that has substantially different terms, the original liability should be derecognised and a new liability recognised. [IAS 39.40]

A profit or loss on the exchange, or transfer, of a financial liability should be recognised directly in the income statement and is calculated as being the difference between the carrying amount of the financial liability extinguished and any consideration (cash paid or another liability assumed) given by the entity. [IAS 39.41]

13 Hedging Transactions

Hedging is a risk management technique. It is where an entity tries to reduce the impact of future potential losses or costs.

Illustration 5

Alpha enters into a contract to acquire a new piece of machinery from Beta, an overseas entity. The machinery costs R$100,000 and is payable in one year's time. Alpha's operating currency is CU and the current exchange rate is CU1: R$2.

Alpha has the exchange risk associated with the contract. To eliminate this risk Alpha enters into a forward contract to acquire R$100,000 in one year's time at the current exchange rate.

In one year's time when Alpha has to pay R$100,000 to Beta for the machinery, it can exercise the forward contract. Alpha will therefore have paid CU50,000 for the machinery regardless of whether the exchange rate has moved.

Hedge accounting is where the related changes in fair value of a financial asset or financial liability are offset against each other in some way. In order to use hedge accounting an entity will have a hedging instrument and a hedged item.

The 'hedged item' is an asset or liability, or a transaction that exposes the entity to risks in the changes in fair value or future cash flows. In order for the item, or transaction, to be classified as a hedged item for accounting purposes it should be specifically designated as being hedged. In the illustration above, the payment of the R$100,000 to Beta is the hedged item. [IAS 39.9]

The 'hedging instrument' is a financial instrument (which may be a derivative) that is designated as being the hedging instrument *"whose fair value or cash flows are expected to offset changes in the fair value or cash flows of a designated hedged item"*. In the illustration above, the forward contract to buy the foreign currency is the hedging instrument. [IAS 39.9]

All derivatives may be identified as hedging instruments, but a non-derivative financial asset or liability may be a hedging instrument only where it is hedging foreign currency risk. For accounting purposes only, hedging instruments should involve external parties to the entity.

An entity may designate a proportion of a hedging instrument to a hedged item.

Hedging relationships fall under three categories: [IAS 39.86]

- a fair value hedge, which hedges the exposure to changes in fair value of an item or transaction;

- a cash flow hedge, which hedges the exposure to changes in expected cash flows; and

- a hedge of a net investment in a foreign operation as defined in IAS 21 *The effects of changes in foreign exchange rates.* Such hedges reduce the exposure of an entity where it has overseas operations and is accounted for as if it were a cash flow hedge.

13.1 Qualifying for hedge accounting

A hedging relationship only qualifies for hedge accounting if a number of stringent conditions are met: [IAS 39.88]

- an entity should formally designate and document a hedging relationship when it is entered into. The formal documentation should include the identification of the hedged item, the hedging instrument and the risks that are being hedged;

- the hedging instrument should be 'highly effective' in offsetting the changes in fair value or cash flows of the hedged item and should be capable of being measured reliably;

- for a forecast transaction that is classified as a cash flow hedge, the occurrence of the transaction should be highly probable and lead to exposure to differences in resulting cash flows; and

- the hedge is continually assessed for effectiveness and determined actually to have been highly effective.

The effectiveness of a hedge is the level to which a hedging instrument offsets the changes in fair value or cash flows in their entirety. For a hedge to be classified as effective, IAS 39 requires that it should be within the range of 80-125%.

Illustration 6

An entity has entered into a hedging relationship. At the year-end the entity assesses the fair value of the hedged item and hedging instrument, and the following gains and losses arise:

Hedged item – gain of CU500

Hedging instrument – loss of CU600

The effectiveness of the hedge is calculated as:

CU600 / CU500 = 120% - the hedge is therefore assessed as being highly effective.

13.2 Hedge accounting

13.2.1 Fair value hedge

If a fair value hedge meets the conditions for hedge accounting, then the hedging instrument should be remeasured at fair value, with the gain or loss being reported in the income statement. The gain or loss on the change in fair value of the hedged item that is attributable to the hedged risk should be recognised in the income statement. This treatment applies even if the hedged item is an available-for-sale investment. [IAS 39.89]

13.2.2 Cash flow hedge

A cash flow hedge that meets the criteria for hedge accounting should be split between the proportion of the hedging instrument that is effective and that which is ineffective. The effective proportion should be recognised in equity and any ineffective element should be recognised directly in the income statement to form part of the profit or loss for the period. [IAS 39.95]

Illustration 7

An entity has hedged future cash flows on a financial liability using an interest related derivative. The effectiveness of the hedge has been assessed at 90%. The additional interest costs relating to the derivative are CU20,000.

CU18,000 of the interest costs are recognised in equity. The CU2,000 remaining (the ineffective portion) is recognised in the income statement.

14 Embedded Derivatives

Some contracts that are not themselves financial instruments, may nonetheless have financial instruments embedded in them. For example, a contract to purchase a commodity at a fixed price for delivery at a future date has embedded in it a derivative that is indexed to the price of the commodity. These are known as 'embedded derivatives'.

Embedded derivatives should be separated from the underlying contract, known as the host contract, for accounting purposes where certain criteria apply. The embedded derivative should be separated when: [IAS 39.11]

- it is considered not to be closely related to the host contract. This relationship is assessed based on the characteristics and risks of each of the embedded derivative and the host contract;

- a separate instrument that had the same characteristics and terms as the embedded derivative would be defined as a derivative; and

- the combined instrument (the host contract and the embedded derivative) are not measured at fair value with the changes being recognised directly in the income statement to form part of the profit or loss for the period.

If the embedded derivative meets the criteria for separate recognition, then the resulting host contract should either be accounted for in accordance with the requirements of IAS 39 if it is a financial asset or liability, or another appropriate standard if it is not. [IAS 39.11]

If an embedded derivative meets the criteria to be separated from its host contract but its value cannot be separately measured then it should be measured as a combined financial asset or liability that is held for trading. [IAS 39.12]

15 Disclosure

Disclosures should be made to provide users of the financial statements with an understanding of the effect that financial instruments have had on an entity's financial performance, position and cash flows. IAS 32 requires a number of disclosures to be made that will help meet this objective, although the format of the disclosures may be either narrative or quantitative, or a mixture of both.

15.1 Risk management policies and hedging activities

An entity should describe its financial risk management objectives and policies so that readers are able to place into context the information presented to them. This explanation should include an entity's policy for hedging. [IAS 32.56]

The disclosures should include a discussion of management's policy for controlling risk.

Disclosures relating to items that have been hedged are particularly important, since the offset of profits and losses may hide the true outcome of items.

For all types of hedges, the following disclosures are required, split between the type of hedge: [IAS 32.58]

- a description of the hedge and the financial instruments that are designated as hedging instruments;

- the fair value of the financial instruments designated as hedging instruments at the balance sheet date;

- the nature of the risks that are being hedged; and

- for cash flow hedges, information on the periods in which the cash flows are expected to occur and when the resulting amounts are likely to impact on an entity's profit or loss.

If an entity had any forecast transactions that are now no longer expected to occur this should be disclosed. [IAS 32.58]

Additional disclosures are required when a gain or loss on a hedging instrument in a cash flow hedge has been recognised directly in equity. In such circumstances, an entity should disclose the movements in equity as a result of the transaction, for example an amount that has been recognised in equity in the period, or an amount that has been transferred out of equity. [IAS 32.59]

15.1.1 Interest rate risk

As part of an entity's disclosures on risk, there is a specific requirement to disclose information, split between each class of financial asset and financial liability, about its exposure to interest rate risk. Such disclosures should include details on the contractual repricing and maturity dates (which provide information on the period of time over which interest rates are fixed) of financial instruments and, where applicable, the effective interest rates. [IAS 32.67]

Changes in market interest rates directly affect the cash flows expected to be received or paid under contractually agreed terms in relation to financial assets and liabilities. This is known as cash flow interest rate risk.

If an entity is exposed to interest rate risk from transactions that are not recognised in the financial statements, it is still required to explain the level of risk associated with the transactions. For example, an entity may have entered into a commitment to provide a loan at a fixed interest rate.

These disclosures should be presented in the most appropriate format. For example a tabular format may be appropriate, splitting the information by maturity date, in less than one year, in one to two years and in two to three years.

15.1.2 Credit risk

Credit risk sets out the level of risk that an entity has in relation to the non-recoverability of financial assets recognised in the balance sheet. This information is presented on the basis of an entity's maximum exposure in the event of other parties failing to meet their obligations. An entity is also required to disclose any significant concentrations of credit risk, for example in geographical areas or different parts of the business. [IAS 32.76]

The disclosures in relation to credit risk should be gross of any potential realisation of collateral provided in respect of financial assets. This is to ensure that users can make an assessment of the maximum risk that an entity is exposed to, and to highlight that this may differ from the carrying amounts for the financial assets recognised at the balance sheet date.

15.2 Terms, conditions and accounting policies

The contractual terms and conditions of financial instruments provide information on the amount, timing and level of uncertainty surrounding future cash flows in relation to financial instruments. Disclosure should therefore be made of the nature of an entity's financial instruments, split between financial assets, financial liabilities and equity instruments, including information on the significant terms and conditions. [IAS 32.60]

Although no specific disclosures in respect of terms and conditions are set out, IAS 32 does list a wide range of matters which may warrant disclosure in appropriate circumstances. Such information includes, for example, the date of maturity, early settlement options, the principal amounts, interest or other amounts payable, with the timing of such payments, and foreign currency implications where appropriate.

In accordance with the principles in IAS 1 and IAS 8 *Accounting policies, changes in accounting estimates and errors,* an entity should disclose the accounting policies and methods adopted for reporting the various types of financial instruments. Such information should include an explanation of the recognition and derecognition criteria and the measurement basis applied. [IAS 32.60]

15.3 Fair value

An entity should provide information on the fair value, at the balance sheet date, of financial assets and financial liabilities analysed over their different classes. This information is required to be presented in a way that permits a comparison to be made between the fair values and the carrying amounts recognised in the balance sheet. [IAS 32.86]

The carrying amount in the balance sheet of short-term trade receivables and payables is likely to be a reasonable approximation to fair value, so no fair value information is specifically required.

If an entity cannot measure reliably the fair value of unquoted investments or related derivatives (and they have therefore been measured at cost under IAS 39), this fact should be disclosed, along with the reasons why it is not possible to measure fair value reliably. A description of the financial instruments should also be disclosed and the carrying amount for such items. If possible an entity should also disclose the range of estimates for fair value. [IAS 32.90]

If a financial asset whose fair value could not previously be measured reliably is sold, this should be disclosed, together with the financial asset's carrying amount and any gain or loss made on the transaction. [IAS 32.90]

Information should be disclosed about the methods and significant assumptions used by an entity in determining the fair value of financial assets and financial liabilities. These disclosures should include whether the fair value was determined on the basis of published prices in an active market or estimated by valuation techniques. Where changes in the assumptions used in valuation techniques would significantly impact the measurement of fair value of financial assets and liabilities, this fact should be disclosed along with the potential impact from such changes. [IAS 32.92]

An entity should also disclose the change in fair value recognised in the income statement that resulted from estimates using valuation techniques, rather than by reference to published prices in an active market. [IAS 32.92]

15.4 Other disclosures

Where an entity is required by IAS 39 to continue to recognise a financial asset, even though it has entered into some arrangement to transfer it, a number of disclosures should be made for each class of financial asset so recognised. This information should include: [IAS 32.94(a)]

- the nature of the assets, and the risks and rewards of ownership that the entity continues to be exposed to;
- if the whole of the asset continues to be recognised by the entity, its carrying amount along with that of the associated liability; and
- where part of the asset continues to be recognised, the total amount of the asset, the amount recognised and the carry value of the associated liability.

15.4.1 Collateral

Where financial assets have been pledged as collateral for liabilities, or contingent liabilities, the carrying amount of the financial assets should be disclosed with any significant terms and conditions attaching to them. [IAS 32.94(b)]

15.4.2 Reclassification

Where a financial asset has been reclassified from fair value to one measured at cost (or amortised cost) an entity is required to disclose the reason why it has been reclassified. [IAS 32.94(g)]

15.4.3 Income statement and equity

An entity should disclose material items of income, expenses, gains and losses arising from financial assets and financial liabilities. This information is useful to users of the financial statements, regardless of whether they were included in the profit or loss for the period or as a separate component of equity. [IAS 32.94(h)]

This information should identify the total interest income and total interest expense for financial assets and liabilities that are not measured at fair value with changes being recognised in the income statement, amounts recognised in equity for available-for-sale financial assets and the amount of interest income accrued on impaired financial assets. [IAS 32.94(h)]

Any impairment losses recognised in the income statement for a financial asset should be separately identified for each significant class of financial asset. [IAS 32.94(i)]

15.4.4 Defaults and breaches

Where an entity has defaulted on any amounts in relation to financial instruments for which the lender can demand repayment, the entity should disclose details of those breaches. This information should include disclosure of the amounts recognised in the balance sheet in respect of such defaulted amounts and whether or not the default has been remedied or renegotiated. [IAS 32.94(j)]

16 Chapter Review

The key issues addressed in this chapter are how to define, recognise, measure and report financial instruments.

This chapter has covered:

- an explanation of what is meant by the term financial instruments;

- the main classification of financial instruments;

- the main presentation and disclosure requirements for financial instrument;

- how financial instruments are measured and recognised in their broad categories; and

- the implications of hedging financial instruments.

Chapter 21
CASH FLOW STATEMENTS

1 Business Context

Cash is essential if a business is to continue its operations. Cash, or access to cash, is needed to pay for an entity's outlays on a continuing basis and is a fundamental part of its operating cycle. An entity's operating cycle is the period of time that a normal operating transaction takes to complete within a business, for example the time between the receipt of the order to final payment being made by the customer. If an entity is unable to pay its debts as they fall due, then it risks insolvency.

Cash and liquidity are a different concept to profit. It is possible for a highly profitable entity to have liquidity problems if it does not manage the flow of cash within its business effectively.

Cash is about the liquidity of a business and hence cash flows concern the change in that liquidity. Cash management is not just about surviving; it is about the process of utilising cash resources to their optimal effect.

For an investor to be able to assess the effectiveness of a business, it is important that information is included in the financial statements not only on the entity's performance and financial position but also on its cash flows. When used along side a balance sheet, for example, a cash flow statement provides users with information on the changes in net assets of the entity. An entity may have a strong financial position and good performance during the period, but may also have suffered significant cash outflows. The financial information is therefore not complete without the cash flow information, which may tell a different story to the original assessment of an entity's performance.

2 Chapter Objectives

This chapter covers the preparation and presentation of a cash flow statement as part of an entity's financial statements.

IAS 1 *Presentation of financial statements* sets out the content of an entity's financial statements. It includes the requirement for a cash flow statement to be presented.

On completion of this chapter you should be able to:

- understand the objectives and scope of IAS 7 *Cash flow statements*;

- identify the important terminology and definitions which relate to the presentation of cash flow statements in the financial statements;

- distinguish between cash and cash equivalents, and other assets and liabilities;

- identify the main sections of a cash flow statement and the cash flows relating to each of them; and

- apply knowledge and understanding of IAS 7 through basic calculations.

3 Objectives, Scope and Definitions of IAS 7

3.1 Objective and scope

The objective of IAS 7 is to provide information about the historical changes in cash, and cash equivalents, of an entity. This information is presented via a cash flow statement that classifies cash flows under the headings of: [IAS 7.10]

- operating activities;
- investing activities; and
- financing activities.

The preparation of a cash flow statement as part of an entity's financial statements is required of all entities, with no exceptions. [IAS 7.1]

3.2 What is cash?

The nature of cash may, at first, seem obvious, but cash may be held in many forms. Some forms of cash can be accessed immediately while there is a delay in accessing others.

As defined by IAS 7, cash includes not only cash itself but also any instrument that can be converted into cash so quickly that it is in effect equivalent to cash.

In IAS 7, the cash flow statement seeks to identify changes in:

Classification	Amounts included
Cash	*"Cash in hand and demand deposits".* [IAS 7.6]
Cash equivalents	*"Short-term, highly liquid investments that are readily convertible to known amounts of cash and which are subject to an insignificant risk of changes in value".* [IAS 7.6]

An essential element of a cash equivalent is that it is held for the purpose of meeting short-term cash commitments as they fall due and not for long-term investment purposes. To meet the definition of a cash equivalent, the item should be "readily convertible" which suggests that it has a short maturity of, say, three months or less from the date of acquisition. Cash equivalents may therefore include:

- short term deposits;
- loan notes;
- bank deposit accounts; and
- government securities.

Equity investments should normally be excluded, because, unlike government securities, they are subject to a significant risk of changes in value.

Bank borrowings normally form part of an entity's financing activities, which are discussed below. A bank overdraft, however, is often used as a key element of an entity's daily cash management, for example a positive cash balance may be held at the end of one day with an overdraft the next. In such circumstances the overdraft should be included as a component of cash and cash equivalents.

3.3 Sources and uses of cash

Cash flows are inflows and outflows of cash and cash equivalents (hereafter referred to as 'cash'). [IAS 7.6]

IAS 7 requires sources and uses of cash to be analysed under the following headings: [IAS 7.10]

Headings	Description
Operating activities	"The principal revenue-producing activities" of the entity, together with other activities that are not of an investing or financing nature. [IAS 7.6]
Investing activities	"The acquisition and disposal of long-term assets and other investments not included in cash equivalents". [IAS 7.6]
Financing activities	Activities that change the amount and composition of an entity's equity capital and borrowings. [IAS 7.6]

Illustration 1

The list of transactions and balances set out below should be included in the cash flow headings as shown in the table.

– cash payments to purchase a non-current asset;

– the issue of shares for cash;

– cash received from customers;

– a short-term cash deposit requiring 20 days' notice for its withdrawal;

– a cash repayment of a bank overdraft (assuming the overdraft is used as an integral part of the entity's cash management);

– revaluation of land;

– cash repayment of a loan;

– cash received as commission;

– a bonus issue of shares; and

– cash payment to purchase listed government securities (with a maturity date in one month time).

Operating cash flow	Investing cash flow	Financing cash flow	Cash and cash equivalents
Cash received from customers	Cash payments to purchase a non-current asset	Issue of shares for cash	Short-term cash deposit
Cash received as commission		Cash repayment of a loan	Cash repayment of an overdraft
			Cash payment to purchase listed government securities

Note: the following items are non-cash transactions and would not appear in the cash flow statement:

– the revaluation of land; and

– a bonus issue of shares.

4 Overview of IAS 7 – A Cash Flow Statement

An illustrative pro forma cash flow statement is set out below:

Cash flow statement for the year ended 30 June 2004

	CU000	CU000
Cash flows from operating activities		
Cash generated from operations		10,000
Interest paid		(3,000)
Tax paid		(5,000)
Net cash from operating activities		2,000
Cash flows from investing activities		
Purchase of property, plant and equipment	(1,200)	
Proceeds from sales of property, plant and equipment	100	
Interest received	200	
Dividends received	300	
Net cash used in investing activities		(600)
Cash flows from financing activities		
Issue of ordinary shares	2,000	
Issue of preference shares	1,100	
Issue of non-current interest-bearing borrowings	2,500	
Redemption of non-current interest-bearing borrowings	(1,000)	
Dividends paid	(500)	
Net cash used in financing activities		4,100
Net change in cash and cash equivalents		5,500
Cash and cash equivalents brought forward		3,200
Cash and cash equivalents carried forward		**8,700**

This illustrative example of a cash flow statement shows interest paid as part of operating activities because it is part of the profit or loss reported by the entity in its income statement. However, IAS 7 also permits interest paid to be reported as part of the entity's financing or investing activities. [IAS 7.31]

Interest received and dividends received are shown as part of the investing activities in the illustration set out above; however, they may be reported as part of the operating or financing activities as described above for interest paid. [IAS 7.31]

Dividends paid are shown as part of the financing operations of the entity in the illustration because they relate to the cost of obtaining equity finance. An alternative treatment permitted under IAS 7 is to include them as part of the operating activities of the entity. Although dividends paid are not deducted in the income statement in arriving at the profit or loss for the period, this presentation allows a user to assess the entity's future ability to pay dividends out of its operating activities.

The separate line items set out under the required cash flow headings should represent the major classes of gross cash receipts and payments arising for each of the activities. [IAS 7.21]

Cash flows which relate to a customer rather than to the entity should be reported on a net basis under the relevant cash flow heading. Items shown net may include, for example, cash that is received on behalf of a third party by the entity and is subsequently paid on to that third party. Cash flows should also be presented on a net basis where the related inflow and outflow occurs within a short space of time, the cash flows are large and the maturity dates are short (within three months). An example is the purchase and sale of the same investment. [IAS 7.22]

5 Cash Flows from Operating Activities

The cash flows from an entity's operating activities can be presented using two methods: [IAS 7.18]

- the direct method, which discloses the major classes of gross cash receipts and payments; or

- the indirect method, where the entity starts with the net profit or loss for the period and adjusts it for non-cash transactions, deferrals or accruals of income and expenditure and items that will form part of the entity's investing and financing activities.

5.1 The direct method

The direct method details the actual cash flows that are part of the operating activities of the entity. Such cash flows should therefore include, for example, payments to suppliers, receipts from customers, payments to employees and other payments and receipts made or received as part of the entity's operating activities.

Where this approach is adopted the information will generally be obtained from the entity's accounting records directly.

An alternative approach under the direct method can be used by adjusting each line item in the income statement for non-cash transactions that have occurred during the period and for items that fall under the headings of investing and financing activities.

The nature of the adjustments using this approach is illustrated in the following table:

Income statement item	Examples of adjustments
Revenue	■ Change in trade receivables
Cost of sales	■ Relevant part of depreciation charge ■ Change in inventories ■ Change in trade payables on purchases
Operating expenses	■ Relevant part of depreciation charge ■ Changes in accruals/prepayments ■ Change in trade payables on operating expenses

Illustration 2

Extracts from the draft financial statements of Delta for the year ended 31 December 2003, are set out below:

Income statement

	CU	CU
Revenue		250,000
Cost of sales Opening inventories	30,000	
Purchases	218,000	
Closing inventories	(52,000)	
		(196,000)
Gross profit		54,000
Other operating expenses (all cash costs except for depreciation of CU11,000)		(21,600)
Profit from operations		32,400

Balance Sheet extracts	31 Dec 2003	31 Dec 2002
	CU	CU
Trade receivables	68,000	23,000
Trade payables	21,600	42,800

The cash from operations for Delta for the year ended 31 December 2003 using the direct method is:

	CU
Cash from customers (250,000 + (23,000 - 68,000)) (Revenue plus the movement in trade receivables)	205,000
Cash to suppliers (218,000 + (42,800 - 21,600)) (Purchases plus the movement in trade payables)	(239,200)
Other cash operating expenses (21,600-11,000) (Other cash operating activity expenses adjusted for non-cash items, e.g. depreciation)	(10,600)
Cash outflow from operating activities	(44,800)

Note: This illustration highlights how an entity can have profits from operating activities but an outflow of cash from those activities.

5.2 Indirect method

The indirect method of calculating the cash flows from an entity's operating activities makes adjustments to the net profit or loss for the period. The adjustments are for non-cash transactions, deferrals or accruals of income and expenditure and for items that will form part of the investing and financing activities of the entity. [IAS 7.18]

Illustration 3

Using the information from Illustration 2 above, the cash generated from operations for Delta for the year ended 31 December 2003 using the indirect method is:

	CU
Profit from operating activities	32,400
Depreciation charge (adjust for non-cash expenses)	11,000
Increase in inventories (52,000-30,000) (adjust for the movement in inventories)	(22,000)
Increase in trade receivables (68,000-23,000) (adjust for the movement in trade receivables)	(45,000)
Decrease in trade payables (21,600-42,800) (adjust for the movement in trade payables)	(21,200)
Cash outflow from operating activities	(44,800)

This gives the same solution as the direct method.

The adjustments for movements in inventories, trade receivables and payables are to reverse out the effect of accruals accounting (recording income when it becomes receivable rather than when the cash is received).

The presentation of the net cash flows of the entity for its operating activities may be presented by showing movements during the period in inventories and operating receivables and payables.

5.3 Taxation

Although profit-based taxes may relate to items throughout the cash flow statement, it may not be practicable to identify separately the elements of tax which relate to each of the three components of the cash flow statement. As a result, tax will normally be reported as part of an entity's operating activities, although it may be split between the relevant headings where it is practicable to do so. [IAS 7.35]

The cash flow in relation to tax should be separately identified in the cash flow statement and where it has been allocated between the different headings, a total should be disclosed. [IAS 7.35]

6 Cash Flows from Investing Activities

Cash flows arising from investing activities are important as they provide information on the level of investment that an entity has made in assets that it will hold and use in its business on an ongoing basis.

Examples of cash flows arising from investing activities include:

- cash paid to acquire, or a receipt from the sale of, an item of property, plant or equipment;

- cash paid to acquire, or a receipt from the sale of, an intangible asset, such as a brand or trademark;

- cash paid to acquire, or a receipt from the sale of, a separate business;

- cash paid to acquire, or a receipt from the sale of, an equity or debt instrument in another entity, such as a joint venture; and

- cash given as an advance or loan to another entity, or the repayment of such items.

Cash inflows or outflows arising from the sale or acquisition of a business should be shown as a net figure and identified separately in the cash flow statement. As listed above, such cash flows form part of an entity's investing activities. [IAS 7.39]

It is important to remember that when an asset is sold, not only will there be a cash inflow from the proceeds of the sale but the entity will also make a profit or loss on the transaction. The profit or loss itself is not a cash flow and therefore does not form part of the cash flow statement. It is the cash proceeds received on the sale that are reported in the cash flow statement.

Illustration 4

An item of plant was disposed of for cash proceeds of CU1,000. The carrying amount of the item of plant at the date of the sale was:

	CU
Cost	3,000
Less: Accumulated depreciation	1,300
Carrying amount	1,700

A loss of CU700 (the difference between the proceeds of CU1,000 and the carrying amount of CU1,700) should be recognised in the income statement and the non-current asset should be removed from the balance sheet. This loss should be excluded when calculating cash flows from operating activities for the cash flow statement.

The CU1,000 cash proceeds received should be recognised in the cash flow statement as an investing activity – "proceeds from sale of property, plant and equipment".

The cash flows that occur as a result of making an acquisition of a business, or from disposal of a business, have a direct impact on the entity's cash flows reported in the period and its likely future cash flows. Such information should therefore be separated out, so that a user of the financial statements is able to make a better assessment about cash flows that are likely to be ongoing and those that are not. IAS 7 specifically requires the following information to be disclosed in aggregate for acquisitions and sales of businesses, including subsidiaries, made during the period: [IAS 7.40]

- the total proceeds from a sale of businesses or the consideration paid to acquire businesses, separately identifying the proportion that is cash;

- the amount of cash that is included in the businesses being purchased or sold; and

- a summary of the assets and liabilities, other than cash, of the businesses acquired or disposed of.

7 Cash Flows from Financing Activities

Financing activities change the amount and composition of an entity's equity capital and borrowings. Such activities are included under a separate heading in the cash flow statement because this analysis provides useful information on the amount of cash generated by the entity that will be needed to service its financing activities. Examples of financing activities are:

- cash proceeds received from issuing shares in the entity;

- cash paid to redeem shares in the entity;

- cash proceeds received from issuing debt instruments, such as debentures, bonds or long-term borrowings;

- cash paid to repay debt instruments; and

- the capital element in finance lease payments made during the period.

As discussed above, dividends paid by an entity may also form part of an entity's financing activities depending on the analysis chosen.

It is important to remember that it is cash movements that are reflected in the cash flow statement, so, for example, where shares are issued above their par value, the amount recorded in the cash flow statement is a single figure for the total cash received (being the par value and any share premium recognised). The same principle applies to dividends paid by an entity, since dividends recognised elsewhere in the financial statements may include amounts that have been proposed and declared at the balance sheet date, although not yet paid. The cash flow statement only recognises the actual outflow of cash to investors.

Illustration 5

An entity has declared preference dividends for the year of CU7,000 (based on its 7% CU100,000 irredeemable preference shares in issue).

At the start of the year, there was a balance of CU3,500 for preference dividends payable.

At the end of the year no amount was owing to preference shareholders in respect of dividends.

The preference dividend paid for the year is not simply the CU7,000 declared, as this amount needs to be adjusted for any opening and closing balances.

	CU
Opening balance	3,500
Declared in the year	7,000
Less: Closing balance	-
Dividend paid	10,500

8 Sundry Items

8.1 Foreign currency cash flows

Where cash flows arise in a foreign currency they should be translated into the entity's functional currency at the exchange rate on the date that the cash flow occurred. [IAS 7.25]

Accounting for foreign currency transactions is dealt with in IAS 21 *Accounting for the effects of changes in foreign exchange rates*. The translation of foreign currency cash flows should be consistent with the application of IAS 21. The average exchange rate for the period may be used as an approximation to the actual exchange rate although an entity is not permitted to use the rate at the balance sheet date to translate foreign currency cash flows.

Where an entity has a foreign subsidiary, its cash flows should be translated to the functional currency at the exchange rates on the dates that the cash flows occurred. [IAS 7.26]

8.2 Non-cash transactions

Investing and financing transactions that do not impact on cash, for example the conversion of debt to equity, should not be included in the cash flow statement. The effect of such transactions should be disclosed elsewhere in the financial statements as appropriate. [IAS 7.43]

8.3 Additional disclosures

An entity should disclose the components of cash and provide a reconciliation between this and the corresponding items in the balance sheet. [IAS 7.45]

If an entity has any significant cash balances that are restricted in some way and therefore are not available for use by the entity this should be explained. [IAS 7.48]

Other disclosures are required where such additional information is relevant to users in their understanding of an entity's financial statements. Additional useful disclosures may include, for example, the amount of an entity's undrawn borrowings and a split of cash flow information to identify the flows that are needed to maintain an entity's current operating capacity and those which increase its capacity.

9 Chapter Review

This chapter has been concerned with cash flow statements. In particular it has focussed on identifying and disclosing the key elements of a cash flow statement.

This chapter has covered:

- the objectives, scope, definitions and disclosure requirements of IAS 7;

- cash flows arising from operating activities;

- cash flows arising from investing activities; and

- cash flows arising from financing activities.

Chapter 22
SEGMENT REPORTING

1 Business Context

Most multinational entities sell a number of products and services in different markets or geographical locations which may be regarded as different segments. The total profitability of an entity will depend on the performance of each of these segments. For some entities the key segments will be based on products and services, for others it will be by geographical area. In each case, the separate management and performance measurement of individual segments is essential, as while one product or geographical area may be performing well, another may be failing.

While management will have access to performance data on each separate part of the business, the published income statement only reports the aggregate performance of the entity. Overall profitability is important, but additional information is needed by external users to understand fully the businesses hidden below this top level reporting.

IAS 14 *Segment reporting* provides the link between the business operations and the main components of the financial statements by requiring information to be disaggregated into each major product or geographical area. Investors can therefore make better assessments of the performance of each part of the business, leading to a better understanding of the business as a whole.

A related business issue occurs when an entity closes or discontinues a part of its overall business activity. Management will have assessed the impact of the closure on its future profitability, but users of the financial statements, be they investors or other stakeholders, will want to make their own assessment. IFRS 5 *Non-current assets held for sale and discontinued operations* provides an analysis not of future profit but of the contribution of the discontinued element to the current year's profit (or loss), i.e. the part that will not be included in future years' profits.

Showing information about segments and discontinued operations separately allows users of financial statements to make relevant future projections of cash flows, financial position and earnings-generating capacity.

2 Chapter Objectives

This chapter deals with the requirement to produce information on the entity's different segments, business or geographical, in accordance with IAS 14. It also deals with the part of IFRS 5 about the reporting requirements where the entity has discontinued operations during the period.

On completion of this chapter you should be able to:

- demonstrate a knowledge of the objectives and scope of IAS 14;
- demonstrate a knowledge of the important terminology used when identifying and disclosing segmental information;
- understand how to identify reportable segments;

- demonstrate a knowledge of the key disclosures required for reportable segments;

- understand the definition of discontinued operations according to IFRS 5; and

- demonstrate knowledge of the key disclosures required for discontinued operations.

3 Objectives, Scope and Definitions of IAS 14

The objective of IAS 14 is to set out principles for reporting financial information by segment to help users better understand how an entity has performed in past periods. In addition, users should be able to assess the entity's risks and returns in order to make an informed judgement about the overall business operations.

A segment can generally be thought of as a distinguishable component of the entity that is subject to risks and returns which are different from those of the entity's other components. [IAS 14.9]

IAS 14 should be applied by entities whose equity and debt are publicly traded or are in the process of issuing equity or debt in public securities markets. [IAS 14.3]

Other entities are encouraged to apply IAS 14. Where an entity chooses to disclose segmental information on a voluntary basis, it should do so in accordance with the requirements of the standard. [IAS 14.5]

If an entity is required to present segment information and it prepares both consolidated and entity only financial statements, the segmental information is only required in the consolidated statements. If, however, the equity of a subsidiary, associate or joint venture entity of the group is traded publicly then the entity should meet the requirements of IAS 14 in its individual financial statements. [IAS 14.6, 14.7]

4 Overview of IAS 14

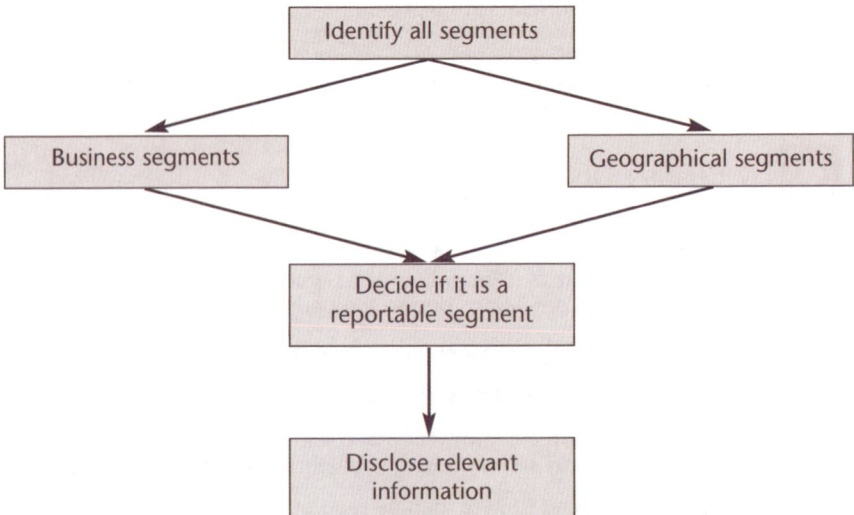

Identify all segments

Business segments

Geographical segments

Decide if it is a reportable segment

Disclose relevant information

5 Segment Reporting

5.1 Identifying segments

IAS 14 makes a distinction between business and geographical segments. Business segments are identified by reference to the different goods and services provided by an entity, for example general retail and financial services. The distinguishable components may provide individual goods or services, or a group of related goods or services. It is, however, a requirement that the risks and returns of each component are different from those of other such segments. [IAS 14.9]

The entity will need to consider the different operations of the business in relation to, for example, the nature of the products or the production process used, whether goods are sold to different classes of customer, whether different distribution systems are used and whether there are any regulatory requirements that only apply to part of the entity's operations.

Geographical segments arise when an entity is engaged in the provision of goods and services in different economic environments. The identifiable components again need to have risks and returns different to those of components operating in different geographical regions. IAS 14 identifies a number of considerations that should be assessed to help identify different geographical segments. These considerations include an assessment of the economic and political conditions, of whether special risks are associated with operating in a particular area and the impact of currency risk and of any exchange control regulations. In addition, it will be appropriate to consider the distance between operations and the nature of the relationships between operations in different areas. [IAS 14.9]

The risks and returns of an entity may be influenced by both the locations in which the products are manufactured and the locations of the customers that the goods are sold to. IAS 14 therefore allows geographical segments to be based on either location.

Segments that have been identified as being important for internal reporting purposes to the board of directors and chief executive officer should form the basis on which segments are reported on an external basis. If, however, the internal reporting structure is not based on the business and geographical split for segments, then such segments should be identified by applying the definitions discussed above. It may be appropriate to consider operations at a lower level than that reported for internal purposes where segments do not meet the definitions described above. [IAS 14.31, 14.32]

5.2 Reportable segments

A reportable segment is either a business or geographical segment that has been identified in accordance with the criteria set out above and meets certain size criteria as described below. [IAS 14.9]

Although identifiable segments will generally be reported separately, it may be possible to group segments together where, for example, the individual segments are substantially similar. Such an assessment should be made with specific reference to similarities in their long-term performance and in the factors that were considered when defining segments. [IAS 14.34]

A segment is considered to be reportable if the majority of its revenue is earned from external customers and it meets one of the specified size tests detailed below. [IAS 14.35]

The focus on sales to external customers avoids the need to report internal transactions (such as those that occur between different business divisions). However, the nature of some businesses, for example entities operating in the oil industry, means that vertically integrated activities are reported separately for internal reporting purposes. In such circumstances separate reporting externally is encouraged. If the entity does not do so, then selling segments should be combined with buying segments to identify segments that do meet the IAS 14 criteria. If no such reasonable basis exists then a selling segment should be identified as an 'unallocated' reconciling item. [IAS 14.41]

The first requirement in relation to a reportable segment is that the majority of its revenue is earned from external customers. There are then three separate size tests:

- segment revenue (including internal sales) as a percentage of total entity revenue (including internal sales);

- segment profit or loss as a percentage of total entity profit or loss; and

- segment assets as a percentage of total entity assets. This comparison is made on a gross basis.

If any one of these tests results in a percentage of 10% or more, then the segment is reportable.

A segment that does not meet the size thresholds may still be reported separately on a voluntary basis. The thresholds just determine when a segment is required to be reported separately. A number of similar internally reported segments that individually do not meet the size criteria may be combined and reported as one segment. [IAS 14.36]

Where a segment was separately reported in the previous period, it should continue to be reported separately even if the thresholds are not met in the current period, where the segment has been identified as being of continuing significance. Equally, where a segment meets the 10% threshold in the current period it should be separately reported for both the current and the previous period even if it was not separately reported in the previous period, assuming that it is practicable to do so. [IAS 14.42, 14.43]

If the reportable segments that have been identified as meeting one of the 10% thresholds do not together represent 75% of the entity's (or group's) external revenue, then additional segments are required to be reported even though they do not meet any of the thresholds. This overall size test is to ensure that all entities present a sufficient level of information regarding their individual activities to ensure that users of the financial statements can make informed economic decisions. [IAS 14.37]

5.3 Reporting formats - primary and secondary formats

Illustration 1

A quoted entity, reports six different types of business to its chief executive.

In the most recent financial year, the sales of these six, as a percentage of total sales (including those to internal customers), were as follows:

Business type	% internal	% external	% total
1	0	40	40
2	0	20	20
3	12	6	18
4	0	9	9
5	0	8	8
6	0	5	5
	12	88	100

The reportable segments are:

Business type	% internal	% external	% total	Notes
1	0	40	40	**reportable segment** because all sales are to external parties and 40% total > 10% threshold test
2	0	20	20	**reportable segment** because all sales are to external parties and 20% total > 10% threshold test
3	12	6	18	**not reportable** (despite 18% total > 10% threshold) because the majority of sales are internal
4	0	9	9	**reportable segment** (despite 9% total < 10% threshold) because all sales are to external parties and the entity needs to report 75% of consolidated, (i.e. external) sales
5	0	8	8	**not reportable** (8% total < 10% threshold)
6	0	5	5	**not reportable** (5% total < 10% threshold)
	12	88	100	

The override rule comes into play: 75% of the 88% external sales is 66%, so business types 1 and 2 are insufficient; business type 4 is also needed.

The main source of an entity's risks and returns, i.e. its different products and services or its different locations, should be used to identify its primary reporting format for segment information. Once the primary reporting format has been identified the other set of segmental information becomes its secondary reporting format. So if geographical segments are the primary reporting format, business segments will be the secondary. [IAS 14.26]

The structure and focus of internal management reporting should be used to identify the primary and secondary reporting formats. If, however, an entity's risks and rewards are strongly affected by both its products and services and its geographical areas then the primary reporting format is considered to be by business segment. Where internal reporting is not based on a business or geographical basis, then management should use the risks and rewards analysis to determine the primary reporting format. [IAS 14.27]

5.4 What has to be reported?

Since the purpose of disclosing segmental information is to provide additional information to the users of the financial statements, information should be presented using the accounting policies adopted for the presentation of the financial statements of the entity. [IAS 14.44]

The disclosure requirements differ for the primary and secondary formats. The main disclosure requirements for each reportable segment are summarised in the table below: [IAS 14.49 – 14.72]

	Primary	Secondary
Segment revenue: internal	yes	
Segment revenue: external	yes	yes
Segment result	yes	
Segment assets	yes	yes
Segment liabilities	yes	
Segment acquisitions of non-current assets	yes	yes
Segment depreciation/amortisation	yes	
Significant other non-cash expenses forming part of segment expenses	yes	

Segment revenue is that directly attributable to the segment and an allocation on a reasonable basis of total revenue of the entity (or group) reported in the income statement that is directly attributable to a segment. Segment revenue should include both sales to external parties and to other reported segments; it will also include the entity's share of revenue from joint ventures where these are accounted for by using the proportional consolidation basis. Where a share of the entity's associates and joint ventures profits or losses are included in consolidated revenue, then the segment revenue will include a share of these also. [IAS 14.16]

Segment expenses are those directly attributable to the segment and an allocation on a reasonable basis of the expenses that result from the normal operating activities of the entity. Such amounts exclude interest and tax, as well as general administrative expenses which arise at the entity level rather than at a segment level. Segment expenses also specifically exclude losses arising on the sale of investments and an entity's share of losses arising from associates or joint ventures that have been equity accounted for. [IAS 14.16]

The segment result is simply segment revenue less segment expenses.

Segment assets and liabilities are those operating assets and liabilities that are used by the segment in its operating activities. Such assets and liabilities will be either directly used by the segment or allocated to segments on a reasonable basis. Segment assets and liabilities do not include tax recoverables or payables. This may mean that there are centrally held assets and liabilities that are not allocated to any specific segment. Also, where assets are jointly held by more than one segment, they should only be allocated to individual segments if the related revenues and expenses are also allocated. [IAS 14.16, 14.47]

Illustration 2

An entity operates in several business segments including retailing. The leasehold shop premises and inventories held within those shops can be allocated to the retailing segment. The entity's head office assets, tax assets and liabilities and borrowings cannot be apportioned between the retailing and other segments. Distribution and warehousing facilities could be apportioned on a reasonable basis between those segments that use the assets.

In addition to these disclosures an entity is encouraged to identify any significant amounts that have been included in segment revenue and expense for its primary reporting format. This disclosure is designed to provide additional information on the performance of a segment. [IAS 14.59]

Segment cash flow information is encouraged by IAS 7 *Cash flow statements*. Where such information is provided, the disclosures in respect of non-cash amounts, such as depreciation, are not required. [IAS 14.63]

As part of the primary reporting format disclosures, a detailed reconciliation with the full financial statements should be provided for the main line items in the segmental information, for example revenue, results, assets and liabilities. [IAS 14.67]

Where an entity's primary reporting format is by geographical segment based on the location of assets and these locations are not similar to the locations of the entity's customers then the entity should also disclose revenue to external parties based on customer location. This additional breakdown of segment revenue is only required where the customer-based geographical segment revenue is 10% or more of total entity revenue. Similar disclosures are required where the primary segment disclosures are based on customer-located geographical segments and the location of the segment assets is different. [IAS 14.71, 14.72]

It is possible that an internally reported business or geographical segment may represent 10% of total external revenue but is not included as a reportable external segment because the majority of its sales are to internal customers. In this case this fact should be disclosed along with revenue split between internal and external sales. [IAS 14.74]

Inter-segment sales should be measured at the actual amount at which the transfers took place. This pricing basis should be disclosed along with any changes in this basis during the period. [IAS 14.75]

Any changes in the accounting policies for segment reporting that significantly affect the segment reporting should be highlighted and comparative segment information restated to reflect this change where practicable to do so. If this leads to a change in the identification of segments and the comparative segments have not been restated because it is not practicable to do so then the old and new segment basis should both be reported in the year of change. This is to ensure that some useful comparison can still take place. [IAS 14.76]

6 Discontinued Operations: IFRS 5 - Presentation and Disclosure

6.1 Discontinued operations

Investors need to evaluate the financial effects of discontinued operations on future operations, IFRS 5 provides information to assist them in doing this.

Disclosure is required when an entity discontinues a component of its activities. Disclosure of a discontinued operation is often made before the component is discontinued i.e. when it is classified as held for sale.

A component of an entity comprises operations and cash flows that can be clearly distinguished, operationally and for financial reporting purposes, from the rest of the entity.

A discontinued operation is a component of an entity that either has been disposed of or is classified as held for sale. The component should represent a separate major business line or geographical area of the entity's operations. The effective closure of the component should be part of a single plan.

6.2 Disclosure

The objective of the disclosures is to provide users of the financial statements with sufficient information so that they are able to evaluate the financial effect of discontinued operations. [IFRS 5.30]

The discontinued operation's profit or loss after tax should be disclosed as a single figure on the face of the income statement. A break down on the face of the income statement or within the notes to the financial statements should show the revenue, expenses, pre-tax profit or loss, the related income tax expense and the profit or loss on asset disposals.

An entity should also disclose for a discontinued operation the net cash flows attributable to the operating, investing and financing activities of that operation.

6.3 Prior periods

Results in the income statement reported for prior periods should be restated so that they reflect all operations that have been discontinued by the end of the current year.

Where adjustments are made to amounts that were presented as part of discontinued operations in a prior period, they should be separately disclosed as part of discontinued operations in the current period and the nature of such adjustments explained. Adjustments may become necessary where there was some element of uncertainty as to, say, the disposal price. The assets and liabilities of a discontinued subsidiary in the prior period balance should not be reclassified as held for sale.

Illustration 3

An entity has classified a subsidiary as held for sale during the current year. It is not necessary for the subsidiary to have been previously reported as a separate business segment for it to be separately presented as a discontinued operation. A separate subsidiary is a component of the entity as its operations and cash flows are capable of being separately identified both operationally and for financial reporting purposes. By being classified as held for sale it meets all the criteria of a discontinued activity.

The prior period income statement and note disclosures shall be re-presented so that they relate to all operations discontinued by the current year end. But the assets and liabilities of the subsidiary in the prior period balance sheet are not reclassified as held for sale.

6.4 Reclassification

Reclassification from events occurring after the balance sheet date is not permitted by IFRS 5. Where the criteria for discontinuance are satisfied after the balance sheet date, the operation cannot be retrospectively classed as a discontinued operation. But details of the discontinuance should be disclosed in the notes to the financial statements.

7 Chapter Review

This chapter has been concerned with segment reporting and discontinued operations. Key issues relating to IAS 14 have been the identification of reportable segments and the nature of the disclosure requirements. Key issues relating to IFRS 5 have been the identification of discontinued activities and the required disclosure and presentation requirements.

This chapter has covered:

- the objective and scope of IAS 14;

- the nature of segmental reporting;

- an overview of IAS 14;

- reportable segments and reporting formats;

- segment disclosure requirements;

- identification of discontinued activities; and

- disclosure and presentation of discontinued activities in accordance with IFRS 5.

Chapter 23
INTERIM REPORTING

1 Business Context

Financial information is used by interested parties to assess an entity's financial performance and position, its ability to generate future cash flows and its liquidity. The better the quality of the information available and the more frequently it is made available, the more informed are the decisions investors can make leading to greater market efficiency. Good quality interim accounting information may assist timely feedback on analysts' predictions of profits for the current year to date.

While other standards address the quality of information in the annual report, IAS 34 *Interim financial reporting* deals with interim reporting and ensures that this information is relevant and reliable.

2 Chapter Objectives

This chapter deals with the preparation of interim reports under IAS 34. The standard does not require the preparation of interim financial statements; it looks at the information that should be presented if such a statement is prepared. National regulators often require the preparation of interim statements where an entity's equity or debt is publicly traded. IAS 34 specifies the minimum content that should be included in an interim report that is described as conforming to international standards and sets out principles on recognition and measurement.

On completion of this chapter you should be able to:

- demonstrate a knowledge of the objectives, scope and terminology of IAS 34;

- understand the key items contained within interim financial reports and the form of those reports;

- determine the current and comparative interim reporting periods required by IAS 34;

- apply recognition and measurement criteria to interim financial reports;

- demonstrate an understanding of the types of estimates that are permitted in interim financial reports; and

- apply IAS 34 knowledge and understanding in particular circumstances through basic calculations.

3 Objectives, Scope and Definitions of IAS 34

The objectives of IAS 34 are to prescribe:

- the minimum content to be included in a set of interim financial reports; and

- the recognition and measurement principles for an interim period.

An interim financial report is defined as being a financial report containing either a complete set of financial statements (as described in IAS 1 *Presentation of financial statements*) or a set of condensed financial statements for an interim period. [IAS 34.4]

An 'interim period' is any financial reporting period which is shorter than a full financial year. [IAS 34.4]

IAS 34 does not set out which entities should be required to publish interim financial reports, nor how frequently interim reports should be produced (thus while half-yearly or quarterly interim reports are usual, any period of less than a year can be used) nor how soon after the end of an interim period interim reports should be produced. However, the IASB encourages publicly traded entities to prepare interim financial information in accordance with IAS 34. It also encourages the preparation of interim reports at least at the end of the first half of a financial year, with this information being presented within 60 days of end of this period.

However, where governments, or other regulators, require entities to publish interim financial reports, then IAS 34 determines the nature and minimum content that should be included in them.

4 Contents and Form

4.1 Contents

An interim financial report should, as a minimum, include: [IAS 34.8]

- a condensed balance sheet;

- a condensed income statement;

- a condensed statement showing either:

  - all changes in equity; or

  - changes in equity other than those arising from capital transactions with owners and distributions to owners;

- a condensed cash flow statement; and

- explanatory notes.

4.2 Form

An entity may choose to publish a complete set of financial statements for an interim period. Where a complete set of financial statements is prepared it should be in accordance with IAS 1 rather than IAS 34 even if it is for an interim period. However, it is more likely that an entity will choose to publish condensed information in its interim financial statements as it is less onerous to prepare. [IAS 34.9]

'Condensed' means that each of the headings and sub-totals presented in the entity's most recent annual financial statements are required, but there is no requirement to include greater detail unless this is specifically required by IAS 34. Generally there is no requirement to update detailed notes presented in the last full financial statements because a user will have access to this previously published information. However, an entity should provide additional line items and headings if their omission would be misleading to users of the interim information. [IAS 34.10]

IAS 34 requires an entity to present both basic and fully diluted earnings per share (EPS) figures, calculated for the interim period, on the face of the income statement. [IAS 34.11]

4.3 Selected explanatory notes

As mentioned above, relatively insignificant updates to the information presented in the notes to the most recent full financial statements are not required in an interim report. A user of the financial statements will have the last set of financial statements and a comparison of these with the condensed reports presented in the interim statement should provide enough information to ensure that an informed decision about the current financial position of the entity can be made. However, some information is essential to the understanding of the interim report and therefore IAS 34 does require that it is presented in the notes to the interim report. This information should normally be prepared on a year-to-date basis (i.e. by treating the interim period as distinct in its own right rather than as part of a longer period). Other information should be presented if the omission of such information would affect the economic decisions of users of the information.

Information presented and measured during an interim period is based on the facts for that interim period. The overriding goal is for a user of the interim report to understand the information that is presented within it on a stand alone basis.

The use of estimates is inherent in the preparation of all financial information, including that contained in an interim report. Where an estimate made in an interim period changes significantly in the following interim period, but no separate financial information has been presented for the following interim period, an entity should explain this change in the full financial statements. This additional disclosure is only required where the change is significant, for example where the original assessment of a fall in the value of an asset has changed due to the outcome of an event that happened in the remaining part of the financial year. [IAS 34.26]

The explanatory information required to be presented in the notes to the interim financial statements is set out below. [IAS 34.16]

- In preparing an interim report an entity should apply the same accounting policies and methods of computation that were followed and used for the preparation of its most recent annual financial statements. This provides consistency of measurement and presentation and assists comparability. An entity is required to disclose this fact clearly in the interim report. Where it has been necessary to adopt a different policy or method, for example following the publication of a new international standard, this should be fully explained, providing a description of the nature and effect of the change. Where an entity has changed its accounting policy during an interim period it should restate comparative interim period results in line with IAS 8 *Accounting policies, changes in accounting estimates and errors.* [IAS 34.43]

- Many businesses are seasonal in nature or go through cycles; for example, a retail outlet selling ice-cream will make the majority of its sales during the summer months. An interim period which only covers the winter months is likely to be very different to one covering the summer months for such an entity. Information should therefore be disclosed to explain this difference. In seasonal businesses an entity is encouraged to present additional comparative information as well as that set out in the next section.

- An entity should disclose items that are unusual in nature, size or incidence in the current period, or occurred in the prior period where they impact the current interim period in a way that might affect the economic decisions made by a user of the interim report.

- Where an entity is required to present segmental information in its annual financial statements as required by IAS 14 *Segmental reporting*, it should report the segmental results, including identifying segmental revenue, for its business or geographical segments as appropriate.

- An entity is required to disclose information on significant events that have occurred after the end of the interim period in the same way as it does in its full financial statements.

- An entity should include information on the effect of any changes in composition of the entity during the interim period. Such changes might include, for example, the acquisition or disposal of a significant subsidiary, a discontinued operation being identified or the restructuring of the entity's main businesses.

- Additional information is also required in relation to changes in the capital structure of the entity; this might be through a share issue or the repayment of debt. Information in relation to an entity's contingent liabilities or contingent assets should be updated for changes since the last annual balance sheet date and any dividends paid during the period should be disclosed.

If an entity's interim financial reports have been prepared to comply with IAS 34, this fact should be disclosed. [IAS 34.19]

5 Reporting Periods

Interim reports should include interim financial statements (condensed or complete) for periods as follows: [IAS 34.20]

Statement	Current interim period	Comparative
Balance sheet	At end of the current interim period	At end of the immediately preceding financial year
Income statement	For: • the current interim period; and • cumulatively for year-to-date (where the interim period is not on a year-to-date basis)	For the comparable interim periods: • same interim period; and • cumulatively for year-to-date of the immediately preceding financial year
Statement of changes in equity	Cumulatively for year-to-date	Year-to-date of the immediately preceding financial year
Cash flow statement	Cumulatively for year-to-date	Year-to-date of the immediately preceding financial year

Illustration 1

An entity has a 31 March financial year end, and is about to present its half-yearly interim financial statements for the six months to 30 September 2003.

The relevant dates for which each interim financial statement needs to be prepared for the current period and for the comparative period(s) are:

Statement	Current interim period	Comparative
Balance sheets: as at	30 September 2003	31 March 2003
Income statements: 6 months ending	30 September 2003	30 September 2002
Statement of changes in equity: 6 months ending	30 September 2003	30 September 2002
Cash flow statement: 6 months ending	30 September 2003	30 September 2002

6 Recognition and Measurement

There are two possible approaches to recognition and measurement in interim financial statements:

- *the discrete approach*: where each interim period stands alone as an independent reporting period; or

- *the integral approach*: where each interim period is seen as part of the larger accounting year to which it belongs, where revenues and costs would be recognised as a proportion of the annual totals.

In most circumstances IAS 34 requires the discrete approach, i.e. year-to-date basis. As a result, the entity should apply the same accounting policies in its interim financial statements as in its annual financial statements making measurements for the interim period on a year-to-date basis. This basis may result in a different accounting treatment being used in the full financial statements compared with that for the interim period as a result of events that occur following the interim period. [IAS 34.28]

Revenues that are received, or costs that are incurred, only at certain points in time within a financial year should not be spread over the full year by anticipating or deferring them; instead they should be recognised as they become receivable or are incurred. As an example, if it is appropriate to accrue a government grant throughout the year, then a consistent treatment should be followed during the interim period. [IAS 34.37, 34.39]

Illustration 2

An entity's accounting year ends on 31 December each year and it is currently preparing interim financial statements for the half year to 30 June 2004. It has a contractual agreement with its staff that it will pay them an annual bonus equal to 10% of their annual salary if the full year's output exceeds 1 million units. Budgeted output is 1.4 million units and the entity has achieved budgeted output during the first six months of the year. Annual salaries are estimated to be CU100 million, with the cost in the first half year to 30 June being CU45 million.

It is probable that the bonus will be paid, given that the actual output already achieved in the year is in line with budgeted figures, which exceed the required level of output. So a bonus of CU4.5 million should be recognised in the interim financial statements at 30 June 2004.

Illustration 3

An entity's accounting year ends on 31 December 2004, and it is currently preparing interim financial statements for the half year to 30 June 2004.

The price of its products tends to vary. At 30 June 2004, it has inventories of 100,000 units, at a cost per unit of CU1.40. The net realisable value of the inventories is CU1.20 per unit at 30 June 2004. The expected net realisable value of the inventories at 31 December 2004 is CU1.55 per unit.

The value of the inventories in the interim financial statements at 30 June 2004 is the lower of cost and NRV at 30 June 2004. This is:

$$100,000 \times CU1.20 \qquad = \qquad CU120,000$$

Although a year-to-date approach is generally applied for the preparation of interim reports, IAS 34 requires that income tax should be accrued based on the entity's best estimate of what the weighted average annual tax rate will be. However, the taxable profit is that for the interim financial reporting period only (i.e. it is not a proportion of the annual profit).

Illustration 4

An entity's accounting year ends on 31 December 2004, and it is currently preparing interim financial statements for the half year to 30 June 2004.

Its profit before tax for the 6 month period to 30 June 2004 is CU6 million. The business is seasonal and the profit before tax for the six months to 31 December 2004 is almost certain to be CU10 million. Income tax is calculated as 25% of reported annual profit before tax if it does not exceed CU10 million. If annual profit before tax exceeds CU10 million the tax rate on the whole amount is 30%.

The taxation charge in the interim financial statements is based upon the weighted average rate for the year. In this case the entity's tax rate for the year is expected to be 30%. The taxation charge in the interim financial statements will be CU1.8 million.

7 Use of Estimates

The preparation of both annual and interim financial reports relies on the use of estimates in measuring assets and liabilities. The measurement procedures in any period should be designed to ensure that the resulting estimates are reliable. It is often the case that the preparation of an interim financial report will require a greater use of estimation methods than the preparation of the annual financial reports. [IAS 34.41]

IAS 34 sets out a number of examples where different estimation methods are used at the interim period compared with an entity's financial year-end, for example:

- *Inventories*: At the year-end it is best practice to perform a full stock take to ensure that the level of inventories recorded in the financial statements is accurate. However, such a procedure is not necessarily required at the interim reporting date.

- *Contingencies*: While contingencies should be disclosed in interim reports, it is not always necessary to obtain formal reports from experts (on such matters as litigation and technical claims) in order to verify the amount of such contingencies at the interim date.

- *Provisions*: The inclusion in the financial statements of certain provisions, such as those for warranties or environmental damage, may require the use of experts. Whilst experts may be engaged to assist with the full year-end estimates, at the interim period it may be appropriate instead to update the information that was provided at the previous year end.

8 Chapter Review

The key issues covered in this chapter deal with recognition, measurement and disclosure in interim financial statements. IAS 34 does not require the preparation of interim financial statements but it does specify the minimum content of such reports where they are prepared and the principles to be applied within them.

This chapter has covered:

- the objectives, scope and terminology of IAS 34;

- the form and content of interim financial reports;

- interim reporting periods;

- recognition and measurement criteria in interim financial reports; and

- the calculation of estimates in interim financial reports.

Chapter 24
EARNINGS PER SHARE

1 Business Context

A key performance measure of an entity is its earnings per share (EPS) figure. It is an important element of the price earnings ratio which is often used for business valuation purposes. However, EPS is only as good as the basis on which it has been calculated. If there were no guidelines setting out how such a measure should be calculated then entities would have the ability to derive a measure that presented a favourable position even where this was not the reality.

Put simply, EPS is calculated as reported profits divided by the number of shares in issue. Although entities adopt different accounting policies which may affect their reported profits, they are required to calculate the number of shares in a consistent manner. Setting such guidelines minimises an entity's ability to report an EPS figure that has been adjusted to fit particular circumstances. Consistency of calculation improves an entity's financial reporting and aids the ability of users to make useful comparisons between different entities.

2 Chapter Objectives

On completion of this chapter you should be able to:

- understand the purpose of earnings per share and the objective of IAS 33 *Earnings per share;*

- demonstrate a knowledge of the calculation of basic EPS;

- be able to adjust EPS for changes in the number of shares resulting from, for example, a bonus issue;

- understand what diluted and adjusted EPS figures are; and

- demonstrate the disclosure requirements within IAS 33.

3 Objectives, Scope and Definitions of IAS 33

The objective of IAS 33 is to set out principles for the calculation and presentation of EPS, to improve performance comparisons between different entities in the same reporting period and between different reporting periods for the same entity. Since EPS is a measure of performance based on the reported profits of the entity, it is important to appreciate that entities may have adopted different accounting policies in calculating their profits.

IAS 33 applies to entities whose ordinary shares are publicly traded or are in the process of being issued in public markets. Where an entity presents both group financial statements and individual entity financial statements, EPS disclosures are only required in the consolidated financial statements. However, an entity is permitted to disclose EPS information in the entity's individual financial statements. [IAS 33.2, 33.4]

4 Basic Earnings Per Share

An entity is required to calculate and present a basic EPS amount based on the profit or loss for the period attributable to the ordinary equity holders of the parent entity. If an entity has reported 'continuing operations' separately then it is also required to report a basic EPS figure based on the continuing profit or loss for the period. [IAS 33.9]

If an entity has discontinued operations during the period an EPS figure should be calculated based on these results. [IAS 33.68]

Basic EPS is calculated by dividing the relevant profit or loss (the numerator) by the weighted average number of ordinary shares outstanding (the denominator) during the period. [IAS 33.10]

$$\frac{\text{Net profit (loss) for the period attributable to ordinary shareholders}}{\text{Weighted average number of ordinary shares outstanding during the period}}$$

Shares should generally be included in the weighted average number of shares from the date the consideration for their issue (this is generally the date of their issue) is receivable.

4.1 Calculating earnings

To arrive at the profit or loss attributable to the ordinary shareholders it is necessary to deduct any dividends or other financing costs in relation to preference shares. Such adjustments will include the financing cost associated with any redemption premium payable on preference shares. The dividends on redeemable preference shares are usually included in the income statement as finance costs in accordance with IAS 32 *Financial instruments: disclosure and presentation*. Where a dividend has not been declared in respect of non-cumulative preference shares, no deduction should be made. However, where an entity has cumulative preference shares, one year of dividend should be deducted regardless of when the dividend is actually declared and paid. [IAS 33.12]

Illustration 1

An entity's income statement shows a profit after tax of CU10,000. The entity has two classes of preference share capital in issue:

- CU10,000 8% redeemable preference shares which are classified as debt within the financial statements. The related dividend has been included in the income statement as a finance cost.

- CU5,000 10% irredeemable preference shares which are classified within equity. The related dividend is included in the statement of changes in equity.

The redeemable preference share dividend has already been deducted in arriving at the profit after tax. The irredeemable preference dividend of CU500 needs to be deducted to arrive at the profit attributable to ordinary shareholders of CU9,500.

4.2 Calculating the weighted average number of ordinary shares

The weighted average number of ordinary shares is used in the calculation of the basic EPS figure. This takes into account changes in the number of shares during the period. The starting point is the number of shares that were outstanding at the beginning of the period. This is then adjusted for shares issued or cancelled during the period. Where the number of shares has changed during the period a time weighting factor should be applied, being the number of days that the shares were outstanding as a proportion of the total number of days in the period.

Illustration 2

An entity has 10m ordinary shares in issue at 1 January 2003. Its year end is 31 December. During 2003 the following events occur:

1 April 2003   2m shares are issued to acquire a subsidiary;

1 October 2003   4m shares are issued to raise cash to repay borrowings.

The weighted average number of ordinary shares is calculated as follows.

Number of shares outstanding at the beginning of the period

10m x 12/12   = 10.0m

2m additional shares issued 1 April as consideration for the acquisition, in existence for the remaining 9 months of the year

2m x 9/12   =   1.5m

4m additional shares issued 1 October for cash, in existence for the remaining 3 months of the year

4m x 3/12   =   1.0m

Weighted average number of shares outstanding = 10.0 + 1.5 + 1.0 = 12.5m

The share issues in Illustration 2 both result in an increase in the entity's resources, in the form of cash and profit-earning net assets respectively. As these additional resources were only available for part of the accounting period, the number of shares has been time weighted proportionately.

But where there has been a change in the number of shares without a corresponding change in the resources of the entity, as with a bonus issue, for example, the weighted average number of shares should be adjusted by assuming that this new number of shares had always been outstanding. This adjustment therefore assumes that the new issue of shares had occurred at the beginning of the earliest period reported. The EPS calculation for comparative periods reported should also be adjusted in respect of such issues.

Examples of where the number of shares change but there is no corresponding change in resources include:

■ *a bonus issue* (or stock dividend). This is where shares are issued to current shareholders for no consideration, i.e. shares given for free. In a stock dividend, shares are issued to the shareholders rather than the entity paying out a cash dividend. In such circumstances the number of shares increases but there is no change to the entity's resources (assets); and

■ *a share split*. This is where the entity splits each share that is currently in issue. For example, an entity currently has 1,000 CU10 shares in issue. The entity is reorganising its funding and therefore wishes to split the shares into CU5 units. Following the share split there will be 2,000 CU5 shares in issue. The resources of the entity have not changed.

Illustration 3

At 1 January 2003 an entity had in issue 20m ordinary shares.

During 2003 the following events took place:

31 May 2003: issue of 6m shares for cash.

30 September 2003: 1 for 2 bonus issue.

Net profit for the year ended 31 December 2003 was CU8m.

EPS for 2003

Weighted average shares:

Weighted average number of shares at the beginning of the year

20m x 12/12 = 20.0m

6m shares issued for cash on 31 May, in existence for 7 months

6m x 7/12 = 3.5m

1 for 2 bonus issue on 30 September – as no additional resources were received, adjust number of shares for the complete period

■ For shares outstanding at the beginning of the year: 20m x $^1/_2$ x 12/12 = 10.0m

■ For shares issued on 31 May: 6m x $^1/_2$ x 7/12 = 1.75m

Weighted average number of shares for the period is:

20.0m + 3.5m + 10.0m + 1.75m = 35.25m

Earnings per share for 2003:

CU8m / 35.25m = CU0.227

5 Diluted Earnings Per Share

IAS 33 also requires an entity to disclose a diluted EPS figure. A diluted EPS figure takes account of any convertible instruments such as convertible preference shares already in issue presenting a performance measure setting out the effect that these will have on the basic EPS calculation if conversion occurs. A dilution is basically a reduction in the EPS figure (or increase in a loss per share) that will result on the conversion of convertible instruments in issue as a result of more shares being in issue. [IAS 33.5]

5.1 Calculation of earnings

The starting point in calculating the profit or loss used in the diluted EPS figure is that for basic EPS. However, following the conversion of the convertible instruments, the entity will no longer have to pay out the financing costs on the convertible instruments. Holders will instead be entitled to participate in the net profit attributable to the ordinary equity holders, through their holdings of the additional shares. Therefore, the net profit should be increased by the financing costs no longer payable on these convertible instruments.

5.2 Calculation of the weighted average number of shares

The weighted average number of shares is that used for basic EPS plus the number of shares that would be issued if the convertible instruments were converted. It is assumed that the conversion took place at the beginning of the earliest period reported, i.e. they had always been in existence. [IAS 33.36]

The conversion of all instruments with the potential to be ordinary shares should be assumed. This embraces not only convertible debt or preference shares but also, for example, share options. All such instruments are included in the calculation if their presumed conversion would lead to a dilution in basic EPS (a decrease in EPS or increase in a loss per share). To establish whether such instruments are dilutive their conversion should be determined using the profit or loss from continuing operations. [IAS 33.41]

Where dilutive share options are held, the proceeds received from their exercise is presumed to have been from the issue of shares at the average market price. If the number of shares from this calculation is less than the actual number of shares required to be issued on exercise then the additional shares are assumed to have been issued for free. [IAS 33.45]

6 Presentation and Disclosure

An entity is required to present both the basic and diluted EPS figures for profit or loss from continuing operations on the face of the income statement. The basic and diluted EPS figures should be presented with equal prominence for all periods reported i.e. comparative figures are also required. The EPS figures are required even where the entity has made a loss during the period, in which case the reported figures will represent a loss per share. [IAS 33.66]

In addition, if the entity has discontinued operations during the period then a basic and diluted EPS figure should be reported based on the discontinued results of the entity. This figure may be presented either on the face of the income statement or as part of the notes. [IAS 33.68, 33.69]

An entity should disclose the following with respect to the basic and diluted EPS figures:

- the amounts used as the numerator in both calculations and a reconciliation of those amounts to the reported profit or loss attributable to the parent entity for the period;

- the weighted average number of ordinary shares used as the denominator for both calculations; and

- a reconciliation of the weighted average number of shares used in the basic EPS calculation to that used for diluted EPS. Individual adjustments should be separately identified in the reconciliation. [IAS 33.70]

If share transactions have taken place after the balance sheet date and the number of shares would have changed significantly from those used in the calculations had the issue taken place before this date, then this fact should be disclosed.

An entity is permitted to report an EPS figure that has been adjusted for specific events in addition to the basic and diluted EPS figures. Examples of such additional EPS figures might be to remove one-off profits or losses that have arisen during the period from, say, the sale of a large piece of machinery. In these circumstances the entity may wish to report a more 'steady' EPS figure. If such additional EPS figures are reported then they should be calculated based on the same weighted average number of shares as for the basic and diluted EPS figures. If the profit or loss figure used in the calculation is not a line item on the face of the income statement then a reconciliation to such an item should be presented. Additional EPS figures should be presented in the notes to the financial statements. [IAS 33.73]

7 Chapter Review

EPS is one of the key performance measures of an entity and its main purpose is to allow users of the financial statements to compare one entity with another in the confidence that both are using the same reporting guidelines.

This chapter has covered:

- understanding the role of EPS as a performance measure;

- demonstrating the calculations required to derive a basic EPS figure;

- understanding the diluted EPS figure; and

- knowing the presentation and disclosure requirements in IAS 33.

Chapter 25
RELATED PARTY DISCLOSURES

1 Business Context

It is generally assumed that directors attempt to promote the interests of the shareholders in their dealings with other entities.

Given the variety of stakeholders who have interests in an entity, there is a risk that some relationships will lead to conflicting interests. Examples might include transactions between entities under common control, for example a parent and a subsidiary, or transactions between an entity and its directors. In these circumstances the normal rules of commercial arrangements may not apply and thus the reported performance of the entity may be distorted.

A conflict of interest may arise where a director seeks to promote his or her self-interest rather than that of the shareholders. In these circumstances, the two parties to the transaction are said to be related to each other and transactions that take place between them to be related party transactions.

Some related party transactions are difficult to identify, for example where no price is charged for the transaction, such as the provision of management services, for free, by a parent to a subsidiary. Another example is where a newly acquired subsidiary terminates long-standing trading arrangements on the instructions of its new parent. It is difficult to identify this 'non-trading' as a related party transaction.

Corporate governance structures seek to control such relationships. As part of this process, IAS 24 *Related party disclosures* aids transparency by requiring disclosure in the financial statements of any such relationships and the transactions stemming from them.

2 Chapter Objectives

This chapter explains the disclosure requirements of IAS 24 in relation to related party transactions. IAS 24 contains no recognition or measurement requirements; it merely requires disclosure of the nature of related party relationships and of any transactions between such parties.

On completion of this chapter you should be able to:

- understand the scope and objectives of IAS 24 on related party disclosures;

- interpret the important terminology and definitions which relate to the identification of related party relationships and transactions;

- understand and demonstrate a knowledge of the key principles concerning related party disclosures in the financial statements; and

- apply knowledge and understanding of IAS 24 in particular circumstances, through the application of its principles to given scenarios.

3 Objectives, Scope and Definition of IAS 24

3.1 Objectives

The principal objective of IAS 24 is to ensure that an entity's financial statements contain the disclosures necessary to draw attention to the possibility that its financial position, and profit or loss, may have been affected by the existence of related parties and by related party transactions.

IAS 24 not only requires transactions with key management personnel, for example the directors, to be disclosed but also ensures that important information about the rewards and incentives available to them are clearly set out in the financial statements.

Knowledge of related party transactions, any outstanding balances with a related party and the nature of related party relationships may affect the assessment of an entity's operations by users of the financial statements. Such assessments are likely to include the risks and opportunities facing an entity.

Related party relationships are, however, a normal feature of commerce and business, so IAS 24 does not attempt to prevent such relationships or impute revised values to related party transactions.

The key emphasis of IAS 24 is that appropriate disclosure is made.

3.2 Scope

IAS 24 should be applied in identifying whether a related party relationship exists and whether related party transactions have taken place in the period. Its application is also required in identifying whether there are any outstanding balances between the entity and a related party. The standard also sets out the circumstances in which disclosures are appropriate and what those disclosures should be. [IAS 24.2]

IAS 24 requires the disclosure of related party transactions and outstanding balances with related parties in the separate financial statements of a parent entity. Such disclosures should also be made in the financial statements of an investor in a joint venture and a venturer where appropriate. [IAS 24.3]

Related party transactions and outstanding balances arising from transactions with other entities in a group are disclosed in an individual entity's financial statements, although such intra-group transactions are eliminated on consolidation in the financial statements of the group.

3.3 Related parties

A party may be related to an entity in a number of ways. Some related party relationships are easier to identify than others. For example a joint venture undertaking of an entity is related to that entity, as are the key management personnel of an entity or its parent.

The term 'key management personnel' includes the directors but goes much wider to include any person who has authority or responsibility for running the business. Because such personnel are key to the successful operation of the entity, the definition of a related party extends to the close members of their family and any entity that is controlled, jointly controlled or significantly influenced by either the key management personnel or a close member of their family. [IAS 24.9]

Control is the ability to obtain benefits by governing the financial and operating policies of an entity. Joint control is the sharing of control through a contractual arrangement and significant influence is the ability to participate, rather than control, the financial and operating policy decisions. [IAS 24.9]

Close members of family of an individual are family members who may be expected to influence, or be influenced by, that individual in their dealings with the entity. Examples of close family members include the individual's domestic partner and any dependants of the individual or of his or her partner. [IAS 24.9]

Other relationships that are specifically identified as being a related party include a post-employment benefit plan for the benefit of the entity's employees. [IAS 24.9]

4 Substance over Form

In identifying a related party relationship, attention should be directed to the substance of the relationship rather than focusing on its legal form. For example, two entities that have a common director are not necessarily related parties nor are two venturers purely because they share joint control over a joint venture. Significant volumes of business with a customer or supplier do not necessarily create a related party relationship with them.

Illustration 1

Mint is an entity that complies with the minimum requirements of IAS 24. The following relationships have been identified:

(1) Toffee is a separate entity in which one of Mint's junior managers owns 10% of the share capital.

This is not a related party. A junior manager is unlikely to be a member of 'key management personnel' in Mint and with only a 10% holding in Toffee is unlikely to have significant influence over it.

(2) The daughter of a director of Mint.

The daughter is a related party. The director is a related party as a member of 'key management personnel' and his or her daughter falls within the definition of close family members.

(3) A director of Mint owns 60% of the share capital of another entity called Chocolate.

Chocolate is a related party as it is under the control of a member of 'key management personnel'.

(4) Miss Butterscotch owns 25% of the share capital of Mint.

Miss Butterscotch is probably a related party since a 25% shareholding is likely to provide her with the ability to exert significant influence. This will depend, however, on who owns the remaining 75% holding.

(5) A director of Mint is also a director of Sugar (which is independent of Mint) but is not a shareholder in either entity.

If the director is one amongst many on the board of Sugar and there are no other directors on both the boards of Mint and Sugar, then it is unlikely that there is common control or influence. The act of merely being a director on both boards does not mean that the second entity is automatically a related party of the first entity. There is probably no related party relationship.

(6) Cream is an entity owned by the niece of the finance director of Mint.

The niece is not a sufficiently close relative of Mint's finance director for Cream to constitute a related party.

5 Related Party Transactions

A related party transaction is defined as a transfer of resources, services or obligations between related parties, regardless of whether a price is charged. [IAS 24.9]

In simple terms this covers any transaction between two related parties even if the transactions takes place at a full arm's length price, i.e. a market price. Contrast this with the common practice whereby employees receive goods or services at reduced prices or for free; if the employees fall within the definition of key management personnel, such transactions will be between related parties and the entity will need to disclose them.

IAS 24 is based on the principle that it is the identification of the related party relationship that triggers the disclosure requirements.

6 Disclosures

IAS 24 requires an entity to disclose the relationship between an entity and its parent and subsidiaries. This relationship is seen as so important to users of the financial statements that disclosure is required irrespective of whether there have been any transactions between the group entities. [IAS 24.12]

In addition, an entity is specifically required to disclose the name of its parent and, if different, the ultimate controlling party. If the financial statements of the parent or ultimate controlling party are not publicly available the entity is required to identify the next most senior parent in the group that does have financial statements available to the general public. [IAS 24.12]

An entity should also disclose in all circumstances the compensation, being the consideration in exchange for their services, received by key management personnel of the entity in total and for each of the following five categories: [IAS 24.16]

- short-term employee benefits, for example salary and holiday pay;

- post-employment benefits, for example pensions;

- other long-term benefits, for example long-service awards or sabbatical leave;

- termination benefits; and

- share based payment transactions, for example shares and share options.

A number of disclosures are required where related party transactions have taken place during the period. These disclosures are designed to provide users of the financial statements with relevant information about the transactions so that the effect of them on the financial performance of the entity can be understood. Such disclosures should include the nature of the relationship, the amount of the transactions, the amount of any balance outstanding at the year-end and the terms and conditions attaching to any outstanding balance, for example whether security or guarantees have been provided and what form the payment will take. If an amount has been charged to the income statement for non-recoverability of an outstanding balance this should be disclosed. [IAS 24.17]

Transactions between related parties may be on an arm's length basis. This does not however negate the requirement to disclose the transactions.

These disclosures should be presented separately for different categories of related parties, although items of a similar nature may be disclosed together. Where aggregation results in key information necessary to understand the effect of the transactions on the financial statements being unavailable, separate disclosure should be made. [IAS 24.22]

The different categories for which separate disclosures are required are identified as: [IAS 24.18]

- the parent;
- entities with joint control, or significant influence, over the entity;
- subsidiaries;
- associates;
- joint ventures in which the entity is a venturer;
- key management personnel of the entity or its parent; and
- other related parties.

Although information is required about the nature of related parties there is no requirement to identify them specifically by name.

Illustration 2

Pinot is a entity that complies with the minimum requirements of IAS 24.

The disclosures that would be required by IAS 24 in the financial statements of Pinot, in respect of each of the following transactions are shown below.

(1) Pinot sells goods on credit to Chablis, which is an entity owned by the son of one of the directors of Pinot. At the year end there was a receivable of CU100,000 owing from Chablis to Pinot. The CU100,000 was expensed to the income statement as it was considered as being non-recoverable. Debt collection costs incurred by Pinot were CU4,000.

The ownership of Chablis makes it a related party of Pinot. Disclosure of the nature of the relationship, any transactions during the period and the fact that the CU100,000 balance was considered to be non-recoverable and therefore charged to the income statement. There is no requirement to disclose the debt collection costs of CU4,000, or the names of Chablis, the director of Pinot or his or her son.

(2) Pinot purchased goods from Merlot for CU600,000, which was deemed to be an arm's length price. Pinot owns 40% of the ordinary share capital of Merlot.

Merlot is almost certainly a related party of Pinot, as a result of Pinot's significant influence through the 40% shareholding. Despite being at an arm's length price, the value of the transaction should be disclosed (aggregated with similar transactions during the year if appropriate). If Pinot discloses that the related party transactions were made on terms equivalent to market price transactions, this should be substantiated. The nature of the relationship, but no names are required to be disclosed.

(3) An amount of CU90,000 is due to one of Pinot's distributors, Shiraz.

A distributor is not a related party so no disclosure is required.

(4) A house owned by Pinot, with a carrying amount of CU200,000 and a market value of CU450,000, was sold to one of its directors for CU425,000. Pinot guaranteed the loan taken out by the director to purchase the property.

The nature of the relationship, details of the amount and nature of the transaction should be disclosed, along with the fact that Pinot is guaranteeing the loan of a related party. If payment is outstanding at the year-end then the amount should be disclosed although the director does not need to be named.

7 Chapter Review

This chapter has covered:

- the scope and objectives of IAS 24 on related party disclosures;

- the important terminology and concepts which relate to the identification of related party relationships and related party transactions; and

- the key requirements concerning related party disclosures in financial statements.

Chapter 26
CONSTRUCTION

1 Business Context

Construction contracts are common in certain industries, such as the building and aerospace industries where entities enter into contracts for the construction of a substantial asset that takes a considerable amount of time to complete. Such contracts may extend over several years.

Few entities can afford to wait until the end of the contract before being paid by the customer. In practice, stage payments for work completed are agreed within the overall contract and partial payment is received from the customer.

Similarly, if profit was only recognised at the end of each contract, then reported profits in the financial statements would not represent the value of work achieved in an accounting period. It is therefore necessary to divide the overall contract over the total time it takes and to recognise an appropriate part of the contract costs, revenues and profit each period.

2 Chapter Objectives

This chapter deals with the accounting and disclosure requirements in IAS 11 *Construction contracts.*

On completion of this chapter you should be able to:

■ demonstrate a knowledge of the objectives and scope of IAS 11;

■ demonstrate a knowledge of the important terminology and definitions which relate to the valuation of construction contracts;

■ demonstrate an understanding of the key principles relating to the valuation of construction contracts and the allocation of contract costs and revenues to accounting periods; and

■ apply this knowledge and understanding in particular circumstances through basic calculations.

3 Objectives, Scope and Definitions of IAS 11

The objective of IAS 11 is to prescribe the accounting treatment of the revenues received and costs incurred in a construction contract.

IAS 11 defines a construction contract as one specifically negotiated for the construction of an asset, for example a building, pipeline or ship, or a combination of assets that are closely related in terms of their design, technology and function or their ultimate purpose or use. Services that are directly related to the construction of an asset, for example project management, meet the definition of a construction contract, as does a contract for the demolition of an asset. [IAS 11.3]

The dates on which a construction contract starts and ends usually fall in different accounting periods, so the principal concern is how to allocate revenue and costs to the different accounting periods to reflect the reality of the construction activity as it takes place.

IAS 11 applies only to the contractor, i.e. the entity carrying out the work; it does not apply to the customer for whom the work is being carried out. The customer will usually account for the constructed asset in accordance with IAS 16 *Property, plant and equipment*. [IAS 11.1]

There are two distinct types of construction contract:

- *fixed price contracts:* where the revenue arising is fixed, either for the contract as a whole or on units of output, at the outset of the contract. Under such contracts there is an element of certainty about the revenue accruing, but not about the costs which will arise; and

- *cost plus contracts:* where costs will be recoverable plus some agreed element of profit. Under such contracts there is a high degree of certainty about the profit arising although there is no certainty about either the revenue or the costs.

The distinction between the two types of contract is particularly important when deciding the stage at which contract revenues and expenses should be recognised.

IAS 11 will generally be applied to individual construction contracts; but in order to reflect economic reality it will occasionally be necessary to aggregate several contracts together or break a large contract down into smaller ones.

If one contract covers the construction of a number of individual assets that have been separately tendered for it may be appropriate to treat the construction of each asset as a separate contract. To be treated separately the acceptance of each proposal should not be reliant on the acceptance of the other proposals and it should be possible to identify the costs and revenues relating to each asset. [IAS 11.8]

A number of individual contracts should be aggregated if the individual contracts have been negotiated as one, the contracts are closely interrelated with an overall profit margin and they are performed at the same time or consecutively. [IAS 11.9]

Where a contract entered into for the construction of a single asset contains a clause that provides for the construction of an additional asset at the option of the customer, the second asset should be treated as a separate contract if its design or function differs significantly from the asset under the original contract or if the price is separately negotiated. [IAS 11.10]

4 Contract Revenue and Contract Costs

4.1 Contract revenue

This section looks at how total contract revenue should be built up over the life of the contract. It does not deal with the timing of recognition through its allocation to accounting periods, which is discussed later.

Contract revenue is the total amount of consideration receivable under the contract. This will therefore include revenue due from the originally agreed contract and from any subsequent changes (variations) in the contract provided that they have been agreed i.e. the amounts are known and are recoverable. [IAS 11.11]

In the early stages of a contract, the contract revenue will often be an estimate of what the final amount will be, as it may be dependent on the outcome of future events. Contract revenue may alter where it is possible for the contractor to make claims against the customer, or a third party, for costs that were not originally included in the contract.

4.2 Contract costs

Contract costs should include the costs that directly relate to a contract, for example costs of materials used in the construction, site labour costs, the cost of hiring equipment and depreciation of equipment used in the contract. In addition, contract costs will include an allocation of costs incurred to carry out contract activity in general, for example insurance and construction overheads. It is appropriate to allocate these costs to each contract on a systematic and rational basis. [IAS 11.16]

If other costs are identified as being specifically recoverable under a particular contract, these should also form part of the construction costs of that contract. [IAS 11.16]

5 Recognition of Contract Revenue and Costs

5.1 Stage of completion

The principal objective of IAS 11 is to recognise contract revenue and costs in each accounting period to reflect the stage of completion of the contract. In order for contract revenue and costs to be recognised, the entity should be able to measure reliably such amounts. [IAS 11.22]

The stage of completion approach avoids the mismatch between costs being recognised as they are incurred and revenue only being recognised when the contract is completed. This would not reflect commercial substance, since the contractor earns revenues as the project activity progresses. The stage of completion method is often referred to as a percentage of completion method.

Under this method, contract costs should be expensed in the period in which the work that gives rise to them is completed and the associated revenue should be recognised to match the work completed. Costs may also be incurred in relation to work that will be carried out in a future period; these should be deferred on the balance sheet as an asset, assuming that they are recoverable under the contract, and are usually referred to as 'contract work in progress'.

The stage of completion of a contract can be assessed in a number of ways. Examples included in IAS 11 are:

- measurement of the costs incurred to date on work performed as a proportion of the total estimated costs under the contract;

- surveys of work completed. This may be appropriate where a specialised asset is being constructed or where it is likely that significant costs will be incurred in the earlier stages of the project although this does not match the level of completion of the asset; and

■ measurement of the physical completion to date as compared with the total asset. This may be appropriate for the construction of buildings.

5.2 Reliable measurement

As mentioned above, contract revenue and costs should only be recognised where the outcome of the contract can be measured reliably. Where contract revenue has been recognised but the recovery of the amount subsequently looks unlikely, an expense should be incurred to represent a bad debt rather than an adjustment being made to revenue.

IAS 11 distinguishes between the two types of contract in terms of the criteria to be met for measurement to be reliable.

■ For a *fixed price contract* the contractor should be able to measure reliably the total contract revenues and be able to identify and measure reliably both the costs that have been incurred and those that will be incurred to complete the project. The contractor should also assess whether it is probable that payment will be received under the contract. [IAS 11.23]

■ Under a *cost plus contract* the outcome of the contract is capable of reliable measurement where it is probable that the contractor will receive payment for the revenues under the contract and the costs can be both clearly identified and are themselves reliably measurable. [IAS 11.24]

Illustration 1

The following information relates to a contract.

Contract details:	CU000
Estimated contract revenue	100
Costs to date	48
Costs to complete	32
Total estimated costs	80

Based on the stage of completion method, the contract revenue and costs are:

Stage of completion	55%	

Income statement:	CU000	
Revenue	55	(55% of CU100,000)
Cost of sales	44	(55% of CU80,000)
Profit	11	

Illustration 2

The following information relates to a cost plus contract obtained by a business with a 30 June year end:

	2003	2004
	CU000	CU000
Cumulative costs incurred on work to date	100	150
Agreed profit as a percentage of costs	20%	20%

The outcome of the contract can be estimated reliably at both year ends.

To prepare the income statement for each of the two years, the business calculates the costs incurred, assesses the profit that should be recognised and inserts revenue as the balancing figure. In the second year deductions are made for values already recognised in the income statement.

2003

Costs	CU100,000
Profit	CU100,000 x 20% = CU20,000
Revenue	Costs + profit = CU100,000 + CU20,000 = CU120,000

2004

Costs	CU150,000 to date, less CU100,000 recognised in 2003 = CU50,000
Profit	CU50,000 x 20% = CU10,000
Revenue	Costs + profit = CU50,000 + CU10,000 = CU60,000

Where the outcome of the project cannot be measured reliably, which may be the case during the early stages of construction, then revenue should only be recognised to the extent that costs are recoverable, although the costs should be recognised as an expense as they are incurred. As the project progresses the likelihood of being able to assess reliably the outcome of the project will improve, to the point where the stage of completion method should be used to assess the revenue and costs that should be recognised. [IAS 11.32, 11.35]

Illustration 3

A business is not able to measure reliably the outcome of a contract, but estimates that all costs incurred are recoverable from the customer. The following details are available:

Contract details:	CU000
Estimated contract revenue	100
Costs to date	30
Costs to complete	45
Total estimated costs	75

The contract revenue and costs are:

Stage of completion	25%	

Income statement:	CU000	
Revenue	25	(25% of CU100,000)
Cost of sales	25	
Profit	Nil	

5.3 Loss making contracts

Where the revenue and costs in a contract have been assessed and it is expected that a loss will be incurred, that loss should be recognised as an expense immediately. The loss should not be deferred until the project is completed or spread over the period of the contract. [IAS 11.32, 11.36]

This means that when a loss has been identified, there is no need to estimate the contract's stage of completion.

Illustration 4

The following details relate to a contract expected to be loss making:

Contract details:	CU000
Estimated contract revenue	100
Costs to date	72
Costs to complete	48
Total estimated costs	120
Stage of completion	60 %

The revenue and costs are:

Income statement:	CU000	
Revenue	60	(60% of CU100,000)
Cost of sales	72	
Loss	12	
Realisation of full contract loss	8	((CU100,000 - CU72,000 - CU48,000) + CU12,000)
Expected contract loss	20	

6 Disclosure

A break down of amounts recognised in respect of construction contracts should be disclosed. Such amounts include the amount of contract revenue recognised in the period, the total costs incurred to date (i.e. on a cumulative basis rather than for the period) and the aggregate profits recognised to date. [IAS 11.39, 11.40]

The entity should clearly explain the methods used to determine both contract revenues and the stage of completion. [IAS 11.39]

Amounts recognised in the balance sheet in relation to the contract should also be disclosed, including the gross amounts due from customers and recognised as an asset and any amounts that are due to the customer that have been recognised as a liability at the balance sheet date. [IAS 11.42]

Other disclosable amounts which may occur under a contract are any advances received from customers and any retentions, being amounts held back by the customer as security for any rectification work required, under the contract. [IAS 11.40]

7 Chapter Review

This chapter has been concerned with the key issues relating to construction contracts, including how profits are accounted for over the accounting periods in which construction work is performed.

This chapter has covered:

■ the objectives, scope, definitions and disclosure requirements of IAS 11;

■ what can and can not be treated as contract costs under IAS 11;

■ the requirement that contract revenues and contract costs (and therefore contract profit) should be recognised once the outcome of the contract can be estimated reliably;

■ the application of the recognition criteria to fixed price and cost plus contracts;

■ how to deal with contract revenues and costs under the stage of completion method when the outcome can be measured reliably; and

■ the requirement to recognise contract losses immediately.

CHAPTER 27
RETIREMENT BENEFIT PLANS

1 Business Context

Retirement benefit plans (otherwise called 'pension schemes', 'superannuation schemes' or 'retirement benefit schemes') are important economic entities in most developed economies. Collectively, they are financially significant because they are major suppliers of funds for corporate financing and exert substantial economic influence over capital markets through their investment policies.

Retirement benefit plans exist for the benefit of the employees that are members of the plans and hold funds invested by both the employer and its employees. Due to the nature of retirement benefit plans they are normally set up as stand alone legal entities to meet this separate duty of accountability to their members rather than to the shareholders of the entity employing the members.

Recent scandals involving the misappropriation of retirement benefit plan assets have highlighted the importance of relevant, timely reporting by retirement benefit plans.

2 Chapter Objectives

This chapter covers the accounting and disclosure requirements of IAS 26 *Accounting and reporting by retirement benefit plans*. IAS 26 does not consider the accounting for pension costs in the employing entity's financial statements which is covered in IAS 19 *Employee benefits*.

On completion of this chapter you should be able to:

- understand the nature and scope of IAS 26;

- interpret the important terminology and definitions which relate to the financial statements of retirement benefit plans;

- understand and be able to distinguish between defined contribution plans and defined benefit plans; and

- demonstrate knowledge of the principal disclosure requirements of IAS 26.

3 Objectives, Scope and Definitions of IAS 26

The objective of IAS 26 is to provide useful and consistently produced information on retirement benefit plans for members of the plans and other interested parties.

IAS 26 should be applied in the preparation of financial reports by retirement benefit plans. [IAS 26.1]

Although it is commonplace for a retirement benefit plan to be set up as a separate legal entity run by independent trustees, plan assets may be held within the entity employing the plan's members. IAS 26 applies in both sets of circumstances. In the latter case IAS 26 still regards the retirement benefit plan as a reporting entity separate from the employing entity.

The preparation of a retirement benefit plan's financial report should be in accordance with not only IAS 26 but also all other international standards to the extent that they are not overridden by IAS 26.

IAS 26 does not cover:

■ the preparation of reports to individual participants about their retirement benefit rights; or

■ the determination of the cost of retirement benefits in the financial statements of the employer having pension plans for its employees and providing other employee benefits.

'Retirement benefit plans' are *"arrangements whereby an entity provides benefits for its employees on or after termination of service (either in the form of an annual income or as a lump sum), when such benefits, or the employer's contributions towards them, can be determined or estimated in advance of retirement from the provisions of a document or from the entity's practices"*. [IAS 26.8]

There are two main types of retirement benefit plan, although it is also possible to have a hybrid of the two:

(1) *defined contribution plans* (sometimes called 'money purchase schemes'). These are retirement plans under which payments into the plan are fixed. Subsequent payments out of the plan to retired members will therefore be determined by the value of the investments made from the contributions that have been made into the plan and the investment returns reinvested [IAS 26.8]; and

(2) *defined benefit plans* (sometimes called 'final salary schemes'). These are retirement plans under which the amount that a retired member will receive from the plan during retirement is fixed. Contributions are paid into the scheme based on an estimate of what will have to be paid out under the plan. [IAS 26.8]

The following diagram outlines the relevant relationships (it is also relevant to IAS 19).

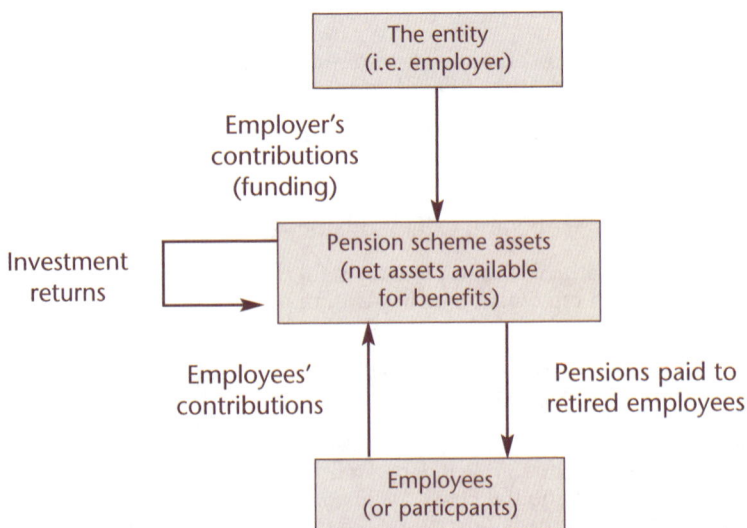

3.1 Key Concepts

'Funding' represents the employer's contributions paid to the fund in order to meet the future obligations under the plan for the payment of retirement benefits.

'Participants' are those employees who will benefit under the plan. (i.e. employees and retired employees). [IAS 26.8]

The 'net assets available for benefits' are the assets less liabilities of the plan that are available to generate future investment income that will increase the plan's assets. These net assets are calculated before the deduction of the actuarial assessment of promised retirement benefits. [IAS 26.8]

4 Defined Contribution Plans

A defined contribution plan is where the annual pension payable to retired employees (i.e. participants) is based upon the accumulated value of the assets in the employee's fund.

The assets in the pension plan are funded by contributions made into the plan and investment returns on those assets. Contributions may be made by the employer, the employee or both parties.

A financial report prepared for a defined contribution plan should contain: [IAS 26.13]

(1)   a statement of the net assets in the plan that are available to meet the benefits payable under the plan; and

(2)   a description of the funding policy of the plan.

The objective of the plan's financial report is to provide information about the plan itself, for example that it is being run with the members' best interest in mind, and to set out the performance of the investments in the plan. The performance of the investments will directly affect the retirement benefits that are paid out under the plan and hence such information will be of particular interest to the participants of the plan.

A defined contribution plan report will typically include:

- a description of the significant activities for the reporting period, along with details of any changes that have been made to the plan and the effect of these changes on the plan;

- a description of the plan's membership, terms and conditions;

- financial statements containing information on the transactions and investment performance for the period as well as presenting the financial position of the plan at the end of the period; and

- a description of the investment policies.

5 Defined Benefit Plans

Under defined benefit plans the annual pensions payable to retired employees (i.e. the participants) are based upon a formula, for example using the number of years' service and the employee's final salary.

The level of payments ultimately to be paid out of the fund is uncertain as they depend upon such factors as life expectancy and future investment returns. The expertise of an actuary is used to estimate these uncertain future events to ensure that based on the assets in the plan and the expected future contributions to be made, the pension scheme is adequately funded to meet its future obligations. The future obligations are measured as the actuarial present value of promised retirement benefits, which is more precisely defined as being the present value of the expected payments by a retirement benefit plan to existing and past employees, attributable to the service already rendered. [IAS 26.8]

A related concept is 'vested benefits' which are benefits payable regardless of whether the participants in the plan continue in the entity's employment. [IAS 26.8]

If the estimated expected obligations payable under a plan exceed the assets (i.e. there is a deficit), then the employer may have to make additional contributions to ensure the retirement plan is adequately funded. If assets exceed obligations (i.e. there is an excess), then the employer may be able to reduce its future contributions payable.

A defined benefit plan report should contain a statement showing the net assets that are available for the payment of benefits, the actuarial present value of promised retirement benefits, identifying which of these benefits are vested and which are not, and the resulting surplus or deficit in the plan. This information may alternatively be presented by providing a statement of the net assets of the fund that are available to pay future benefits, together with a note disclosing the actuarial present value of promised retirement benefits and those benefits which are vested and those which are not. This actuarial present value information may be contained in an accompanying actuarial report, rather than in the statement of net assets. [IAS 26.17]

A defined benefit plan's report should provide participants with information about the relationship between the future obligations under the plan and the resources within the plan that are available to meet those obligations. A typical report will therefore include:

- a description of significant activities for the reporting period along with details of any changes that have been made to the plan and the effect of the changes on the plan;

- a description of the plan's membership, terms and conditions;

- financial statements containing information on the transactions and investment performance for the period as well as presenting the financial position of the plan at the end of the period;

- actuarial information, including the present value of the promised retirement benefits under the plan and a description of the significant actuarial assumptions made in making those estimates; and

- a description of the investment policies.

6 All Retirement Plans

6.1 Valuation of assets

Retirement benefit plan investments should be carried at fair value, which for marketable securities is market value. Where an estimate of fair value is not possible, for example where the plan has total ownership of another entity, disclosure should be made of the reason why fair value is not used. [IAS 26.32]

6.2 Disclosure

The report of all retirement benefit plans should also include the following information: [IAS 26.34]

- a statement of changes in the net assets that are available in the fund to provide future benefits; and
- a summary of the plan's significant accounting policies.

The statement of changes in the net assets available to provide future benefits should disclose a full reconciliation showing movements during the period, for example contributions made to the plan split between employee and employer, investment income, expenses and benefits paid out.

Information should be provided on the plan's funding policy, the basis of valuation for the assets in the fund and details of significant investments that exceed a 5% threshold of net assets in the fund available for benefits. Any liabilities that the plan has other than those of the actuarially calculated figure for future benefits payable and details of any investment in the employing entity should also be disclosed.

General information should be included about the plan, such as the names of the employing entities, the groups of employees that are members of the plan, the number of participants receiving benefits under the plan and the nature of the plan, i.e. defined contribution or defined benefit. If employees contribute to the plan, this should be disclosed along with an explanation of how the promised benefits are calculated and details of any termination terms of the plan. If there have been changes in any of the information disclosed then this fact should be explained.

Illustration 1

The following summarises some of the key requirements of IAS 26 for:

(A) defined contribution plans;

(B) defined benefit plans; or

(C) all retirement plans.

	(A)	(B)	(C)
(1) Investments to be carried at fair value wherever possible			Yes
(2) Recognition of the actuarial present value of promised retirement benefits		Yes	
(3) A statement of changes in net assets available for benefits			Yes
(4) No requirement for an actuarial report	Yes		

7 Chapter Review

This chapter has been concerned with the accounting and reporting requirements of retirement benefit plans. A key distinction made in IAS 26 is between 'defined contribution' and 'defined benefit' plans. These different types of funds are subject to different obligations and disclosure requirements.

This chapter has covered:

- the nature and scope of IAS 26;

- the important terminology and concepts which relate to the financial statements of retirement benefit plans;

- the major attributes of defined contribution plans and defined benefit plans; and

- the principal disclosure requirements of IAS 26, distinguishing between those that apply to the different types of plan or to all retirement plans.

Chapter 28

BANKS AND SIMILAR INSTITUTIONS

1 Business Context

Banks, and similar financial institutions, represent a significant and influential sector of business worldwide. A banking institution is different compared with many other organisations in a number of ways. Stakeholders of a banking institution tend to be much more widely spread than is the case with other organisations since most individuals and organisations make use of banks, as lender or borrower. Banking institutions operate in a heavily regulated industry and the risks associated with such entities are different from entities operating in say the retail or manufacturing sectors. Banking institution can also be differentiated from other entities due to the nature of their assets and liabilities.

As a result of being largely unique in nature, banks and other similar financial institutions are required to comply with a number of accounting standards which apply only to them and their special circumstances. IAS 30 *Disclosures in the financial statements of banks and similar financial institutions* deals with the disclosure requirements for such entities. Additional disclosure is deemed essential to ensure that users of the financial statements understand the performance and operations of banking institutions; for example a bank may be exposed to significant liquidity risk, i.e. the risk of having insufficient funds to carry on its normal operations.

2 Chapter Objectives

This chapter sets out the disclosure requirements of IAS 30. This standard supplements other IFRS which also apply to banks unless they are specifically exempted.

IAS 30 deals only with disclosure and presentation requirements and does not prescribe methods of recognition and measurement.

On completion of this chapter you should be able to:

- understand the nature and scope of IAS 30;

- interpret the important terminology and definitions which relate to the financial statements of banks; and

- demonstrate knowledge of the principal disclosure requirements of IAS 30.

3 Scope and Definitions of IAS 30

The presentation and disclosure requirements of IAS 30 apply to the financial statements of banks and similar financial institutions (subsequently referred to as banks). [IAS 30.1]

The term 'bank' includes all entities that are financial institutions, where:

■ their principal activities are to accept deposits and borrow money with the objective of lending and investing; and

■ which are within the scope of banking and similar legislation.

IAS 30 applies to the preparation of both the separate financial statements and the consolidated financial statements of a bank.

4 Accounting Policies

All entities are required by IAS 1 *Presentation of financial statements* to disclose their principal accounting policies used in the preparation of their financial statements. Because of the unique nature of banks IAS 30 sets out what the key accounting policies should include:

■ the recognition of the principal types of income;

■ the valuation of investment and dealing securities;

■ the distinction between those transactions and other events that result in the recognition of assets and liabilities on the balance sheet and those transactions and other events that only give rise to contingencies and commitments;

■ the basis for the determination of impairment losses on loans and advances and for expensing uncollectible loans and advances; and

■ the basis for the determination of charges for general banking risks and the accounting treatment of such charges.

A bank should also disclose the policy by which it expenses uncollectible loans and advances in its income statement. [IAS 30.43]

5 The Income Statement

To ensure that the income statement is presented in a consistent manner across all such entities in the industry, and to present the information in the most appropriate manner, IAS 30 requires the income statement of a bank to be presented by grouping income and expenses according to their nature. The income statement should disclose amounts for the principal types of income and expenses. [IAS 30.9]

All international standards need to be applied in the preparation of a set of financial statements by a bank, not just those that specifically relate to banking institutions.

Specific disclosures are required by IAS 30 of the following items, either on the face of the income statement or in the notes to the financial statements of a bank: [IAS 30.10]

- interest and similar income;

- interest expense and similar charges;

- dividend income;

- fee and commission income;

- fee and commission expense;

- gains less losses arising from dealing securities;

- gains less losses arising from investment securities;

- gains less losses arising from dealing in foreign currencies;

- other operating income;

- impairment losses on loans and advances;

- general administrative expenses; and

- other operating expenses.

5.1 Offsetting

Offsetting of assets and liabilities or income and expenditure is not generally permitted under IFRS since it leads to less information being presented and does not generally aid understanding. This general prohibition is equally relevant for banking institutions. There are, however, certain instances where offsetting of related amounts aids understanding, for example in the application of hedge accounting and dealings in foreign currencies. IAS 30 therefore permits offsetting to be applied in hedge accounting under IAS 39 *Financial instruments: recognition and measurement* and in specific instances identified in IAS 32 *Financial instruments: disclosure and presentation.* [IAS 30.13]

6 The Balance Sheet

Consistent with the approach for the presentation of the income statement, a bank should present its balance sheet by grouping together assets and liabilities by their nature. The assets and liabilities should be presented in an order that reflects their relative liquidity. [IAS 30.18]

In addition to complying with the requirements of international standards generally, banks should comply with IAS 30's specific requirement that certain information should be presented on the face of the balance sheet or in the notes to the financial statements in relation to a bank's assets and liabilities as set out below. [IAS 30.19]

6.1 Assets

The presentation of assets should include: [IAS 30.19]

- cash and balances with the central bank;

- treasury bills and other bills eligible for rediscounting with the central bank;

- government and other securities held for dealing purposes;

- placements with, and loans and advances to, other banks;

- other money market placements;

- loans and advances to customers; and

- investment securities.

6.2 Liabilities

The presentation of liabilities should include: [IAS 30.19]

- deposits from other banks;

- other money market deposits;

- amounts owed to other depositors;

- certificates of deposits;

- promissory notes and other liabilities evidenced by paper; and

- other borrowed funds.

The classification between current and non-current items is not presented separately because the nature of a bank's operations means that most of its assets and liabilities can be realised or settled in the near future.

6.3 Fair values

The fair value should be disclosed of each class of financial assets; loans and receivables, held-to-maturity investments, financial assets at fair value and available-for-sale assets and liabilities, as required by IAS 32. [IAS 30.24]

7 Other Disclosures

7.1 Contingencies and commitments

A number of disclosures are required for banks in relation to any contingencies or commitments that they may have. This information is particularly important since it sets out information about possible future expenditure that the bank may incur and hence the effect on future liquidity. Such amounts are often large and therefore may have a significant impact on a bank's risks. Although IAS 37 *Provisions, contingent liabilities and contingent assets* applies to banks a number of specific additional disclosures are required by IAS 30 as detailed below. [IAS 30.26]

Information should be provided on the nature and amount of commitments to extend credit, where such commitments cannot be withdrawn without the risk of the bank incurring significant penalties. [IAS 30.26]

Disclosure should be made for contingent liabilities and commitments as a result of entering into off-balance sheet items. Such items include: [IAS 30.26]

- direct credit substitutes;

- certain transaction-related contingent liabilities, for example warranties and stand-by letters of credit; and

- short-term self-liquidating trade-related contingent liabilities arising from the movement of good.

7.2 Maturities of assets and liabilities

An analysis should be provided of assets and liabilities by their relevant maturity groupings. This information should be presented based on their outstanding period of maturity at the balance sheet date. Such maturity groupings include up to one month, one to three months, three months to a year, one to five years and over five years. [IAS 30.30]

This analysis should be based on the contractual maturity dates of the items and the maturity periods presented should be the same for assets and liabilities. [IAS 30.30]

7.3 Concentrations of assets, liabilities and off-balance sheet items

Significant concentrations of a banks assets and liabilities, including off-balance sheet items, should be disclosed. Such disclosures should be made, for example, by geographical area or customer group or on another appropriate basis based on the concentration of risk. [IAS 30.40]

These disclosures are required in addition to the requirement to disclose segmental information by business or geographical area as required by IAS 14 *Segment reporting.*

7.4 Losses on loans and advances

Due to the nature of a bank's business it is likely to incur a relatively large number of uncollectible debts. To understand fully the risks associated with the bank's ongoing business and the effect that such unrecoverable amounts have on its liquidity, disclosure is required of such amounts.

A bank should provide details of its provision for impairment losses on loans and advances (i.e. a decrease in the recoverable amount of an asset). This information should disclose all movements during the period including amounts charged to the income statement for impairment losses on unrecoverable loans and advances, and any credits for amounts subsequently recovered. [IAS 30.43]

In addition, the aggregate amount of the provision for impairment losses on loans and advances should be disclosed at the balance sheet date. [IAS 30.43]

Where a bank has provided for losses in relation to loans and advances in addition to impairment losses as discussed above (this may be permitted under local legislation) these amounts should not be reported as part of the profit or loss for the period. Such amounts, or their reversal, should instead be recognised against retained earnings and separately identified. [IAS 30.44]

7.5 Banking risk

There may be instances, such as local legislative requirements, where an entity is required to make a provision for general banking risks. Provisions of this general nature are not permitted under the application of IAS 37 and therefore should not be reflected in the income statement for the period. The impact of any changes in such provisions should therefore be recognised separately within equity, as appropriations of, or increases in, retained earnings. [IAS 30.50]

7.6 Assets pledged as security

It is common in some national jurisdictions for liabilities to be secured by an entity's assets. If a bank has pledged certain assets against its liabilities this fact should be disclosed. The disclosures should include details of the nature and carrying amount of the assets that are securing the liabilities. [IAS 30.53]

7.7 Acting as trustee

If a bank acts as trustee, in an official capacity, the assets of the trust should not be included in the bank's financial statements, as they do not represent assets that belong to the bank. Where such activities are significant, the bank should disclose this fact and provide an indication of any potential liability that may arise as a result of failing adequately to carry out its responsibilities in its capacity as trustee.

7.8 Related party transactions

The disclosure of related party transactions as required by IAS 24 *Related party disclosures* is particularly important and relevant for the full understanding of a bank's financial statements. For this reason, IAS 30 reiterates the disclosures that would be appropriate to comply with the requirements of IAS 24, for example the nature of any related party relationship and the types of transactions that have taken place.

8 Chapter Review

This chapter has been concerned with the disclosures and presentation in the financial statements of banks and similar institutions.

This chapter has covered:

- the nature and scope of IAS 30 on banks;

- the important terminology and definitions which relate to the financial statements of banks; and

- the principal disclosure requirements of IAS 30.

Chapter 29
INSURANCE

1 Business Context

An insurance entity assesses the risks from which another party wishes to be sheltered and prices an insurance contract accordingly. Where in making that assessment, an insurance entity decides that the risks in the contract are potentially too great for it to take on alone it has the ability to offload some of the risk by selling it on to another insurer. The second insurer will take a share in the premium income, but will also share in the associated risks in the contract. This is known as reinsurance.

There are a number of underlying complex issues in relation to insurance contracts with the overriding one being uncertainty, resulting from the underlying risks that an insurance entity is exposed to. IFRS 4 *Insurance contracts* attempts to provide a framework within which a common set of reporting principles are set out to provide relevant information that will assist a user's understanding of the entity's financial statements.

2 Chapter Objectives

The objective of this chapter is to set out the requirements of IFRS 4 which represents the first phase of the IASB project on accounting for insurance contracts.

On completion of this chapter you should be able to:

- understand what an insurance contract is;

- appreciate the nature of insurance risk; and

- understand the disclosure requirements relating to insurance contracts.

3 Objectives, Scope and Definitions of IFRS 4

Currently there is a wide range of accounting practices used for insurance contracts and the practices adopted often differ from those used in other sectors. As a result the IASB embarked on a substantial project to address the issues surrounding the accounting for insurance contracts. Rather than issuing one standard that covered all areas, the IASB decided to tackle the project in two phases.

Interim guidance has been issued in phase one of the project in the form of IFRS 4; it is a stepping stone to the second phase of the project. IFRS 4 largely focuses on improving the disclosure requirements in relation to insurance contracts; however it also includes a number of limited improvements to existing accounting requirements.

Although IFRS 4 sets out a number of accounting principles as essentially best practice, it does not require an entity to use these if it currently adopts different accounting practices. An insurance entity is however prohibited from changing its current accounting policies to a number of specifically identified practices.

IFRS 4 specifies the financial reporting of insurance contracts by any entity that issues such contracts, or holds reinsurance contracts. It does not apply to other assets and liabilities held by insurers.

It is important to distinguish between insurance contracts and other contracts that are not covered by IFRS 4 but which might look like insurance contracts. To provide clarification IFRS 4 specifically identifies a number of areas where its provisions do not apply, for example:

■ the provision of product warranties given directly by the manufacturer, dealer or retailer;

■ employers' assets and liabilities in relation to employee benefit plans and obligations under a defined benefit plan;

■ a contractual right, or obligation, that is contingent on the right to use a non-financial item, for example some licences;

■ a finance lease that contains a residual value guaranteed by the lessee, i.e. a specified value for the asset at the end of the lease is guaranteed by the lessee;

■ financial guarantees within the scope of IAS 39 *Financial instruments: recognition and measurement;*

■ contingent consideration that has arisen as a result of a business combination; and

■ insurance contracts that the entity holds as policyholder.

3.1 What is an insurance contract?

Insurance contracts are contracts between two parties, where one party, the insurer, agrees to compensate the other party, the policyholder, if it is adversely affected by an uncertain future event.

An uncertain future event exists where at least one of the following is uncertain at the inception of an insurance contract:

■ the occurrence of an insured event;

■ the timing of the event; or

■ the level of compensation that will be paid by the insurer if the event occurs. [IFRS 4 Appendix B]

Some insurance contracts may offer payments-in-kind rather than compensation payable to the policyholder directly. For example, an insurance repair contract may pay for a washing machine to be repaired if it breaks down; the contract will not necessarily pay monetary compensation.

In identifying an insurance contract it is important to make the distinction between financial risk and insurance risk. A contract that exposes the issuer to financial risk without significant insurance risk does not meet the definition of an insurance contract.

Financial risk is where there is a possible change in a financial or non-financial variable, for example a specified interest rate, commodity prices, an entity's credit rating or foreign exchange rates.

Insurance risk is defined as being a risk that is not a financial risk. The risk in an insurance contract is whether an event will occur (rather than arising from a change in something), for example a theft, damage to property, or product or professional liability. Appendix B to IFRS 4, which forms an integral part of the standard, includes an extensive list of examples of insurance contracts including:

- life insurance and prepaid funeral plans. It is the timing of the event that is uncertain here, for example certain life cover plans only pay out if death occurs within a specified period of time;

- disability and medical cover;

- credit insurance, covering the policyholder for non-recoverable receivables; and

- travel cover to provide against any loss suffered whilst travelling.

Illustration 1

Examples of an insurer taking on insurance risk are:

- An insurance contract issued to a policyholder against the escalation of claims from faulty motorcycles. The fault was discovered a year ago and the extent of total claims is yet to be established. This is an insurance contract since the insured event is the discovery of the ultimate cost of the claims.

- A gas boiler repair service available from a supplier who, for the payment of a fixed fee, will fix the malfunctioning boiler. This is an insurance contract as it is a payment-in-kind contract, with the uncertain event being whether the boiler will break down and the policyholder will be adversely affected.

4 Recognition and Measurement

IFRS 4 exempts an insurer temporarily (during phase one of the IASB's insurance project) from the need to consider the *IASB Framework* in selecting accounting policies for insurance contracts where there is no specific accounting requirement set out in another international standard. However, IFRS 4 expressly:

- requires a test for the adequacy of recognised insurance liabilities – referred to as the 'liability adequacy test';

- prohibits provisions for possible claims under contracts that are not in existence at the reporting date (referred to as catastrophe or equalisation provisions);

- requires an impairment test for reinsurance assets. An impairment is only recognised where after the commencement of a reinsurance contract, an event has occurred that will lead to amounts due under the contract not being recovered in full, and a reliable estimate of the shortfall can be assessed; and

- requires an insurer to keep insurance liabilities on its balance sheet until they are discharged, cancelled or expire, and to present such liabilities without offsetting them against related reinsurance assets.

An insurer recognises its insurance liabilities at each reporting date based on the current estimate of future contractual cash flows, and related items such as handling costs, arising under the insurance contracts. This provision should be reassessed at each reporting date and any identified shortfall should be recognised immediately in the income statement as part of profit or loss for the period. This is the so called 'liability adequacy test'. [IFRS 4.15]

If the accounting policies of an insurer do not demand that a liability adequacy test should be carried out, as described above, then an assessment is still required of the potential net liability (i.e. the relevant insurance liabilities less any related deferred acquisition costs). In these circumstances the insurer is required to recognise at least the amount that would be required to be recognised as a provision under the application of IAS 37 *Provisions, contingent liabilities and contingent assets*.

5 Changing Accounting Policies

An insurer is required to apply the general principles in IAS 8 *Accounting policies, changes in accounting estimates and errors* to any change that it wishes to make in its accounting policies. A change in accounting policy is therefore only permitted where the new policy will provide more relevant and no less reliable information to the users of the financial statements. [IFRS 4.22]

As IFRS 4 is only the first phase of the insurance project, there are a number of relaxations in the application of the standard and how it interrelates to other international standards. For example, IFRS 4 sets out an accounting policy for the remeasurement of designated insurance liabilities to reflect current market interest rates, with any changes being reported directly in the income statement. To encourage insurers to adopt this policy the standard specifically exempts them from having to carry out, and justify, the relevance and reliability test for such a change in policy.

IFRS 4 also identifies a number of accounting policies which may continue to be used if they represent existing practice of an insurer, but which may not be adopted as a new policy because they do not meet the more relevant and reliable test. Such policies include:

- measuring insurance liabilities on an undiscounted basis;

- measuring contractual rights to future investment management fees at an amount that is in excess of their fair value, as implied by a comparison with current fees being charged by other market participants for similar services; and

- using non-uniform accounting policies for the insurance contracts of subsidiaries.

Where an insurer uses excessive prudence (i.e. it is over cautious) in its accounting for insurance contracts there is no requirement to change to a less prudent policy. But an insurer already using sufficient prudence may not change to excessive prudence.

IFRS 4 sets out a number of accounting policies that an insurance entity is permitted to follow, although there is no requirement to do so at present. These relate to future investment margins, shadow accounting, insurance contracts acquired in a business combination or portfolio transfer and discretionary participation features.

6 Disclosures

IFRS 4 requires that information is disclosed in the financial statements of an insurer that identifies and explains amounts that arise from insurance contracts. [IFRS 4.36]

This information should include the accounting policies adopted and the identification of recognised assets, liabilities, income and expense arising from insurance contracts.

More generally, the risk management objectives and policies of an entity should be disclosed, since this will explain how an insurer deals with the uncertainty it is exposed to. [IFRS 4.38]

An entity is not generally required to comply with the disclosure requirements in IFRS 4 for comparative information relating to annual periods beginning before 1 January 2005. However, comparative disclosure is required in relation to accounting policies adopted and the identification of recognised assets, liabilities, income and expense arising from insurance contracts.

7 Chapter Review

This chapter has considered the nature of, and accounting for, insurance contracts.

In summary, this chapter has covered:

- identifying an insurance contract;

- understanding the various forms that an insurance contract may take; and

- setting out the disclosure requirements which help to explain the risks associated with an insurance contract.

Chapter 30
AGRICULTURE

1 Business Context

Accounting practices for the agricultural sector have historically been varied since international standards generally excluded such activities due to their specialist nature. The nature of agricultural activity makes it difficult to apply a traditional cost model since such items are constantly changing through growth and regeneration. Since the use of a historic cost model was not seen as wholly appropriate for accounting for agricultural activity, the IASB issued IAS 41 *Agriculture* based on a fair value model.

The basic business issues in the farming sector have many unique aspects. For example, animals and plants, described as biological assets, have characteristics which are not present in other industries. Another important feature is that government assistance in the agricultural sector is common and is often substantial. Entities in the farming industry are often small or family run but with the increasing awareness of organic produce and fair trade we have seen an expansion of such businesses in recent years.

2 Chapter Objectives

On completion of this chapter you should be able to:

- understand the distinction between biological assets and agricultural produce;

- demonstrate a knowledge of the treatment of biological assets and agricultural produce;

- deal with gains and losses on biological assets and agricultural produce; and

- account for government grants in the agricultural sector.

3 Objectives, Scope and Definitions of IAS 41

IAS 41 sets out the accounting treatment, including presentation and disclosure requirements, for agricultural activity. Agricultural activity is defined as the management of the biological transformation of biological assets for sale, into agricultural produce, or into additional biological assets. Such activities include, for example, raising livestock, forestry and cultivating orchards and plantations. [IAS 41.5]

A biological transformation comprises the processes of growth, degeneration, production and procreation that cause qualitative or quantitative changes in a biological asset. In its simplest form, it is the process of growing something such as a crop, although it also incorporates the production of agricultural produce such as wool and milk. [IAS 41.5]

A biological asset is a living plant or animal. [IAS 41.5]

Agricultural produce is the harvested produce of an entity's biological assets. [IAS 41.5]

IAS 41 considers the classification of biological assets and how their characteristics, and hence value, change over time. The standard applies to agricultural produce up to the point of harvest, after which IAS 2 *Inventories* is applicable. A distinction is made between the two because IAS 41 applies to biological assets throughout their lives but to agricultural produce only up to the point that it is harvested.

IAS 41 includes a table of examples which clearly sets out three distinct stages involved in the production of biological assets. Examples include the identification of dairy cattle as the biological asset, milk the agricultural produce and cheese the product that is processed after the point of harvest. Another example is, vines are the biological asset, grapes the agricultural produce and wine the end product.

IAS 41 does not apply to agricultural lands (IAS 16 *Property, plant and equipment* and IAS 40 *Investment property* apply instead), nor to intangible assets related to agriculture (IAS 38 *Intangible assets* applies).

Illustration 1

Calves and cows are biological assets as they are living animals. Beef and milk are agricultural produce.

Apples are agricultural produce. The related trees and orchards are biological assets.

4 Recognition and Measurement

A biological asset or agricultural produce should only be recognised when: [IAS 41.10]

- the entity controls the asset as a result of past events, for example the acquisition of dairy cattle. The past event is the purchase, and control is obtained as the entity is now the legal owner;

- it is probable that future economic benefits will flow to the entity, because the dairy cattle will produce milk which can be sold or processed into cheese and sold; and

- fair value, or cost, of the asset can be measured reliably.

A biological asset should initially be measured at its fair value less estimated point of sale costs, such as duty and commission to brokers or dealers. [IAS 41.12]

Point of sale costs do not include any costs that are necessary to get the asset to a market, for example transport. Fair value is the amount for which an asset could be exchanged, or a liability settled, between knowledgeable, willing parties in an arm's length transaction. Where an active market exists for a biological asset the quoted price in the market is the appropriate fair value. [IAS 41.8]

Where an active market does not exist, then fair value may be derived by using:

- the most recent transaction in the market, assuming that similar economic conditions exist at the time of the transaction and at the balance sheet date; or

- market prices for similar assets with appropriate adjustments to reflect differences; or

- sector based benchmarks, for example the value of meat per kilogram.

IAS 41 includes the presumption that it will be possible to fair value a biological asset. But if fair value cannot be measured reliably at the time of initial recognition then the biological asset should be recognised at cost less accumulated depreciation and impairment cost (i.e. the decrease in the recoverable amount of an asset). Fair value should then be used as soon as a reliable measurement can be made. [IAS 41.30]

At subsequent balance sheet dates a biological asset should continue to be measured at its fair value. Once a biological asset has been measured at fair value it is not possible to revert to cost.

Agricultural produce should be measured at its fair value, less estimated point of sale costs at the point of harvest. Subsequent measurement is by reference to IAS 2. It will always be possible to fair value the agricultural produce since, by its very nature, there must be a market for it. [IAS 41.13]

Grouping biological assets, or agricultural produce, according to significant attributes, such as age or quality, may help to establish fair value. Such groupings should be consistent with attribute groupings that are used in the market as a basis for pricing, for example, by wine vintage.

Illustration 2

Some biological assets are physically attached to land, for example tree plantations, and it is necessary to value the land and biological assets together as one asset, even though agricultural land is not within the scope of IAS 41. To obtain the fair value of the biological assets, the fair value of the land element should be deducted from the combined fair value.

A farmer wishing to value an apple orchard, in circumstances where there is no separate valuation for the orchard from that for the land on which it is grown, would value it at the combined fair value of the land and orchard, less the estimated fair value of land.

Land is dealt with under IAS 16 or IAS 40.

5 Gains and Losses

Gains or losses arising on the initial recognition at fair value of a biological asset and agricultural produce should be reported directly in the income statement for the period to which they relate, for example a gain may arise on the birth of a calf. Subsequent changes in the fair value will also be reported directly in the income statement. [IAS 41.26]

Gains or losses on the initial recognition of agricultural produce should also be included in the income statement in the period in which they arise. Such gains or losses may arise as a result of harvesting, because the harvested crop may be worth more than the unharvested crop. In this case a gain would arise. [IAS 41.28]

6 Government Grants

An unconditional government grant received in relation to biological assets should be recognised as income when it becomes receivable. [IAS 41.34]

Conditional grants are recognised when the conditions for obtaining the grant are met. It may be possible to recognise part of the grant as some of the conditions are met, for example where an entity is required to farm in a specific location over a number of years. [IAS 41.35]

Government grants recognised during the period should be separately identified and where there are unfulfilled conditions attaching to such grants these should be explained. An indication should be given in the financial statements where there is expected to be a decrease in the amount of government grants received in future periods.

IAS 20 *Accounting for government grants and disclosure of government assistance* applies to government grants relating to biological assets measured at cost less accumulated depreciation and accumulated impairment losses.

7 Disclosure

IAS 1 *Presentation of financial statements* requires biological assets to be separately presented on the face of the balance sheet. [IAS 41.39]

Gains and losses arising on the initial recognition of biological assets and agricultural produce and from changes in fair value of biological assets should be separately disclosed. In addition a description of each group of biological assets is required, with quantification encouraged. [IAS 41.40, 41.41]

IAS 41 encourages the entity to distinguish between consumable and bearer assets, or between mature and immature assets as appropriate. A consumable biological asset is one that is harvested as agricultural produce or sold as biological assets. A bearer biological asset is not a consumable biological asset but one that is self-regenerating rather than harvested for its agricultural produce. For example, livestock intended for the production of meat are consumable biological assets whereas livestock held for dairy farming are bearer assets. Similarly, trees grown for lumber are consumable assets whereas fruit trees are bearer assets.

A description of the nature of activities involving an entity's biological assets by group should be included in the financial statements as well as information on the physical quantity of biological assets and their estimated outputs. [IAS 41.46]

A number of disclosures are required about the fair value of biological assets and agricultural produce. Such disclosures should include details about the methods used to fair value the assets and significant assumptions used as part of that process. Disclosure should also be made of the fair value of agricultural produce harvested. [IAS 41.47, 41.48]

An entity should disclose details of any biological assets where their title is restricted in some way or where the assets have been pledged as security. Any commitment in relation to the purchase or development of biological assets should also be explained. [IAS 41.49]

A full reconciliation should be included of changes in fair value during the period. [IAS 41.50]

Illustration 3

A herd of 5 four year old animals was held on 1 January 2003. On 1 July 2003 a 4.5 year old animal was purchased. The fair values less estimated point of sale costs were as follows:

4 year old animal at 1 January 2003	CU200
4.5 year old animal at 1 July 2003	CU212
5 year old animal at 31 December 2003	CU230

The movement in the fair value less estimated point of sale costs of the herd can be reconciled as follows:

At 1 January 2003 (5 x CU200)	CU1,000
Purchased	CU212
Change in fair value (the balancing figure)	CU168
At 31 December 2003 (6 x CU230)	CU1,380

The entity is encouraged to disclose separately the amount of the change in fair value less estimated point of sale costs arising from physical changes and price changes.

If it is not possible to measure biological assets reliably and they are instead recognised at their cost less depreciation and impairment an explanation should be provided of why it was not possible to establish fair value. A full reconciliation of movements in the net cost should be presented with an explanation of the depreciation rate and method used. [IAS 41.54, 41.55, 41.56]

Additional disclosures are also required in relation to government grants. [IAS 41.57]

8 Chapter Review

This chapter has covered:

- the distinction between biological assets and agricultural produce;

- the importance of market based measures for valuing biological assets and agricultural produce;

- how to recognise assets and produce and the recognition of gains and losses arising; and

- how to deal with government grants in the agricultural sector.

Chapter 31
CONSOLIDATION

1 Business Context

Financial statements normally set out the financial position and performance of a single entity. If that entity is controlled by another entity (its parent) and there are intra-group transactions, then its financial statements may not reveal a true picture of its activities. Consolidated financial statements are prepared on the basis that the group is a single economic entity, by aggregating the transactions and balances of the parent and all its subsidiaries. A group is simply a collection of entities, where one, the parent, controls the activities of the others, its subsidiaries.

The preparation of single entity financial statements would not reflect the economic reality of the financial performance and position under the control of the parent entity.

2 Chapter Objectives

This chapter deals with how an investor entity should report the results of other entities over whose financial and operating policies it has control so that it can obtain benefits from their activities.

A group of entities presents financial information about their activities as if it was a single economic entity, these are known as the consolidated financial statements. IAS 27 *Consolidated and separate financial statements* governs their preparation and is discussed in this chapter. The treatment in the consolidated financial statements for investments giving rise to joint control (under IAS 31 *Interests in joint ventures*) and for those giving rise to significant influence (under IAS 28 *Investments in associates*) are dealt with in separate chapters.

On completion of this chapter you should be able to:

- understand the scope of IAS 27;

- interpret the important terminology and definitions which relate to the preparation of the financial statements of a group of entities;

- understand the key principles relating to recognition and measurement in consolidated financial statements; and

- demonstrate knowledge of the principal disclosure requirements of IAS 27.

3 Objectives, Scope and Definitions of IAS 27

The scope of IAS 27 is wide and should be applied *"in the preparation and presentation of consolidated financial statements for a group of entities under the control of a parent"*. [IAS 27.1]

IAS 27 also addresses the accounting requirements for investments in subsidiaries, jointly-controlled entities and associates in separate financial statements. Separate financial statements are those of an individual investing entity rather than those of the combined group. [IAS 27.3]

IAS 27 does not cover the treatment of a business combination, for example the acquisition of a subsidiary, in the group financial statements. This is set out in IFRS 3 *Business combinations*.

A parent entity can control another entity in a number of ways. The easiest control relationship to identify is where one entity has more than half of the voting rights in another entity. It is not however, a requirement that at least half of the voting rights are held for control to exist. IAS 27 includes a number of examples where control may exist even though the parent does not hold a majority of the voting rights. Such situations include:

- where the parent has the power to control more than 50% of the voting rights, for example by exercising share conversion rights, or where it has the power to govern the financial and operating policies of the other entity through agreement with other shareholders or by statute; or

- where the entity is controlled by its board of directors and the parent has the ability to appoint or remove the majority of the members of that board, or has the power to cast the majority of the votes at such a board meeting.

4 Consolidated Financial Statements

4.1 Presentation

Subject to limited exceptions, IAS 27 requires every parent to prepare a set of consolidated financial statements. [IAS 27.9]

An exception to this requirement arises in circumstances where the shareholders of the parent will gain limited benefit from the preparation of consolidated financial statements at this level. For example where the parent entity is itself a wholly-owned subsidiary. In this scenario the only shareholder is the superior parent entity which will be required to prepare its own consolidated financial statements. This exception also applies where a partially-owned subsidiary has informed the minority interest shareholders (i.e. the shareholders of the subsidiary other than the parent entity) of the proposal not to prepare consolidated financial statements and there were no objections. The ultimate parent (i.e. the top entity in the group), or the intermediate parent if one exists, is required to prepare consolidated financial statements that are publicly available and in accordance with IFRS for this exception to be available. [IAS 27.10]

This exception cannot be utilised where the parent has debt or equity instruments traded on any public market (or is in the process of issuing debt or equity in a public market). In such circumstances its consolidated financial statements are likely to have a wider circulation and therefore should be prepared. [IAS 27.10]

4.2 Scope of consolidated financial statements

Consolidated financial statements are designed to present the group's activities as if they had been undertaken by a single entity. Such financial statements should therefore include, on an aggregate basis, the results and financial position of all subsidiaries of the parent. One exception to this general requirement is where on acquisition an entity meets the criteria to be classified as 'held for sale' under IFRS 5 *Non-current assets held for sale and discontinued operations*. [IAS 27.12]

A subsidiary should not be excluded from the consolidated financial statements because its activities are dissimilar to those of the other entities in the group. This information would instead be presented as additional information in the consolidated financial statements, for example under the business segment analysis required by IAS 14 *Segment reporting*.

The preparation of consolidated financial statements is still generally required where a parent entity is a venture capitalist, mutual fund or unit trust.

4.3 Special purpose entities

IAS 27 requires that an entity is included in the consolidated financial statements where it is controlled by another entity. As explained above, control is usually obtained where the majority of the voting rights in the other entity are held, although it is possible to have control in other circumstances. The identification of control should be established by looking at the substance of the relationship rather than its legal form, for example by identifying which party is gaining the benefits generated by an entity's activities.

It is possible to set up an operating relationship between entities solely for a defined and narrow purpose, for example to effect a lease. Entities used for such purposes are commonly referred to as special purpose entities (SPE) and may be in the form of a trust or partnership rather than an incorporated entity.

What is unique about such entities is that although they may have a governing body, they have restricted decision-making powers which instead lie with the creator of the entity. As a consequence the SPE acts as if it were on 'autopilot'.

Where such entities exist management may have to exercise a significant amount of judgement to identify whether there is effective control over the SPE. Control may exist through the predetermination of the activities of the SPE. Other indicators of control may include where the activities of the SPE are essentially being operated on behalf of another entity or where another entity enjoys the majority of the benefits generated by the SPE.

The Standing Interpretations Committee issued SIC 12 *Special purpose entities* to deal with the treatment of such entities. The SIC requires that where the substance of the relationship is that the SPE is controlled by another entity, that entity should consolidate it in accordance with the requirements of IAS 27.

5 Consolidation Procedures

5.1 Basic approach

The preparation of consolidated financial statements involves the combination of the financial statements of the parent and its subsidiaries on a line-by-line basis. Individual line items are added together for all entities within the group to produce the consolidated figures for the single economic entity. This approach is adopted for all items in the financial statements, for example income, expenditure, assets and liabilities.

A number of further steps are then required to ensure that information is not double counted and that the consolidated financial statements of the group fairly present the results and position of the group as a whole.

The parent entity will have an asset line item in its own financial statements which represents the cost of acquiring an investment in a subsidiary. The cost of the investment is replaced by the results and financial position of the subsidiary on consolidation.

The aggregation of each line item in the balance sheet will lead to equity which represents that of the total of all entities in the group. This will include retained earnings that were generated both before and after a subsidiary was acquired. Retained profits earned before a subsidiary was aquired by its current parent should not be reported as part of the group results. The parent's share of a subsidiary's equity at the time of acquisition should therefore be eliminated.

Any difference between the cost of investment and the parent's share of a subsidiary's equity at the time of acquisition is goodwill, which is recognised in the consolidated financial statements as an asset, in accordance with IFRS 3.

Illustration 1

ABC acquired the entire share capital of XYZ for CU20,000. At that date the equity of XYZ comprised share capital of CU5,000 and retained earnings of CU6,000.

The share capital and pre-acquisition retained earnings are eliminated against the cost of investment in the consolidated financial statements. The difference is goodwill.

		CU
Cost of investment		20,000
Less:		
Share capital	5,000	
Retained earnings	6,000	
		11,000
Goodwill		9,000

The ownership of the profits and net assets of subsidiaries included in the aggregation process should be analysed between the parent entity shareholder and the minority interest. The minority interest is the portion of the results and financial position of subsidiaries that does not belong to the parent. For example, where a parent owns 80% of a subsidiary, the minority interest is the remaining 20%.

The portion of profit or loss and net assets of the group which belongs to the minority shareholders should be presented separately in the consolidated financial statements. [IAS 27.33]

The minority interest is calculated by applying the proportion of shares in the subsidiary that belong to the minority shareholders to the results and net assets of the subsidiary.

Illustration 2

ABC acquired 60% of the share capital of XYZ on 1 January 2003 for CU20,000. At that date the equity of XYZ comprised share capital of CU5,000 and retained earnings of CU15,000.

The profit after tax of XYZ for the year ended 31 December 2003 was CU10,000 and the retained earnings at that date were CU25,000.

The share capital and pre-acquisition retained earnings are eliminated against the cost of investment in the consolidated financial statements. The difference is goodwill.

		CU
Cost of investment		20,000
Less: share of assets acquired		
Share capital	5,000	
Retained earnings	15,000	
Share (60%)	20,000	12,000
Goodwill		8,000

The minority interest in the net assets at year-end is CU12,000 (40% x (CU5,000 + CU25,000)).

The minority interest in the profit for the year is CU4,000 (40% x CU10,000).

The consolidated retained earnings will include ABC's share of the retained earnings since acquisition of CU6,000 ((CU25,000 - CU15,000) x 60%). The pre-acquisition retained earnings were eliminated against the cost of investment.

Generally, where a subsidiary's loss attributable to the minority shareholding in the period is greater than the minority's share of net assets, the excess loss should not be presented as belonging to the minority shareholders. The exception is that if the minority shareholders have a binding obligation to provide additional funding to cover such losses they should continue to be allocated to the minority.

5.2 Adjustments

As the consolidated financial statements present the information for the group as a single entity, any transactions or balances arising between different entities in the group should be eliminated. This treatment is required because the single entity cannot transact business with itself or owe itself money. [IAS 27.24]

Where sales have been made between group entities, these should be eliminated in the revenue and costs of sales lines of the aggregated results of the group. Similarly where balances exist at the year end, the asset and corresponding liability should be eliminated.

A more complex adjustment is necessary where goods are sold between group entities and they are still held by one of the entities at the year-end. Any element of profit created by these internal transactions is not considered to be earned as such as far as the single entity is concerned and should therefore be eliminated. The inventories themselves should be reduced to their original cost to the group.

The full amount of transactions arising within a group should be eliminated even if the seller is a subsidiary in which there is a minority interest.

Illustration 3

PQR owns 60% of STU. The following figures are extracted from their separate financial statements:

PQR   Trade receivables CU280,000, including CU50,000 due from STU

           Trade payables CU220,000, including CU10,000 due to STU

STU   Trade receivables CU125,000, including CU10,000 due from PQR

           Trade payables CU95,000, including CU50,000 due to PQR

The following figures should be included in the consolidated balance sheet of the group.

Trade receivables: CU280,000 – 50,000 + 125,000 – 10,000 = CU345,000

Trade payables: CU220,000 – 10,000 + 95,000 – 50,000   = CU255,000

The intra-group balances should be eliminated in full. Trade receivables and trade payables should only include balances with third parties.

Illustration 4

ABC holds a 75% interest in DEF. At the current year end inventory is held within the group which was purchased from another group entity for CU50,000 at cost plus 25%. The group's consolidated balance sheet has been drafted without any adjustment in relation to this holding of inventory.

The adjustment required to be made to the draft consolidated balance sheet for inventories, the minority interest and retained earnings attributable to the equity holders of ABC are set out below based on the following assumptions:

Assumption 1:   ABC holds the inventory which was bought from DEF

Assumption 2:   DEF holds the inventory which was purchased from ABC

Under both assumptions, the CU10,000 of profit should be taken out of the carrying amount of the inventory (25/125 x CU50,000 = CU10,000). This amount should be removed from the seller's retained earnings.

If non-current assets, such as property, have been sold by one group entity to another, adjustment is necessary to eliminate the unrealised profit or loss on the sale. In addition, the depreciation (i.e. charging an asset's cost over the period in which it will be used by the entity) should be adjusted to the value it would have been had no sale taken place.

5.3 Other requirements

5.3.1 Reporting dates and consistent accounting policies

Since the consolidated financial statements are prepared on the basis that the group is a single economic entity, the financial statements of the parent and its subsidiaries should be made up to the same reporting date. If a subsidiary has a different year-end to it's parent, then it is required to prepare additional financial information for consolidation purposes. Adjustments should be made for significant transactions and events between the subsidiary's reporting date and that of its parent. [IAS 27.26, 27.27]

Where different accounting dates exist for the parent and one of its subsidiaries, the difference in reporting dates should not exceed three months.

It is also essential that uniform accounting policies are applied by all entities in the group. If group accounting policies are not adopted in the subsidiaries' own financial statements, then adjustments should be made to reflect the effect of the group policies for inclusion in the consolidation financial statements. [IAS 27.28]

5.3.2 Ceasing to be a subsidiary

When a parent loses control of a subsidiary, then the subsidiary should be excluded from consolidation from that date. But the results of the subsidiary should be included in the consolidated financial statements up to that date, since this reflects the reality that up until that point the subsidiary was still a group entity.

Once an entity is no longer a subsidiary it should be accounted for as an investment in accordance with IAS 39 *Financial instruments: recognition and measurement.* But if it becomes an associate or joint venture, it should be accounted for in accordance with IAS 28 or IAS 31 respectively. [IAS 27.31]

6 Investor's Separate Financial Statements

For the preparation of the separate financial statements of an entity, i.e. the parent only financial statements rather than the consolidated financial statements, investments in subsidiaries (and associates and joint ventures) should be recognised either at cost or in accordance with IAS 39, at the choice of the entity. If such an investment is classified as 'held for sale' under IFRS 5, then it should be treated in accordance with that standard. [IAS 27.37]

7 Disclosures

A number of disclosure requirements are included in IAS 27 which provide additional information about the nature of the control relationship between the parent and its subsidiaries. These disclosures include: an explanation of the parent / subsidiary relationship where the parent does not hold the majority of the voting rights, an explanation of why even though the majority of the voting rights are held the investor does not have control and an explanation of any significant restrictions on the ability of the subsidiary to transfer funds to its parent, for example by the payment of dividends. [IAS 27.40]

Where a subsidiary does not have the same reporting date as its parent, this fact should be explained along with details on the subsidiary's reporting date. [IAS 27.40]

Where a parent entity does not prepare consolidated financial statements (because it is permitted to use the exception, as explained at the beginning of this chapter) this fact should be disclosed. In addition the parent entity should include the name and country of incorporation (or residence) of the entity in which its results have been consolidated and where the publicly available financial statements can be obtained. A list of significant investments such as subsidiaries, associates and joint ventures, should be provided in the entity-only financial statements with details on the shareholdings held, the country of incorporation and how the investments have been accounted for. [IAS 27.41]

Where separate financial statements have been prepared disclosures are required about investments that are classed as being associates and joint ventures where separate financial statements are prepared. These disclosures detail similar information to that set out above along with an explanation of why the separate financial statements have been prepared, if they are not required by law. [IAS 27.42]

8 Chapter Review

This chapter covered the routine processes by which the consolidated financial statements for a parent and its subsidiaries are prepared as if the various separate legal entities are a single economic entity.

This chapter has covered:

- the scope of IAS 27;

- its requirements as to which entities should produce consolidated financial statements;

- consolidation procedures;

- the requirements in respect of common reporting dates and uniform accounting policies; and

- the disclosure requirements set out in IAS 27.

Chapter 32
HYPERINFLATIONARY ECONOMIES

1 Business Context

Hyperinflationary economies are those with very high rates of general inflation which have such a depreciating effect on the country's currency that it loses its purchasing power at a very fast rate.

This causes particular problems for businesses operating in such economies since money loses its purchasing power at such a high rate that comparisons are at best unhelpful, and potentially misleading. This includes the comparison of results between accounting periods and for similar transactions within the same accounting period.

Thus, where an entity has operations in a hyperinflationary economy it is likely that without restatement the reporting of operating results and the financial position in the local currency will become distorted over time.

There are two types of price changes:

- *general inflation*: being an average increase in a price index of different goods typically purchased. This is a measure of the general purchasing power of money; and

- *specific inflation:* this is a measure of changes in prices of specific types of goods. For example, the price of land and property may be rapidly increasing while inventories may be experiencing only modest increases.

2 Chapter Objectives

This chapter covers the accounting and disclosure requirements for entities operating in hyperinflationary economies in accordance with IAS 29 *Financial reporting in hyperinflationary economies.*

On completion of this chapter you should be able to:

- understand the scope and objectives of IAS 29;

- understand and demonstrate knowledge of the key principles concerning recognition and measurement in hyperinflationary conditions; and

- demonstrate knowledge of the principal disclosure requirements of IAS 29.

3 Objectives, Scope and Definitions of IAS 29

The objective of IAS 29 is to present financial information of an entity operating in a hyperinflationary economy without distorting the entity's actual performance. IAS 29 applies to all entities whose functional currency is that of a hyperinflationary economy. An entity's functional currency is defined in IAS 21 *The effect of changes in foreign exchange rates* as the currency of the primary economic environment in which the entity operates. [IAS 29.1]

IAS 29 only measures general inflation. It adjusts financial statements using a general price index to provide users of the financial statements with more meaningful information and to allow useful comparisons to be made.

IAS 29 does not identify an absolute rate at which hyperinflation is deemed to arise. Instead it lists indicators that suggest that hyperinflation is present. It is a matter of judgement when restatement under IAS 29 becomes necessary.

There is no universally accepted definition of hyperinflation. The only quantitative guidance given in IAS 29 is that a cumulative inflation rate over three years approaching, or exceeding, 100% is indicative of hyperinflation.

Other indications of hyperinflation include the tendency for people to keep their wealth in non-monetary assets (such as property) and monetary amounts being expressed in a stable currency, such as the US dollar, rather than in terms of the local currency.

IAS 29 interacts with IAS 21 in accounting for foreign currencies, however, IAS 29 applies independently of IAS 21 where entities operate in hyperinflationary economies but have no overseas transactions or operations.

4 The Restatement of Financial Statements

4.1 Introduction

IAS 29 requires the primary financial statements of an entity that reports in the currency of a hyperinflationary economy to be expressed in terms of the measuring unit current at the balance sheet date. This requires all values initially measured at an earlier date to be restated by reference to the change in the general price index between the date of initial measurement and the balance sheet date. The same requirement applies whether the financial statements have been prepared using the historical cost basis (i.e. transactions or events are recorded at the amount which was relevant on the day that they took place or occurred, for example actual purchase price) or using a current cost approach (which takes account of changes in asset values). [IAS 29.8]

The restatement using the current measuring unit required by IAS 29 applies to both the current year and to comparative information presented. [IAS 29.8]

4.2 Restatement of historical cost financial statements

4.2.1 The balance sheet

To make the necessary adjustments in the balance sheet it is important to distinguish between:

- *non-monetary items,* such as plant, property, inventories, investments, goodwill and intangible assets. Such items are not fixed in monetary terms; and

- *monetary items,* such as cash, receivables, payables and loans which are fixed in monetary terms.

Non-monetary items are adjusted using a general price index, because they are stated at amounts that were current at the date of their acquisition and not at the balance sheet date. Monetary items are not adjusted as they are already carried at amounts that are current at the balance sheet date.

4.2.2 The income statement

All items in the income statement should be expressed in terms of the measuring unit current at the balance sheet date. This requires all amounts to be restated by applying the change in the general price index from the dates when the items of income and expenditure were initially recorded to the balance sheet date.

4.2.3 Gain or loss on net monetary position

If an entity holds CU1,000 in cash for a year while the price index doubles, then the real value of that cash will fall by CU500 (i.e. half its amount), which represents the loss on the monetary position. The same applies to other monetary assets such as receivables.

Conversely, if an entity owes CU5,000 at the beginning of a year and the price index doubles over the year, the real value of that loan will fall by CU2,500 (i.e. half its value). In this scenario the entity has made a monetary gain of CU2,500.

By adding all monetary assets and liabilities together a gain or loss on the net monetary position can be calculated and should be included in the profit or loss for the period. [IAS 29.9]

The gain or loss may be estimated by applying the change in a general price index for the period to the weighted average of the difference between monetary assets and monetary liabilities.

Illustration 1

An entity in a hyperinflationary economy commenced business on 1 January 2004. It is required to restate its financial statements in accordance with IAS 29. All non-monetary assets were acquired on the first day of trading. There is no depreciation and inventories are purchased on a just-in-time basis.

At 1 January 2004, net monetary assets were CU2,000. Assume profits generate cash evenly over the year.

The relevant indices are:

1 January 2004	100
30 June 2004	110
31 December 2004	120

The following table sets out the amounts recorded in the unadjusted balance sheet and the adjustments required under IAS 29.

Balances at 31 December 2004	Unadjusted balance sheet CU	Adjustment	Inflation adjusted balances CU
Non-monetary assets	10,000	120/100	12,000
Net monetary assets	5,000		5,000
	15,000		17,000
Opening equity	12,000	120/100	14,400
Profit for the year	3,000	120/110	3,273
	15,000		
Loss on monetary assets:			
CU2,000 held all year		(120-100)/100	(400)
CU3,000 generated during year		(120-110)/110	(273)
			17,000

4.3 Restatement of current cost financial statements

4.3.1 The balance sheet

Assets and liabilities recorded on a current cost basis in the balance sheet already reflect the value of current prices and therefore no adjustment is necessary to restate the balance sheet at the year-end.

4.3.2 The income statement

Transactions recorded in a current cost income statement reflect the cost of the transaction at the transaction date. Expenses such as depreciation will be charged at the current value at the time of consumption. It is therefore necessary to adjust all figures in the income statement by the general price index in a similar way to that described above under the historical cost basis.

4.3.3. Gain or loss on net monetary position

The same principles apply for calculating the gain or loss on the net monetary position as that explained above in relation to historical cost accounting.

4.4 Cash flow statement

All items in the cash flow statement should be restated to take account of changes in the general price index.

5 Economies Ceasing to be Hyperinflationary

Where an entity operates in an economy that ceases to be hyperinflationary it is no longer required to apply the requirements of IAS 29. The restated amounts that are recorded in the last reported financial statements should be used as the carrying amounts going forward. There should be no adjustment to restate amounts back to their original value under the appropriate accounting basis. [IAS 29.38]

6 Disclosures

An entity should explain that the financial statements and the comparative information have been adjusted to take account of general inflationary increases by applying the measuring unit current at the balance sheet date. It should also disclose the basis of preparation of its financial statements, for example the historical cost method. [IAS 29.39]

Information on changes in the price index should be disclosed, this should include the rate at the balance sheet date and the movement in the index in the current and previous period. [IAS 29.39]

7 Chapter Review

This chapter has been concerned with financial reporting in hyperinflationary economies.

This chapter has covered:

- the objectives and scope of IAS 29;

- the key principles concerning recognition and measurement in hyperinflationary conditions; and

- the principal disclosure requirements of IAS 29.

Chapter 33
BUSINESS COMBINATIONS

1 Business Context

Entities may increase their market share, diversify their business or improve vertical integration of their activities in a number of ways, including by organic growth or through acquisitions. The acquisition of a competitor may offer rapid expansion or access to new markets and is often seen as more attractive than expansion through organic growth.

The takeover of Airtouch and Mannesman by Vodafone led to it becoming Europe's most valuable company (immediately after the acquisitions) and one of the world's top ten.

To ensure that users of financial statements are able to distinguish between organic growth and growth through acquisition the separation of results is essential and comprehensive disclosures with explanation should be presented.

2 Chapter Objectives

This chapter deals with the treatment of an investing entity ('investor') when it acquires a substantial shareholding in another entity ('investee'). The transaction which brings these two parties together is known as a 'business combination' and creates a 'group' of entities.

The routine processes by which a group of entities annually presents financial information about its activities as those of a single economic entity, are not discussed in this chapter as they are governed by IAS 27 *Consolidated and separate financial statements.*

Situations where the investor gains joint control or significant influence are covered by IAS 31 *Interests in joint ventures* and IAS 28 *Investments in associates* respectively.

On completion of this chapter you should be able to:

- understand the objectives and scope of IFRS 3 *Business combinations;*

- interpret the important terminology and definitions which relate to the treatment of business combinations in financial statements;

- identify the key principles relating to the recognition and measurement of business combinations; and

- demonstrate knowledge of the principal disclosure requirements of IFRS 3.

3 Objectives, Scope and Definitions of IFRS 3

The objective of IFRS 3 is to set out the accounting and disclosure requirements for a business combination. A business combination is simply the *"bringing together of separate entities or businesses into one reporting entity".* [IFRS 3 Appendix A]

In a straightforward business combination one entity will acquire another, resulting in a parent-subsidiary relationship.

In terms of scope, IFRS 3 should be applied to all business combinations, except in the following circumstances where the IASB is in the process of developing separate requirements:

- where two or more quite separate businesses are brought together to operate as one entity in the form of a joint venture;

- where a number of entities that are under common control, (i.e. they are ultimately controlled by the same party) are reorganised as part of a business combination. A typical example is where subsidiaries within a group are moved around the group so that their immediate parent entity changes although the overall parent entity of the group remains the same. Control of an entity is where one party (or a number of parties) has the power over another to *"govern its financial and operating policies so as to obtain the benefits from its activities"*;

- where a business combination involves two or more mutual entities. A mutual entity is defined as being *"an entity other than an investor-owned entity, such as a mutual insurance company or a mutual cooperative entity, that provides lower costs or other economic benefits directly and proportionately to its policyholders or participants"*; and

- where a number of separate entities are brought together by contract as part of a business combination but do not form a reporting entity as a result. An example is where entities come together to form a dual-listed corporation.

Although as originally published on 31 March 2004 IFRS 3 included the above exceptions, a subsequent proposed amendment, if finalised, will remove the exception for combinations by contract or involving mutual entities.

3.1 Purchase method of accounting

All business combinations should be accounted for by the purchase method, whereby: [IFRS 3.14]

- one party to the transaction is identified as the acquirer, with the other being the acquiree. It is assumed that it will always be possible to identify an acquirer;

- the acquirer measures the cost of the business combination; and

- the cost of the business combination is allocated to the identifiable assets and liabilities (including contingent liabilities) acquired.

The application of the purchase method does not result in changes to the measurement or recognition of the acquirer's own assets and liabilities because these items are not part of the purchase transaction.

4 Identifying the Acquirer

The first step in applying the purchase method to a business combination is to identify the acquirer. The acquirer is the party to the transaction that gains control over the other party. [IFRS 3.17]

A combining entity is assumed to have control of another when it acquires more than half of the other entity's voting rights. It is not, however, an essential attribute of control that over half of the voting rights are owned, and there are other circumstances in which control exists, for example where the entity has the ability to appoint or remove the majority of the members of the board of the acquiree. The 'control' concept is discussed in more detail in IAS 27.

In most business combinations the identification of the acquirer is usually clear. However, where this is not the case, IFRS 3 sets out a number of indicators that may help with the identification. These are:

- where the fair value of one entity is significantly greater than that of the other, the larger entity is likely to be the acquirer;

- where one entity has issued shares for cash to effect the business combination, the entity that has undertaken the share issue is likely to be the acquirer; or

- where one of the entities has the ability to select the management team of the combined entity, that party is likely to be the acquirer.

5 Cost of a Business Combination

5.1 General principle

The cost of a business combination is the total of the fair values of the consideration given by the acquirer plus any directly attributable costs of the business combination. [IFRS 3.24]

The consideration paid may take a number of forms, such as:

- cash or other assets given up;

- liabilities assumed, such as taking on the liability for a bank loan of the acquiree. But future losses or other costs expected to be incurred in the future do not form part of the consideration; or

- the issue of equity instruments, such as ordinary shares.

Fair value is the amount which an entity will pay for, say, an asset when it is exchanged between unrelated and willing parties (i.e. not in a forced sale).

Fair value should be measured at the date that the exchange takes place, which in most instances corresponds with the acquisition date. The acquisition date is the date on which the acquirer gains control of the other entity. Where the acquisition is achieved in stages, the date of exchange is the date on which each individual investment is recognised by the acquirer, which may be earlier than the acquisition date.

Where quoted equity instruments are issued as part of the cost of a business combination, their fair value will, except in rare circumstances, be the published price at the date of exchange.

The cost of a business combination should include costs that are directly attributable to the combination. Directly attributable costs are generally professional fees incurred in relation to the combination such as fees paid to accountants, legal advisors and valuation experts. General administrative costs are not directly attributable costs and should therefore be expensed as they are incurred. Costs incurred in issuing debt or equity instruments are an integral part of issuing the capital instruments and are deducted from the carrying amount of those instruments rather than forming part of the cost of the business combination.

Illustration 1

An entity acquires the entire share capital of another entity by issuing 100,000 new CU1 ordinary shares at a fair value of CU2.50. The professional fees associated with the acquisition are CU20,000 and the issue costs of the shares are CU10,000.

The cost of the business combination is CU270,000 calculated as the fair value of the new shares issued (CU2.5 x 100,000) plus the professional fees (CU20,000). The issue costs are deducted from the share premium recorded on issue of the shares.

5.2 Adjustments to the cost of business combinations

In some instances the cost of a business combination may not be known until the outcome of certain future events has been established. For example, an adjustment may be required to the cost where it is contingent on a specified level of profit being maintained or achieved in future periods.

In such cases, the acquirer should include an estimate of these amounts in the cost of the business combination at the acquisition date, assuming that it is probable that the amounts will be paid and it can be measured reliably. Any change in these estimates should be recognised by adjusting the cost of the business combination. [IFRS 3.32]

Illustration 2

P gains control over S in a single acquisition transaction.

The acquisition agreement sets out that as part of the cost of the acquisition an additional 60 million shares will be issued in one year's time if certain performance targets are met. Management believes it is probable that these targets will be met.

At the acquisition date, the published price of P's quoted shares is CU0.50, but it is thought they will fall to CU0.45 in one year's time due to increased competition in the market.

Since it is probable that the targets will be met, the 60m shares should be included in the cost of the business combination as a reliable estimate can be made for their cost.

As per the requirements of IFRS 3, the shares should be valued at their published price at the date of exchange rather than their estimated value, so at CU0.50.

The cost to be included in respect of the share issue is therefore 60m x CU0.50 = CU30m.

6 Allocation of Cost of a Business Combination

6.1 Overview

The cost of an acquisition is compared with the share of the fair value of the identifiable net assets acquired.

Where the cost exceeds the share of identifiable net assets acquired, goodwill is recognised, being the excess.

If the cost of an acquisition is less than the share of identifiable net asset acquired this amount is essentially a discount received by the acquirer and is often referred to as negative goodwill.

6.2 Identification and valuation of net assets acquired

The acquirer shall, at the acquisition date, recognise the acquiree's assets, liabilities and contingent liabilities at their fair value. There is an exception for non-current assets held for sale which should be measured at their fair value less costs to sell, in accordance with IFRS 5 *Non-current assets held for sale and discontinued operations*. Assets and liabilities should be recognised where they meet specific recognition criteria as set out below: [IFRS 3.36, 3.37]

- assets other than intangible assets should be recognised where it is probable that the associated future economic benefits generated by the use of the assets will flow to the acquirer and their fair value can be measured reliably;

- liabilities, other than contingent liabilities, should be recognised where it is probable that an outflow of economic benefits will be required to settle the obligation and their fair value can be measured reliably; and

- for the recognition of an intangible asset or contingent liability its fair value should be capable of being measured reliably.

The identification of intangible assets, for example brands, licences and trademarks, may cause difficulties. Intangible assets acquired as part of a business combination should be separately recognised if they:

- meet the definition of an intangible asset as per IAS 38 *Intangible assets* which requires such assets to be either separable or arise from contractual or other legal rights; and

- their fair value is capable of being measured reliably.

Where the above recognition criteria are met, the fair value of the identifiable assets and liabilities (including contingent liabilities) should be measured as set out in the table below. [IFRS 3, Appendix B]:

Asset, liability or contingent liability	Measure of fair value
Financial instruments that are traded in an active market	Market values
Financial instruments where no active market exists	Estimate the fair value based on comparable instruments of entities with similar characteristics
Receivables	Present value of amounts receivable. Discounting is generally not required for short-term receivables since the effect is not likely to be significant.
Inventories – finished goods	Selling price less: costs of disposal and a reasonable profit allowance for the selling effort of the acquirer
Inventories - work in progress	Selling price of finished goods less: costs of completion, costs of disposal and a reasonable profit allowance for the selling effort of the acquirer
Inventories – raw materials	Current replacement cost
Land & buildings	Market values
Plant & equipment	Market values. If, however, due to the specialised nature of an asset there is no market based value then an estimate should be made using value in use (i.e. an assessment of future cash flows generated by the asset) or depreciated replacement cost (i.e. replacement cost adjusted for the current age and condition of the asset)
Intangible assets	Market values where an active market exists or, if not available, the amount the acquirer would have paid in an arm's length transaction (i.e. a sale between willing and unrelated parties)
Net employee assets or liabilities for defined benefit plans	Present value of the defined benefit obligation less the fair value of any plan assets. The recognition of a net employee asset is restricted to situations where the acquirer can gain benefit from the asset, for example from a reduction in future contributions payable.
Tax assets & liabilities	Amounts receivable or payable when assessed from the perspective of the combined entity i.e. after restating the identifiable assets and liabilities.

Accounts & notes payable, long-term debt, accruals	Present value of amounts to be paid in settling the current obligations. Discounting is generally not required for short-term liabilities since the effect is not likely to be significant.
Onerous contracts (i.e. where the unavoidable costs under a contract exceed the likely benefits expected to arise)	Present value of amounts to be paid
Contingent liabilities	The amount a third party would charge to assume those liabilities

The acquirer recognises the identifiable assets, liabilities and contingent liabilities of the entity acquired at their fair value at the acquisition date. If a minority interest in the acquiree exists, i.e. the acquirer does not acquire 100% of the entity's ordinary shares, then the minority interest should be measured at the minority's proportion of the net fair value of those items.

6.3 Future liabilities not recognised at the acquisition date

There are two types of liability which may arise from a business combination that should not be recognised as liabilities at the date of acquisition.

- The first is the effect of any reorganisation plan which is devised by the acquirer and will only be put into effect once control over the acquiree is gained. This applies even where the acquiree has agreed to implement a restructuring plan once the business combination takes effect. Immediately before the acquisition the acquiree has no present obligation arising from a past event; the event that triggers the obligation is instead the business combination and this has yet to take place.

- The second is the effect of future losses that are likely to be incurred, by either party to the business combination, as a result of the business combination. These are events of a future period and therefore should not be included as liabilities at the date of the acquisition.

6.4 Contingent liabilities

As noted above IFRS 3 requires identifiable contingent liabilities to be recognised as a consequence of a business combination where their amount can be measured reliably.

Following initial recognition at fair value, a contingent liability that is recognised as part of a business combination should be measured at the higher of the amount under IAS 37 *Provisions, contingent liabilities and contingent assets* (which will be nil until such items become liabilities) and their fair value at the acquisition date, less any subsequent amortisation. Without this specific requirement contingent liabilities recognised in such circumstances would fall back to being treated under IAS 37, which would lead to disclosure rather than recognition. [IFRS 3.48]

For contingent liabilities recognised as a consequence of a business combination the disclosure requirements in IAS 37 are still required.

Illustration 3

S discloses in its financial statements that it has a contingent liability of CU15,000.

On the acquisition of S by P on 31 December 2002, the last day of its accounting period, the fair value of this contingent liability is estimated to be CU10,000.

For the next two years there is no change to this estimate, but at the end of 2005, the fair value is re-estimated at CU4,000.

This event is reflected in the consolidated financial statements for the years 31 December 2003 to 2005 as follows:

From 2002 to 2004 the contingent liability will be recognised as a liability in the consolidated balance sheet at CU10,000.

In the 2005 financial statements the amount should be re-measured at CU4,000, while the reversal of CU6,000 will be recognised directly in the consolidated income statement in the year.

7 Goodwill

Goodwill is the excess of the cost of a business combination over the acquirer's interest in the net fair value of the identifiable assets, liabilities and contingent liabilities recognised. It is essentially an amount paid to gain access to the future economic benefits anticipated to be generated from the assets not specifically identified.

7.1 Recognition of goodwill

IFRS 3 requires goodwill resulting from a business combination to be recognised as an asset of the acquiring entity, measured initially as the difference between the cost of the business combination and the identifiable assets and liabilities (including contingent liabilities) recognised. [IFRS 3.51]

After initial recognition goodwill should be carried in the balance sheet at cost, less accumulated impairment losses (i.e. where the recoverable amount of the goodwill falls below its current carrying amount in the balance sheet). Goodwill recognised should be tested for impairment at least on an annual basis in accordance with the requirements of IAS 36 *Impairment of assets.* Goodwill is not permitted to be systematically amortised, for example charged to the income statement on a straight-line basis.

Although recognised as an asset, goodwill should not be revalued and therefore it will either remain in the balance sheet at the value recognised on initial recognition or it will reduce as impairment losses arise.

Illustration 4

ABC acquired an 80% interest in DEF for CU900,000 (including directly attributable costs). The carrying amounts and fair values of DEF plc's identifiable assets, liabilities and contingent liabilities on acquisition were as follows:

	Carrying amounts CU000	Fair value CU000
Tangible non-current assets	375	350
Intangible non-current assets	0	200
Current assets	400	350
Liabilities	(300)	(300)
Contingent liabilities	0	(30)
	475	570

The goodwill and minority interest arising on the business combination are based on the fair values (not carrying amounts) of the assets, liabilities and contingent liabilities which meet the IFRS 3 recognition criteria, even if they have not been recognised by DEF.

	CU000
Cost	900
Share of net assets acquired (80% x CU570)	456
Goodwill	444
Minority interest – 20% of CU570	114

The entity's share of net assets acquired plus the minority interest share equals the total identifiable net assets of the business acquired (CU456,000 + CU114,000 = CU570,000)

7.2 Discount on acquisition

The term 'discount on acquisition', or negative goodwill, is used here to describe the excess of the identifiable net assets recognised in a business combination over the cost of the business combination. IFRS 3 assumes that such an amount will not normally arise and therefore may have arisen as a result of an error in the measurement of the acquiree's net assets or of the cost of the combination. It is generally unusual for a discount to arise since it means that the acquirer paid less than what the business was worth.

IFRS 3 therefore requires that an acquirer reassesses the identification and measurement of the identifiable net assets acquired and the measurement of the cost of the business combination. The treatment of future costs arising in respect of the acquiree is often an area where errors are likely to occur. [IFRS 3.56]

If a discount still remains after the reassessment has been completed then it should be recognised immediately in the income statement in the period in which the business combination took place. This treatment is required since any discount reflects the reality that a bargain purchase was made.

Illustration 5

Assuming the same facts as in Illustration 4 above except that the cost of the business combination was CU400,000 rather than CU900,000.

The 'discount on acquisition' and minority interest arising on this business combination is:

	CU000
Net assets acquired	570
Cost	400
Share of net assets acquired = (80% x CU570)	456
'Discount on acquisition' (negative goodwill)	(56)
Minority interest (20% x CU570)	114

The CU56,000 should be recognised in the consolidated income statement in the year of acquisition.

7.3 Initial recognition and subsequent adjustments

Every effort should be made by an acquirer to complete its assessment of the identifiable assets and liabilities (including contingent liabilities) acquired by the end of the accounting period in which the combination takes place. However, it is sometimes not practicable for the assessment to be finalised in this time scale, especially when the valuation of non-current assets including intangibles is required, or the transaction occurred near the end of the acquirer's accounting period.

In such circumstances, the acquirer is required to make a provisional assessment at the year-end of the identifiable net assets and the cost of the combination. These provisional values should subsequently be finalised within one year of the acquisition date and adjustments should be made directly to the identifiable net assets and cost of the combination, and hence goodwill, accordingly.

Adjustments that subsequently arise following this cut-off date should be recognised as revisions of estimates in accordance with IAS 8 *Accounting policies, changes in accounting estimates and errors* and therefore recognised in the current and future periods. For example, the recovery of a receivable which has been charged to the income statement due to doubts over its recoverability should be recognised as income in the period in which it is recovered. Where an error is identified, retrospective treatment is required in accordance with IAS 8 including the adjustment of goodwill.

The adjustment of provisional figures will generally only relate to the assessment of fair values which cannot be finalised rather than the recognition of additional assets and liabilities due to the outcome of events that took place after the balance sheet date.

8 Disclosures

A business combination may result in substantial changes to both the nature of a group and its performance in future periods. IFRS 3, therefore, requires a large number of detailed disclosures to be made to assist in a user's understanding the impact that a business combination will have in the current and future periods. [IFRS 3.66]

The disclosure requirements, as set out below, has different objectives. In each case even though a detailed list of requirements is set out in the standard, it is made clear that additional disclosures should be presented where the objective of the disclosure is not met.

The first set of disclosures has the objective of requiring disclosure of information about combinations effected during the period or after the balance sheet date. The names of the entities that were party to a business combination during the period should be presented along with the date of the transaction, the percentage of voting equity acquired and the cost of the combination. The cost of the business combination should be broken down into its various elements, for example cash and the issue of shares. If the acquiring entity is planning to dispose of part of the business acquired this should be identified. The amount recognised for the identifiable assets, liabilities and contingent liabilities recognised on acquisition along with their carrying amounts immediately before the combination, where practicable, should be presented.

If an intangible asset did not meet the criteria for separate recognition and was therefore subsumed within goodwill, this fact should be stated.

If a discount was achieved on the acquisition and hence recognised immediately in the consolidated income statement, this amount should be clearly identified.

The disclosures set out above may be aggregated for business combinations that individually will not have a substantial effect on the business.

Where provisional values have been provided in the financial statements of the period in which the business combination arose this fact should be explained along with the reasons why amounts could not be finalised.

The acquiree's profit or loss included in the consolidated financial statements in the year of acquisition should be identified. Where a business acquired has been fully integrated into existing operations it may not be practicable to separate out its results and therefore this fact should be disclosed. Combined results should be presented as if the combination had occurred at the beginning of the period (where practicable). It is hoped that this disclosure will provide useful information to users about the likely future performance of the enlarged group.

The second set of disclosures is specifically aimed at the provision of additional information as to the financial effect that gains, losses and other adjustments relating to the business combinations in the current and previous periods have had in the current period. This information should include, for example, the effect of any gains that have been recognised in respect of the identifiable assets and liabilities of the acquiree or the correction of errors. [IFRS 3.72]

The final set of disclosures provides information surrounding the goodwill recognised during the period. A full reconciliation of movements to the carrying amount of goodwill should be presented, this will include, for example, goodwill recognised during the period and any reductions in asset values as a result of impairments. A number of related disclosures are required regarding the recoverable amount of goodwill as required by IAS 36. [IFRS 3.74]

9 Chapter Review

This chapter has covered:

- the objective and scope of IFRS 3;

- the definitions which are critically important to the understanding of the requirements of IFRS 3;

- the steps in the purchase method of accounting: identify the acquirer, establish the cost of the business combination and the recognition of the net assets acquired, including contingent liabilities at fair value;

- the treatment of goodwill and 'discount on acquisition';

- initial accounting and subsequent adjustments; and

- the disclosure requirements of IFRS 3.

CHAPTER 34
ASSOCIATES

1 Business Context

Investments can take a number of different forms. Typically where one entity acquires the majority of the voting rights of another, it gains control. However, outright control is not always the most appropriate form of investment for an entity to have. There may be circumstances where although an entity does not have the expertise to efficiently control another entity, the business in which it operates is still of significant importance to it. In such circumstances an investor may instead decide to obtain sufficient ownership of the entity to have the power to influence decisions of its governing body (its board of directors) but not to have control over it.

Investments that meet these criteria will generally be classed as associates. As the investor has what is described as significant influence over the investee, it is appropriate to report its share of the investee's results rather than just the dividends receivable; after all, it is partly answerable for the investee's performance.

2 Chapter Objectives

IAS 27 *Consolidation and separate financial statements* and IFRS 3 *Business combinations* deal with the parent-subsidiary relationship where the investee is under the control of the investor. They cover the requirements in relation to the bringing together of two parties and the subsequent presentation in the consolidated financial statements on the basis that the two entities are treated as a single economic entity.

This chapter deals with the financial reporting by an investing entity when it has significant influence over its investee. In such circumstances the investee is described as an 'associate' of the investor.

On completion of this chapter you should be able to:

- understand the objectives and scope of IAS 28 *Investments in associates*;
- interpret the important terminology and definitions which relate to such investments;
- understand the key principles relating to the recognition and measurement of such investments;
- demonstrate knowledge of the principal disclosure requirements of IAS 28; and
- apply knowledge and understanding of IAS 28 in particular circumstances through basic calculations.

3 Objectives, Scope and Definitions of IAS 28

IAS 28 sets out the accounting requirements when an entity has an investment in an associate. The standard does not apply where the investor is a venture capital organisation or where the investment is owned by a mutual fund or unit trust (or similarly structured entity) and such investments have been accounted for using a fair value approach under IAS 39 *Financial instruments: recognition and measurement.* [IAS 28.1]

An associate is defined as an entity over which the investor has significant influence. For an investment to meet the definition of an associate it should not be a subsidiary, where the investor has control, or a joint venture, where the investor has joint control. [IAS 28.2]

Significant influence is defined as the power to participate in the financial and operating policy decisions of the investee without having control or joint control over those policies. [IAS 28.2]

The assessment of significant influence is a matter of judgement. IAS 28 includes practical guidance to assist management in making that assessment. For example, where an investor has at least 20% of the voting power in another entity, IAS 28 presumes that this size of holding is enough to give rise to significant influence over that entity. Conversely, where less than 20% of the voting rights are held, the investor is presumed not to have significant influence over the investee. However, the nature of each investment should be carefully assessed as both of these presumptions may be overruled. It is important to consider not only an investor's current shareholding but also any potential holding which could result from share options or warrants that are immediately exercisable (i.e. the right to acquire shares immediately).

IAS 28 provides a list of factors that normally indicate that significant influence is present. These factors include:

- where the investor has a representative on the board of directors or on an equivalent body;

- where the investor actively participates in the policy-making processes of the entity, including the level of dividends to be paid;

- where a number of significant transactions take place between the investor and the investee;

- where members of management move between the two entities; or

- where the investor provides essential technical information to the entity.

There are exceptions from compliance with IAS 28. Where the investment is classified as 'held for sale' in accordance with IFRS 5 *Non-current assets held for sale and discontinued operations,* it should be treated in accordance with that standard. IAS 28 does not apply if the investor is not required to prepare consolidated financial statements under IAS 27. [IAS 28.13, 28.14]

In addition, an exception applies where the investor is a wholly owned subsidiary (or partially owned but the minority interest shareholders have been notified of the intention not to apply the requirements of IAS 28 and they have not objected) and the investor does not have debt or equity instruments traded in a public market (nor is in the process of issuing debt or equity in a public market) and the investor's parent prepares consolidated financial statements that are publicly available and are prepared in accordance with IFRS. [IAS 28.13]

4 Equity Method of Accounting for Associates

Subject to the exceptions referred to above, associates should be accounted for using the equity method. If the relationship changes such that the investor gains control, or joint control, over the entity then it should be treated in accordance with IAS 27 or IAS 31 *Interests in joint ventures* respectively. If the ability to exercise significant influence is lost then the investment should cease to be equity accounted for and the requirements of IAS 39 should be applied. [IAS 28.13, 28.18]

Where the investor ceases to have significant influence, the carrying amount of the associate at this date is deemed to be the cost for initial recognition of the investment as a financial asset under the requirements of IAS 39. [IAS 28.19]

Under the equity method of accounting, the investment in the associate is initially recognised at cost and is subsequently adjusted in each period for changes in the investor's share of net assets of the associate. The investor's reported profit or loss for the period will include its share of the associate's reported profit or loss for the period, presented as a single line item. [IAS 28.2]

Where the parent and a number of its subsidiaries have an interest in a single entity, the group's share in the investment is determined by adding together all the interests held by group entities.

An investor's interest in an associate should be presented in the balance sheet as a single line under non-current assets. [IAS 28.38]

Illustration 1

Pecs has a number of wholly owned subsidiaries and a 40% interest in the share capital of Abs. These shares were acquired three years ago when the balance on Abs' retained earnings was CU100.

	Pecs group CU	Abs CU
Investment in Abs	120	–
Other assets	1,080	650
	1,200	650
Liabilities	(200)	(150)
	1,000	500
Share capital	300	100
Retained earnings	700	400
	1,000	500

The consolidated balance sheet of Pecs should incorporate Abs using the equity method of accounting. The carrying amount of the investment is calculated as:

Cost of investment	CU120
Share of post acquisition profit	
(40% x (400 − 100))	CU120
	CU240

Consolidated balance sheet

	Pecs group CU	
Investment in Abs	240	
Other assets	1,080	
	1,320	
Liabilities	(200)	
	1,120	
Share capital	300	
Retained earnings	820	(Pecs 700 plus share of Ab's post acquisition profit, 120)
	1,120	

Illustration 2

The consolidated income statement of Pecs and its subsidiaries and the income statement of Abs for the year ended 31 December 2004 are shown below.

	Pecs group CU	Abs CU
Turnover	1,100	600
Cost of sales	(200)	(150)
Gross profit	900	450
Expenses	(130)	(150)
Profit from operations	770	300
Finance income	90	–
Finance costs	(40)	(10)
Profit before tax	820	290
Tax	(270)	(70)
Net profit for the year	550	220

The consolidated income statement of Pecs will only include its share of the profit after tax of Abs.

	Pecs group CU	
Turnover	1,100	
Cost of sales	(200)	
Gross profit	900	
Expenses	(130)	
Profit from operations	770	
Finance income	90	
Finance costs	(40)	
Share of profits of associates	88	(40% of Abs profit after tax))
Profit before tax	908	
Tax	(270)	
Net profit for the year	638	

4.1 Procedures to be used

The procedures used in the preparation of the consolidated financial statements in accordance with IAS 27 are used in the application of equity accounting.

Where transactions take place between an investor and its associates, adjustment should be made to eliminate any internally generated profit or loss that arises. The amount eliminated is only the element that relates to the investor's share, since this is the amount that is essentially internally generated by the group.

Illustration 3

If an investor held a 30% share in an associate and made a profit of CU100 from a sale of inventory to the associate, then only CU30 (i.e. the investor's share) would be eliminated from the reported profit.

As equity accounting does not involve the aggregating of the individual asset and liability balances with those of the parent and subsidiaries, the receivables and payables balances due from and to associates is not eliminated.

At the acquisition date the investment in the associate should be recognised at its cost. This represents the share of the fair value of the net assets acquired and the future economic benefits attributable to assets which cannot be separately identified and recognised i.e. goodwill. Fair value is generally market value, although where no market exists for the transfer of such items, fair value may need to be assessed using a different basis. The calculation of fair values is consistent with the application of IFRS 3 *Business combinations*.

If the goodwill is a positive figure it should be included as part of the carrying amount of the investment. If the cost was less than the fair value of the net assets acquired, then a discount was achieved on the purchase (which is unlikely to occur in practice). The discount should be included as part of the investor's share of the associate's profit or loss for the period in which the investment was made.

The associate's most recent set of financial statements should be used for equity accounting purposes. If the associate's reporting date is different to that of the investor, then financial statements at the investor's reporting date should be prepared, unless it is impracticable to do so. The additional financial statements should be based on the associate's financial statements prepared at its last reporting date and adjusted for significant events that have occurred during the period between the two dates. The reporting dates should not be more than three months different to each other. [IAS 28.24, 28.25]

The associate's accounting policies should be consistent with those of its investor. Where the main accounting policies are different an adjustment should be made to the associate's financial statements for equity accounting purposes. [IAS 28.26]

If an associate makes losses then the investor should equity account for these in the same way as it recognises profits, by reducing the carrying amount of the share of the associate's net assets. If, however, losses continue the carrying amount of the associate should only be reduced as far as nil. Any excess loss should only be recognised by the investor as a liability where it has an obligation to make payments on behalf of the associate. If the associate makes profits in future periods the investor should resume equity accounting for its share.

4.2 Impairment losses

The requirements of IAS 39 should be applied to determine whether an impairment loss should be recognised in respect of the investment. An impairment arises where the recoverable amount of the asset has fallen below its current carrying amount. Where IAS 39 indicates that an impairment has arisen, IAS 36 *Impairment of assets* should be applied to assess its size.

The recoverable amount of the investor's share in an associate is determined by considering the net realisable value (i.e. net selling price) of the investment and its value in use. The value in use is determined either by estimating the present value (i.e. taking into account the time value of money) of the future cash flows that are expected to be generated by the associate or by estimating the present value of the expected future dividend stream.

5 Investor's Separate Financial Statements

An interest in an associate should be accounted for in the individual financial statements of the investor by applying the requirements of IAS 27 for separate financial statements. [IAS 28.35]

6 Disclosures

IAS 28 requires a number of detailed disclosures to be made about an entity's investment in its associates. Such disclosures include the fair value of an associate where published price quotations are available and summarised financial information of the associate. The summarised financial information should include the main items in the associate's financial statements, including assets, liabilities, revenue and profit or loss for the period. [IAS 28.37]

Where an investor has overruled the presumption that significant influence exists once the 20% holding of voting rights has been achieved, this fact should be disclosed along with the reason why a holding of less than this has led to the investor having a significant influence or why a holding of more than 20% has not. [IAS 28.37]

The associate's reporting date should be disclosed and if this is different from that of the investor, the reason why this date has been used. If there are any significant restrictions on the associate's ability to transfer funds to the investor, then this should be disclosed. Where an associate has made significant losses that have led to the investor's share of the associate's net assets being recorded as nil with the entity no longer recognising those losses, then the amount of any unrecognised losses should be disclosed. [IAS 28.37]

Where the equity method of accounting has not been used for the recognition of an investment in an associate, this fact should be disclosed along with summary financial information about the associate. [IAS 28.37]

Where the investor has a share in the associate's contingent liabilities, accounted for in accordance with IAS 37 *Provisions, contingent liabilities and contingent assets*, the amount should be disclosed. [IAS 28.40]

7 Chapter Review

This chapter has been concerned with the accounting requirements for an investment which gives rise to significant influence over an investee.

This chapter has covered:

- the scope of IAS 28;

- the critically important definitions of an associate and significant influence;

- the method of accounting for associates; and

- the disclosure requirements of IAS 28.

Chapter 35
JOINT VENTURES

1 Business Context

Investments can take a number of different forms. Typically where one entity acquires the majority of the voting rights in another, it gains control. However, in some industries and in particular circumstances, it is more beneficial to share such investments with other interested parties. By sharing the investment each investor contributes different skills; alternatively the arrangement benefits all parties through reduced costs. Such arrangements are commonly known as joint ventures.

Joint venture arrangements are quite common in the investment property sector. For example, British Land plc reported 12 active joint ventures holding £2.4billion of properties in its financial statements for the year ended 31 March 2004. Such arrangements were said to provide British Land access to properties that were not otherwise on the market and to reduce the risks associated with property investment and development.

2 Chapter Objectives

This chapter deals with the financial reporting by an investing entity where it has joint control over another entity. In such circumstances the investee is described as a 'joint venture' of the investor.

On completion of this chapter you should be able to:

- understand the objectives and scope of IAS 31 *Interests in joint ventures*;

- interpret the important terminology and definitions which relate to such investments;

- understand the key principles relating to the recognition and measurement of such investments;

- demonstrate knowledge of the principal disclosure requirements of IAS 31; and

- apply knowledge and understanding of IAS 31 in particular circumstances through basic calculations.

3 Objectives, Scope and Definitions of IAS 31

IAS 31 sets out the accounting requirements in relation to interests in joint ventures and the appropriate recognition of joint venture assets, liabilities, income and expenses in the financial statements of investors. [IAS 31.1]

A joint venture is where two, or more, parties (described as venturers) act together under contractual arrangements to carry out activities that are under their joint control, i.e. the parties agree to share control and to require unanimous agreement for all strategic decisions. Control is the power to govern the financial and operating activities of an economic activity so as to obtain benefits. An entity that invests in a joint venture but does not have joint control is known simply as an 'investor'.

IAS 31 does not apply where the venturer is a venture capital organisation or where the joint venture interest is owned by a mutual fund or unit trust (or similarly structured entity) and such investments have been accounted for under IAS 39 *Financial instruments: recognition and measurement*. Under IAS 39 the investment will be either measured at fair value or classified as a financial asset 'held for trading'. [IAS 31.1]

The presence of a contractual arrangement to share control is the principal factor in determining whether a joint venture relationship exists.

Illustration 1

An entity is set up to build a bridge over a river. Once the bridge is built, the entity will be wound up.

Ten contractors invest in the equity of the entity. Contractors 1 to 6 own 13% each and contractors 7 to 10 own 5.5% each. There exists a contractual arrangement whereby all the strategic financial and operating decisions relating to the bridge building project have to be taken unanimously by contractors 1 to 3 and 7 to 9.

Contractors 1 to 3 and 7 to 9 have joint control over the joint venture entity. Each of them is therefore a venturer in the bridge building entity. Contractors 4 to 6 and 10 are not involved in the contractual arrangement and are therefore only investors in the joint venture.

There are exemptions from compliance with IAS 31 where the joint venture investment is classified as 'held for sale' in accordance with IFRS 5 *Non-current assets held for sale and discontinued operations* and should therefore be accounted for in accordance with that standard. Where the venturer is not required to prepare consolidated financial statements under IAS 27 *Consolidated and separate financial statements* it should treat the joint venture in accordance with IAS 27.

In addition, an exemption applies where the venturer is a wholly owned subsidiary (or partially owned but the minority interest shareholders have been notified of the intention not to apply the requirements of IAS 31 and they have not objected) and the venturer does not have debt or equity instruments traded in a public market (nor is in the process of issuing debt or equity in a public market) and the venturer's parent prepares consolidated financial statements that are publicly available and are prepared in accordance with IFRS. [IAS 31.2]

4 The Three Forms of Joint Venture

In practical terms there are a number of forms a joint venture investment can take, but IAS 31 identifies only three broad types: jointly controlled operations, jointly controlled assets and jointly controlled entities.

4.1 Jointly controlled operations

In a jointly controlled operation a separate entity is not set up, but the parties to the transaction share the activities that are to be carried out. Effectively, the venturers pool resources and provide expertise to the overall operations.

Each venturer will use its own property, plant and equipment in carrying out the activities and will incur its own expenses and liabilities. Each venturer will also be responsible for raising its own finance. The contractual arrangements between the entities which create this form of joint venture investment will normally set out how the revenues and expenses will be shared.

The substance of such an arrangement is that each venturer is carrying on its own activities as essentially a separate part of its own business, since there is no separate entity. The accounting for the joint venture should therefore reflect the economic substance of this arrangement by recognising the assets that the venturer controls. The venturer's own property, plant and equipment that it uses to carry out activities of the jointly controlled operation, any liabilities that it retains obligation for and the expenses that it incurs should be recognised by the entity. Each venturer should also recognise its share of income generated by the jointly controlled operations.

Recognition of these amounts should be included in the individual entity financial statements of each venturer because they are part of its activities. No further adjustment is therefore required in the preparation of the consolidated financial statements. [IAS 31.15]

Illustration 2

An example of a jointly controlled operation is the construction of a new housing estate by a number of independent builders and specialist tradesmen, such as carpenters and plumbers. Each party provides a predetermined amount of labour to the construction and is required to provide the relevant materials and equipment needed to perform the work. Under an agreed contract, each party will receive a specified percentage of the revenue from the sale of the houses. This is an extension of each party's normal operating activities and should therefore be recorded in their individual books and records as such.

4.2 Jointly controlled assets

A joint venture relationship may be established through the use of jointly controlled assets which are used to generate benefits to be shared by each of the venturers. Such arrangements do not involve the creation of a separate entity and the assets may be jointly owned, although the important attribute of such an arrangement is that the assets in question are jointly controlled.

Typically each venturer receives an agreed a share of the benefits generated by the operation of the assets and bears an agreed share of the expenses incurred.

Each venturer in such an arrangement is again essentially using the assets as part of its normal operating activities and should therefore report them as part of those activities in its individual financial statements. In particular, a venturer should recognise its share of the jointly controlled assets, any liabilities that the entity has an obligation to meet and a share of the liabilities that are jointly incurred. Jointly incurred expenses and a share of the relevant income and expenses that are earned or incurred jointly should also be recognised by each venturer. [IAS 31.21]

Illustration 3

A common use of jointly controlled assets is by entities in the oil production industry. Typically, they jointly control and operate an oil pipeline. The benefit of such an arrangement is that only one pipeline is needed, with each venturer using the pipeline to transport its own supply of oil and in return paying a proportion of the running costs of the pipeline (i.e. the jointly controlled asset).

No additional adjustments are required in the preparation of the consolidated financial statements since the individual entity financial statements of each venturer already reflect the economic reality of the arrangements.

4.3 Jointly controlled entities

The third broad type of joint venture arrangement is a jointly controlled entity. The identifying factor in this arrangement is that a separate legal entity is set up with ownership being shared by the venturers.

The separate entity may take a number of forms. It may be an incorporated entity, a corporation or a partnership. The importance of the establishment of a separate entity is that it is able to enter into contracts and raise finance in its own right. As a separate legal entity it will also have to maintain its own accounting records and prepare and present its own financial statements.

A jointly controlled entity controls its own assets, incurs its own expenses and liabilities and generates its own income. Each venturer will typically be entitled to a predetermined proportion of the profits made by the joint venture entity.

Illustration 4

Joint venture entities are often set up to pool resources where operations are very similar in a separate line of business. Assets are combined and operated jointly from the joint venture entity. Such entities are particularly common in the telecommunications industry.

Where a venturer has an interest in a jointly controlled entity, it is required to recognise in its consolidated financial statements its share of the entity either by proportionate consolidation or by equity accounting. Proportionate consolidation involves consolidating the venturer's share of the individual line items of the joint venture's financial statements, whereas equity accounting reports the change in the venturer's share of the joint venture entity each period. [IAS 31.30]

4.3.1 Proportionate consolidation

Proportionate consolidation is where the venturer's share of the joint venture's assets, liabilities, income and expenditure is combined line by line with the venturer's own items. [IAS 31.3]

Proportionate consolidation uses the principles used in the full consolidation process required by IAS 27 for the reporting of subsidiaries. The different proportions that are consolidated in respect of a subsidiary and a joint venture represents the different levels of control held by the parent entity. In a subsidiary, the parent has ultimate control and therefore 100% of a subsidiary's net assets and results are consolidated, whereas control is shared in a joint venture, so only the venturer's share is consolidated.

The venturer may present the effects of proportionate consolidation in one of two ways. The first is by combining the proportion of the joint venture results and financial position on a line by line basis with that of the venturer's financial statements. This method results in single figures being presented for each line item. The alternative method is to split each line item between that which relates to the venturer and that which represents the proportion of the joint venture entity.

4.3.2 Equity method

As an alternative to proportionate consolidation a joint venture entity may be accounted for by applying the equity method. The equity method of accounting is used to account for investments in associates under IAS 28 *Investments in associates*. It requires the initial investment to be recorded at cost and adjusted each period for the venturer's share of the change in the net assets and results of the joint venture entity. [IAS 31.3]

IAS 31 permits the use of the equity accounting method although it recommends the use of proportionate consolidation.

A venturer should cease accounting for a joint venture entity under either method when it ceases to have joint control over the joint venture. If the venturer obtains complete control of the joint venture, then it should be accounted for in accordance with IAS 27 from that date.
[IAS 31.36, 31.41, 31.45]

Illustration 5

AB controls a number of subsidiaries and therefore prepares consolidated financial statements.

AB is also a venturer in JV, a jointly controlled entity in which AB owns 25%. AB acquired its share of JV at a cost of CU1m on the creation of JV. At that time JV had net assets of CU4m. Hence, no goodwill was created.

A summarised draft balance sheet of the AB Group (AB and its subsidiaries, but not its interest in JV), and JV is as follows:

	AB group CUm	JV CUm
Non-current assets		
Property, plant and equipment	60	20
Intangibles	30	8
Investment in JV	1	—
Current assets		
Inventories	50	16
Other	80	24
Current liabilities	(90)	(36)
Equity	131	32

	CUm
The equity in AB group plus JV can be calculated as:	
AB group	131
JV post-acquisition ((32 – 4) x 25%)	7
	138

The three layouts for the AB group consolidated balance sheet including JV are as follows:

1 Proportionate consolidation: line by line

	CUm
Non-current assets	
Property, plant and equipment (60 + (25% x 20))	65
Intangibles (30 + (25% x 8))	32
Current assets	
Inventories (50 + (25% x 16))	54
Other (80 + (25% x 24))	86
Current liabilities (90 + (25% x 36))	(99)
Equity - as above	138

2 Proportionate consolidation: share shown separately

		CUm	CUm
Non-current assets			
Property, plant and equipment	own	60	
	JV	5	
			65
Intangibles	own	30	
	JV	2	
			32
Current assets			
Inventories	own	50	
	JV	4	
			54
Other	own	80	
	JV	6	
			86
Current liabilities	own	(90)	
	JV	(9)	
			(99)
Equity – as above			138

3 Equity method of accounting

		CUm
Non-current assets		
Property, plant and equipment	(own)	60
Intangibles	(own)	30
Investment in JV (cost CU1m + share of post-acquisition increase in net assets (per calculation of equity) CU7m)		8
Current assets		
Inventories	(own)	50
Other	(own)	80
Current liabilities	(own)	(90)
Equity – as above		138

Note how the recognition using different methods has a significant effect on the presentation of the financial position of AB.

5 Other Points in IAS 31

5.1 Investor's separate financial statements

An interest in a jointly controlled entity should be accounted for in the individual financial statements of the venturer by applying the requirements of IAS 27 for separate financial statements. [IAS 31.46]

5.2 Transactions between a venturer and a joint venture

Where the venturer sells or contributes assets to a joint venture or purchases assets from a joint venture an adjustment should be made for the amount of any profit generated that reflects a transaction internal to the entity. For example, if a venturer sells an asset to the joint venture for a profit and the asset continues to be held by the joint venture, the proportion of that asset that is consolidated includes an element of profit that was recorded by the venturer. In such circumstances only the profit that relates to the share of the asset that belongs to the other venturers should be retained. [IAS 31.48]

A similar approach should be adopted for the purchase of assets from the joint venture; any profit that has been recognised by the joint venture should not be recognised by the venturer until the assets are sold to an external party. [IAS 31.49]

These adjustments are required for all transactions between a venturer and a joint venture regardless of the form that the joint venture arrangement takes; it is not limited to the creation of a separate joint venture entity.

5.3 Operators of joint ventures

A common feature in the contractual arrangements for a joint venture is to appoint a manager of the joint venture to act on behalf of all the venturers. Such a manager is usually paid a fee. Where such a fee is received it should be treated in accordance with IAS 18 *Revenue*. [IAS 31.52]

If one of the venturers acts as manager this fee should be treated separately from its share of the joint venture profit or loss.

5.4 Investors of a joint venture

An investor in a joint venture arrangement does not share joint control over the joint venture. The investment should be recognised in accordance with IAS 39 as a financial asset or, if the investor has 'significant influence' over the policy decisions of the joint venture, as an associate under IAS 28. [IAS 31.51]

6 Non-monetary Contributions by Venturers

IAS 31 requires that an adjustment is made where transactions take place between the venturer and a joint venture and profit has been recognised where the asset is still held by one of the parties. However, IAS 31 does not specifically mention the treatment required where a venturer contributes a non-cash asset, such as a piece of machinery, to a joint venture entity in return for equity in that joint venture. The Standing Interpretations Committee issued SIC 13 *Jointly controlled entities – non-monetary contributions by venturers* to address this particular issue.

The same principle as described above for the adjustment of transactions between the venturer and the joint venture should be applied in such circumstances. The venturer should only recognise the gain or loss that relates to the other venturer's share. The excluded part represents a transaction by the venturer with itself. Additionally, no part of the gain or loss should be recognised where the significant risks and rewards associated with the non-cash asset have not been transferred to the joint venture entity, where the amount cannot be measured reliably or where the non-cash asset transferred is similar, in its nature, to that contributed by the other venturers.

7 Disclosures

A venturer is required to disclose a list and description of all significant joint ventures that it has an interest in and the proportion of those interests. In addition, where joint venture amounts are not reported separately in the financial statements, the venturer should disclose the aggregate of its share of current assets, long-term assets, current liabilities, long-term liabilities, income and expenditure. [IAS 31.56]

The method under which joint ventures have been recognised should be clearly identified as being either proportionate consolidation or equity accounting. [IAS 31.57]

In addition, a number of disclosures are required in respect of contingent liabilities (unless they are remote) and capital commitments in relation to the joint venture investment. These disclosures include information not only on the venturer's contingent liabilities and capital commitments that have arisen as a result of the joint venture relationship but also on its share of those amounts of the joint venture itself. [IAS 31.54, 31.55]

8 Chapter Review

This chapter has been concerned with the accounting requirements for investments which give rise to joint control over investees.

This chapter has covered:

- the scope of IAS 31;

- the definitions: joint venture, joint control, jointly controlled operations, jointly controlled assets and jointly controlled entities;

- the method of accounting for each type of joint venture;

- proportionate consolidation and the equity method for jointly controlled entities;

- adjustments required for transactions between the venturer and the joint venture; and

- the disclosure requirements of IAS 31.

Chapter 36
FIRST TIME ADOPTION

1 Business Context

Any change in the use of an accounting framework is likely to cause entities transitional problems as they change from one set of standards to another. The purpose of IFRS 1 *First-time adoption of international financial reporting standards* is to establish common guidelines and practices for entities preparing their financial statements for the first time in accordance with International Financial Reporting Standards (IFRS).

IFRS 1 is essentially a road map of how to move from the preparation of financial statements using local Generally Accepted Accounting Practices (GAAP) to using international standards; it reduces uncertainty for users of financial statements and aids transparency. In particular, IFRS 1 means that there will be a clear distinction between changes in reported earnings arising from:

- the underlying economic activity; and
- changes in accounting measurement and recognition criteria.

2 Chapter Objectives

On completion of this chapter you should be able to:

- understand the scope and objectives of IFRS 1;
- understand the key recognition and measurement criteria in IFRS 1; and
- demonstrate knowledge of the key disclosure and presentation issues associated with using international standards for the first time.

3 Objectives, Scope and Definitions of IFRS 1

The objective of IFRS 1 is to ensure that an entity's first IFRS financial statements (and its interim financial reports for any part of the period covered by those financial statements) contain high quality information that is transparent for users whilst ensuring that comparability has not been undermined. IFRS 1 includes a number of choices that an entity can make; although the provision of such choices reduces comparability, the IASB decided that the cost of preparing transitional information in an entity's first IFRS financial statements should not outweigh the potential benefit of including such information.

IFRS 1 applies to the preparation of an entity's first financial statements that are being prepared in accordance with IFRS. In addition, any interim financial reports prepared for part of the period covered by an entity's first IFRS financial statements should also be prepared according to the transitional requirements of IFRS 1.

An entity's first IFRS financial statements are the first annual financial statements in which an entity fully adopts IFRS. An explicit and unreserved statement of compliance with IFRS should be made in those financial statements. If an entity is already applying IFRS but makes changes to its accounting policies, it should follow IAS 8 *Accounting policies, changes in accounting estimates and errors* and not IFRS 1.

4 Recognition and Measurement

4.1 Reporting requirements in the year of adoption

An entity should prepare an opening IFRS balance sheet at the date of its transition to IFRSs. This is the beginning of the earliest period for which comparative financial information is presented and is the starting point for its adoption of IFRS.

An entity should choose its accounting policies based on the latest versions of international standards current at its reporting date i.e. the end of the latest period covered by its first IFRS financial statements. Once selected, these accounting policies should be applied to all periods reported. Earlier versions of standards should not be used in the comparative periods. The latest standards are used since these contain the most up to date information and therefore provide the best accounting treatment. [IFRS 1.7]

Illustration 1

An entity has a 31 December accounting year end and intends to prepare its financial statements to comply with IFRS for the first time in the year to 31 December 2005. The entity reports one year of comparative information.

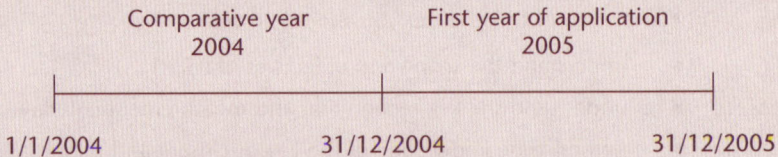

Comparative year 2004	First year of application 2005

1/1/2004	31/12/2004	31/12/2005

The date of transition to IFRS is 1 January 2004.

The 'opening IFRS balance sheet' at 1 January 2004 should be restated in accordance with IFRS current at 31 December 2005, as the basis for the 2004 comparative information.

Subject to some exemptions, which are mentioned briefly later, an entity should restate information on an IFRS basis as if the entity had always followed international standards.

Action	Example
Recognise all assets and liabilities as required by IFRS. This may require the recognition of items not previously recognised.	Development costs expensed in the income statement under local GAAP may need to be capitalised if they meet IFRS recognition criteria.
Derecognition of assets and liabilities that do not meet IFRS recognition criteria but have been recognised under existing GAAP.	General provisions previously recognised under an entity's local GAAP may not be permitted under IAS 37 *Provisions, contingent liabilities and contingent assets*.
Reclassification of items recognised under previous GAAP as one type of asset, liability or component of equity under a different classification.	Redeemable preference shares currently classified as equity may need to be reclassified as liabilities.
Apply IFRS in **measuring** all recognised assets and liabilities. This may result in the restatement of the carrying amount of assets and liabilities.	Deferred tax balances may have been discounted to present value under an entity's local GAAP. IAS 12 *Income taxes* does not permit the discounting of deferred tax and therefore the amount will need to be remeasured on an undiscounted basis.

Illustration 2

An entity is a first-time adopter of IFRS. It has previously reported under local generally accepted accounting practices (GAAP). The entity has identified the following items as requiring a different treatment in the opening IFRS balance sheet.

1. An intangible asset acquired two years ago which was not recognised as an asset under local GAAP but which meets IFRS recognition criteria. The asset should be recognised in the opening balance sheet.

2. Development costs recognised under local GAAP in the opening balance sheet do not meet IFRS recognition criteria. The development costs should be charged to retained profit and removed from the opening balance sheet.

4.2 Exemptions

As explained above, on first time adoption of IFRS an entity is required to restate its results as if it had always followed international standards. A number of exemptions are, however, permitted on a cost / benefit basis, i.e. where the cost of preparing such information is likely to be in excess of any benefit achieved from restating it.

There is a risk that when information is restated the outcome of events which affect restated items is used to refine that information. This is discussed further below in relation to the use of estimation techniques. IFRS 1 includes a number of prohibitions on the use of retrospective application where this is thought to be a particular issue.

The exemptions in IFRS 1 are briefly set out below.

- *Business combinations* – an exemption from having to apply IFRS 3 *Business combinations* to all past business combinations is provided. An entity is however permitted to apply IFRS 3 to a past business combination but if it does so, then all subsequent combinations should be restated under IFRS 3.

- *Fair value or revaluation as deemed cost* – an entity adopting the cost model for property, plant and equipment under IAS 16 *Property, plant and equipment* is permitted to use fair value at the date of transition to IFRS. This value is then 'frozen' (becomes deemed cost) within the IFRS financial statements. This approach is also permitted for investment properties and intangible assets. A past valuation may also be used as deemed cost provided that it is broadly similar to fair value (or depreciated cost).

- *Employee benefits* – an entity is not required to split out all past actuarial gains and losses in a retirement benefit plan since it was created, even if it is going to use what is essentially a deferral method for future gains and losses (known as the "corridor") in IAS 19 *Employee benefits*.

- *Cumulative translation differences* – IAS 21 *The effects of changes in foreign exchange rates* requires an entity to identify translation differences that have not been reported in the income statement, for later recognition. The exemption permits all such translation differences to be deemed to be zero at the date of transition.

- *Compound financial instruments* – a compound financial instrument is where it has attributes of both a liability and equity. International standards require that the two elements are separated; the exemption does not require the separation where the liability element is no longer outstanding.

- *Timing of adoption in groups* – where a parent and its subsidiaries adopt international standards at different times, elections are permitted that simplify the adoption process in the subsidiaries' separate financial statements.

4.3 Estimates

Once an entity has chosen its IFRS accounting policies, it may need to revisit estimates that have been made under its existing accounting framework. The entity should consider whether such estimates meet the measurement criteria under international standards. In reassessing estimates an entity should not take into account information that has come to light since the relevant financial statements were prepared. For example, an entity should make estimates under IFRS at the date of transition to IFRS as if they had been calculated using IFRS at the date of their orginal assessment. Subsequent information should be considered in the same way as non-adjusting events under IAS 10 *Events after the balance sheet date* unless there is evidence that the original estimates contained errors. [IFRS 1.31]

New estimates may need to be made at the date of transition to IFRS. Where this is the case, these estimates should be made based on information that existed at the date of transition.

5 Presentation and Disclosure

5.1 Comparative information

To comply with IAS 1 *Presentation of financial statements* an entity is required to report at least one year of comparative information.

Entities may have presented historical summaries of financial information for periods before the first period for which full comparative information is presented, for example a three or five year summary income statement. Such summaries are not required to be restated to comply with the recognition and measurement requirements of IFRS. However, where such summaries are presented and have not been restated under IFRS the information should be clearly identified as being prepared under a different accounting framework. Although it is not necessary to restate this information, the main adjustments that would be required if it were restated under IFRS should be identified and explained. No quantification is necessary.

5.2 Explanation of transition

An entity should explain how the transition from its previous GAAP to IFRS has affected the financial statements in relation to its financial performance and position and cash flows. [IFRS 1.38]

5.2.1 Reconciliations

To assist with the requirement to explain the transition in an entity's first IFRS financial statements, an entity is required to present a number of reconciliations, these include:

- a reconciliation of equity (i.e. the balance sheet) reported under previous GAAP to that reported under IFRS for the date of transition to IFRS. In addition, a reconciliation of equity should be provided for the previously reported figures that were for the latest period presented in the entity's most recent annual financial statements under previous GAAP to IFRS. For example, for an entity that adopts IFRS for the first time in its financial statements for the year to 31 December 2005 and presents one year of comparative information, a reconciliation of its balance sheet as at 1 January 2004 and 31 December 2004 should be presented;

- a reconciliation of the profit or loss reported under previous GAAP for the latest period in the entity's most recent annual financial statements to its profit or loss under IFRS for the same period. Using the example above, this will be a reconciliation of the income statement for the period ending 31 December 2004;

- where the entity reported a cash flow statement under previous GAAP, the main adjustments made to restate the comparatives should be explained; and

- additional disclosures should be presented in relation to any impairment losses (i.e. the reduction in an asset's recoverable amount below its balance sheet carring amount) or reversals of impairment losses recognised for the first time when preparing its opening IFRS balance sheet.

6 Chapter Review

This chapter has been concerned with the procedures necessary in the introduction of IFRS for the first time.

This chapter has covered:

- the objectives and scope of IFRS 1;

- the key recognition and measurement criteria in IFRS 1; and

- the key disclosure and presentation issues in adopting IFRS for the first time.